Judicial Review

JUDICIAL REVIEW

Ian McLeod LLB BA
Solicitor
Department of Law
London Guildhall University

ISBN 1 872328 76 8

Published by Barry Rose Law Publishers Ltd
Chichester
England

TABLE OF CONTENTS

CHAPTER 10: DELEGATION

CHAPTER 11: FETTERING DISCRETION BY CONTRACT AND ESTOPPEL

CHAPTER 12: NATURAL JUSTICE - THE REQUIREMENT OF FAIRNESS

APPENDIX

INTRODUCTION

My aim in writing this book has been to produce a modern and practical account of the principles underlying the process of judicial review. Accordingly, although I have cited old authority where it seemed essential to do so, I have tried wherever possible to use recent cases both to establish and to illustrate the principles.

My desire to make the book practical, and more particularly my perception of the needs of busy and often under-resourced practitioners, has had a number of consequences.

First, I have given many of the cases a fairly full treatment. with substantial quotations from many of the leading judgments.

Secondly, I have included an Appendix containing the full texts of Order 53 of the Rules of the Supreme Court and ss.29-31 of the Supreme Court Act 1981, as well as substantial extracts from the European Convention for the Protection of Human Rights and Fundamental Freedoms.

Thirdly, I have structured the material in terms of the most frequently encountered practical problems, rather than in accordance with the more abstract theories of politico-legal science.

Those actually involved in making or defending an application for judicial review may obtain up-to-date practical advice on matters such as fees from the Crown Office (tel. 071-936 6000 ext. 6205) from whom a copy of the current version of a leaflet containing Notes, issued at the direction of the Lord Chief Justice, may also be obtained.

In the interests of readability I have excluded case references from the text, although in most instances I have included the year in which each case was reported. However, I have omitted even this date where there is rapid repetition of citation.

The material in Parts A and B of the Appendix is Crown copyright. The Council of Europe regards the European Convention on Human Rights as a public document in which there is no copyright.

At a more personal level, my major source of support in writing this book has undoubtedly been my wife Jacqui, whose skills in word-processing, proof-reading and organizing the Table of Cases, combined with a singularly patient temperament, have been invaluable.

I have tried to state the law as it was on December 1, 1992.

Ian McLeod.

Judicial Review

TABLE OF CASES

CHAPTER 1

THE CONSTITUTIONAL CONTEXT OF JUDICIAL REVIEW

A: Introduction

Judicial review may be described in general terms as "the process by which the courts exercise a supervisory jurisdiction over the activities of public authorities in the field of public law" (Lewis, *Judicial Remedies in Public Law,* 1992, p.6). The fact that review is supervisory rather than appellate in nature means that a useful starting point is the distinction between appeal and review.

B: The Distinction Between Appeal and Review

Appeal is a means of challenging *a decision*, while review is a means of challenging *the way in which the decision was made.* One major practical consequence of the distinction is that in the case of an appeal the appellate body is not only being asked to say whether the decision was right or wrong, but can also generally substitute its own decision. In the context of review, however, the supervisory body is not called upon to say whether it agrees with the merits of the decision, and therefore, even if it upholds the challenge, it cannot substitute its own decision, but can at best merely quash the original decision, compel it to be re-made in a lawful fashion, and make an order prohibiting future illegality.

There are innumerable judicial protestations underlining the importance of the distinction between appeal and review. Two will suffice to illustrate the point.

The case of *Chief Constable of the North Wales Police v. Evans* (1982) concerned a challenge to the exercise of a chief constable's disciplinary functions. The Court of Appeal seems to have lost sight of the distinction between appeal and review, as a result of which it was brought sharply to heel by the House of Lords, where Lord Brightman said:

"There is ... a wider point than the injustice of the decision-making process of the chief constable. With profound respect to the Court of Appeal, I dissent from the view that 'Not only must [the probationer constable] be given a fair hearing, but the decision itself must be fair and reasonable.' If that statement of the law passed into authority without comment, it would in my opinion transform, and wrongly transform, the remedy of judicial review. Judicial review, as the words

1

imply, *is not an appeal from a decision, but a review of the manner in which the decision was made.* The statement of law which I have quoted implies that the court sits in judgment not only on the correctness of the decision-making process but also on the correctness of the decision itself." (Emphasis added.)

In *R. v. Devon County Council ex parte G.* (1988) Lord Donaldson M.R. emphasized the consequential limitation on the role of the court. The case involved a dispute between a parent and a local education authority over the (non-)availability of free school transport. The Master of the Rolls said:

"Let me stress the role of the courts in this controversy. The school which the applicant attends, the parish council, Devon ratepayers and the media are all fully entitled to say that, if they were members of the education committee, the applicant would, of course, have been provided with free transport. And they have done so. Judges do not enjoy such a freedom. In judicial review proceedings such as these, their role is much more limited. They can only consider whether (a) the council misapplied the relevant law or (b) it reached a decision which no council properly applying the law could reasonably have reached."

The case of *Dabek v. Chief Constable of Devon and Cornwall* (1990) must be mentioned as representing a deviation from the clear-cut distinction between appeal and review, but there is no doubt that the decision is an oddity and it must not be taken as casting doubt on the established principle. The facts involved an appeal to the High Court against the Crown Court's decision to uphold the chief constable's revocation of a shotgun certificate. Farquharson L.J. said that in appeals of this sort the court should not seek to substitute its own judgment as to the merits of the case, but should confine itself to considering whether there were grounds on which the chief constable and the Crown Court could have made their respective decisions.

The concept of appeal being entirely statutory, it follows that statute establishes the availability or non-availability of appeal in specific cases. The concept of review being essentially a common law concept, it follows that the courts decide on its availability, with the principles emerging on a case-by-case basis. In *Council of Civil Service Unions v. Minister for the Civil Service* (1984), which is more usually known as the *GCHQ* case, Lord Diplock indicated the scope of judicial review thus:

"The subject matter is a decision ... or else a refusal to make a decision.

"To qualify as a subject for judicial review the decision must have consequences which affect some persons (or body of persons) other than the decision-maker, although it may affect him too. It must affect such other person either:

(a) by altering rights or obligations of that person which are enforceable by or against him in private law; or

(b) by depriving him of some benefit or advantage
which either (i) he had in the past been permitted by the decision-maker to enjoy and which he can legitimately expect to be permitted to continue to enjoy until there has been communicated to him some rational ground for withdrawing it on which he has been given an opportunity to comment; or (ii) he has received assurance from the decision-maker will not be withdrawn without giving him first an opportunity of advancing reasons for contending that they should not be withdrawn ...

"For a decision to be susceptible to judicial review the decision-maker must be empowered by public law (and not merely ... by agreement between private parties) to make decisions that, if validly made, will lead to administrative action or abstention from action by an authority endowed by law with executive powers, which have one or other of the consequences mentioned in the preceding paragraph. The ultimate source of the power is nearly always nowadays a statute or subordinate legislation made under a statute, but ... may still be ... 'the prerogative'."

C: The Courts Exercising Jurisdiction in Judicial Review

1. Introduction

For almost all practical purposes, the jurisdiction in relation to applications for judicial review is exercised solely by the High Court. Civil cases are usually heard by a single judge of the Queen's Bench Division, and criminal cases are usually heard by a two, or sometimes three, judge Divisional Court.

The jurisdiction in relation to applications for leave to apply for judicial review is exercised by a single judge where the application is *ex parte* and is dealt with on the papers, irrespective of whether the matter to which it relates is civil or criminal. Oral *ex parte* applications for leave to apply are dealt with by a single judge in civil cases and by a Divisional Court in criminal cases.

There appears to be no magic in the distinction between a single judge and a Divisional Court. In *R. v. Secretary of State for the Home Department ex parte Chinoy* (1992), Bingham L.J., speaking as part of a two member Divisional Court, said:

> "We exercise, for all practical purposes, the same jurisdiction as a single judge."

The generality of the proposition that the High Court has sole jurisdiction is, however, subject to one qualification.

In *Chief Adjudication Officer v. Foster* (1991) the Court of Appeal held itself to have a quasi-original jurisdiction, which entitles it to consider and decide judicial review issues which are relevant to an appeal, even though the issues were not, or could not validly have been, raised in the court below. The court acknowledged that this aspect of its jurisdiction would arise only rarely.

There is one other situation in which the Court of Appeal may appear to be exercising a jurisdiction in judicial review. Where the Court of Appeal is required to decide whether a decision of an inferior decision-maker was subject to judicial review or to appeal, and it decides in favour of judicial review, the court may forthwith reconstitute itself as a Divisional Court of the Queen's Bench Division of the High Court in order to dispose of the case (see e.g. *R. v. Miall* (1992), discussed further at p.135). Clearly, however, in this situation the court has become a Divisional Court, and therefore it does not represent a genuine exception to the general rule that it is the High Court which exercises exclusive juridiction.

2. Precedent in Judicial Review

It might appear that one necessary consequence of the non-appellate nature of judicial review is that the jurisdiction is one at first instance, and indeed the High Court so held in *R. v. Greater Manchester Coroner ex parte Tal* (1984). The consequence of this in terms of the doctrine of precedent would be to free the court from the principles of self-bindingness which the Court of Appeal formulated for its own use in *Young v. Bristol Aeroplane Co.* (1944), and which the High Court adopted for the purposes of its appellate jurisdiction in *Huddersfield Police Authority v. Watson* (1947). However, the courts have expressed their unease with this potential freedom.

In *Hornigold v. Chief Constable of Lancashire* (1985) it was said that the decision in *Tal* had been intended to provide a sensible basis on which the Divisional Court should approach its own previous decisions, and had not been intended to provide a charter under which parties were free to reargue points which had previously been argued before another Divisional Court, simply in the hope that the second court might be persuaded to reach a different conclusion. The court was anxious that the effect of allowing such arguments to be advanced would be to upset the legal stability which the doctrine of precedent was said to be designed to maintain.

The court went on the say that departure from one of its own previous decisions could be justified only if that decision was plainly wrong. Additionally, an advocate seeking such departure must be able, at the outset of his argument, to indicate how he intends to persuade the court of the wrongness of the earlier decision.

Similarly, in *R. v. Secretary of State for the Home Department ex parte Bagga and Others* (1989) Woolf L.J. displayed a marked lack of enthusiasm for the flexibility adopted in *Tal*. Having had regard to a number of earlier decisions of the Divisional Court, he proceeded to grant applications for judicial review on the basis of those decisions, without hearing argument as to their correctness. Counsel for the Home Secretary agreed to reserve his arguments for the Court of Appeal.

In passing, it may be useful to observe that in *R. v. Greenwich London Borough Council ex parte Lovelace and Another (No. 2)* (1992) the Court of Appeal held that the Divisional Court is a court of first instance for the purposes of the Legal Aid Act 1988, at least in those cases where it is dealing with applications for judicial review of decisions of bodies other than courts and tribunals. Obviously, however, the binding authority of *Greenwich* is limited to the statutory context within which it was decided, and it can be of only indirect relevance to the doctrine of precedent, and the court specifically left open the question of whether the High Court is a court of first instance when dealing with applications for judicial review in respect of inferior courts.

3. Setting Aside the Grant of Leave
Where leave to apply has been granted, the respondent can apply to have the leave set aside, but such applications will only rarely be granted, as further discussed at p.48.

4. Avenues of Renewal and Appeal
There is no appeal as such against an initial refusal of leave to apply, but in civil cases where the initial application has been dealt with on the papers the application may be renewed before either a single judge, or exceptionally a Divisional Court, with a further avenue of renewal or appeal therefrom to the Court of Appeal. If the initial application has been

dealt with orally, the renewed application is made directly to the Court of Appeal. There is no progression in any case, either by way of renewal or appeal, to the House of Lords.

In criminal cases an application may be renewed before a Divisional Court, irrespective of how the initial application has been made, but there is no further progression therefrom.

After the substantive hearing, in civil cases appeal lies, as of right, to the Court of Appeal. In criminal cases appeal lies, with leave, directly to the House of Lords.

D: Constitutional Fundamentals

The scope of judicial review will be explored throughout this book, but one persistent theme, sometimes explicit and sometimes implicit, will be the constitutional propriety of the court's intervention in the political process. If the case-law is to be seen as a reasonably coherent whole, and not simply - in Tennyson's memorable phrase - "a wilderness of single instances", it is therefore appropriate to begin with a brief survey of some fundamental doctrines of the British constitution. Three particularly relevant matters are the legislative supremacy of Parliament, the rule of law, and the separation of powers.

1. The Legislative Supremacy of Parliament

According to Dicey, "the very keystone of the law of the Constitution" is that

"Parliament ... has ... the right to make or unmake any law whatever; and further, that no person or body is recognized by the law of England as having a right to override or set aside the legislation of Parliament."

In *Pickin v. British Railways Board* (1974) Lord Reid emphasized that once a Bill has received the Royal Assent, and therefore become an Act, the courts have no power other than to interpret and apply it. Although this proposition now requires some qualification in the context European Community law, and more particularly in the light of *R. v. Secretary of State for Transport ex parte Factortame Ltd. (No.2)* (1991), it remains valid in general terms.

2. The Rule of Law

Turning to Dicey again, the rule of law has three elements, the first of which is

"the absolute supremacy or predominance of regular law as opposed to the influence of arbitrary power, [with the resulting exclusion of] the existence of arbitrariness ... or even of wide discretionary authority on the part of the government."

The second element is the importance of ensuring that

"every man, whatever be his rank or condition, is subject to the ordinary law of the realm and amenable to the jurisdiction of the ordinary tribunals [sc. courts]".

The third element is that the British constitution is

"the result of the judicial decisions determining the rights of private persons in particular cases brought before the courts."

Dicey's influence has been enduring, even though, whatever the position may have been in Victorian England, none of these three propositions can be uncritically endorsed a century or so later.

For example, when considering Dicey's first point, it must be remembered that in practical terms there not only is, but also must be, significant scope for the exercise of discretion in the exercise of governmental powers. This is not necessarily inconsistent with the idea of the rule of law, provided that there is a legal framework within which any particular discretion must be exercised, coupled with effective remedies if that framework is breached.

Similarly, although Dicey's insistence on the idea of equality before the law may appear to be admirable at a general level, the reality of the matter is that the exercise of power by the State is fundamentally different from the exercise of power by individuals. This fundamental difference springs not only from the extent of State power, but also from the possibilities of enforcement action in the event of non-compliance with the requirements of the State. It is at least arguable, therefore, that the principles of law governing the judicial control of State power should be different from those which apply where only private power is involved. As much of this book will show, there are some respects in which inequality before the law manifests itself in terms of public sector decision-makers being more accountable than their private sector counterparts would be. This is clearly not the kind of inequality Dicey feared.

Thirdly, whilst conceding the substantial historical accuracy of Dicey's description of the British constitution as being judge-made, the post-Diceyan era has seen significant legislative intervention in constitutional matters, such as the Police and Criminal Evidence Act 1984, and the enactment of a wide variety of statutory provisions governing the legal relationships between central and local government.

It will be apparent that the courts may well find themselves dealing with cases where the legislative supremacy of Parliament appears to require one outcome, while the rule of law appears to require another. A classic example is *Customs and Excise Commissioners v. Cure & Deeley Ltd.* (1961).

By s.33 of the Finance (No.2) Act 1940, the Commissioners of Customs and Excise had power to

"make regulations providing for any matter for which provision *appears to them to be necessary* for the purpose of giving effect to the provisions of this Part of this Act and enabling them to discharge their functions thereunder" (Emphasis added.)

In purported exercise of this power the Commissioners made Regulations to the effect that, if the taxpayer failed to deliver a tax return, the Commissioners would have power to determine the amount of tax due. When the company was required to pay tax on this basis, it argued that the Regulations were unlawful, even though an uncritical application of the doctrine of the legislative supremacy of Parliament would simply lead to the conclusion that the regulations were within the scope of the very wide powers which Parliament had chosen to confer on the Commissioners.

Sachs J., who was clearly uneasy about the implications of the extent of the Commissioners' powers in terms of the rule of law, was able to give practical effect to his anxiety by accepting three arguments in favour of the company.

First, the statutory power was to make Regulations relating to the discharge of the Commissioners' functions, whereas the Regulations they had made purported to give themselves the functions of a High Court judge in determining matters of fact and law arising out of disputes between the Crown and the subject. Secondly, the Regulations appeared to exclude the subject's right of access to the courts. Thirdly, the Act itself required payment of tax which was due at law, whereas the Regulations required the payment of tax which the Commissioners thought was due.

In the final analysis, however, it may be that the court has no option but to accept that Parliament has actually conferred extremely wide powers. In *R. v. Secretary of State for Social Services ex parte Stitt* (1991) the High Court acknowledged that a court which detects ambiguity in a statute will lean against an interpretation which would give the executive unbridled power to pass subordinate legislation. Nevertheless, the court went on to say that a statutory provision providing for payments out of the social fund was to be made " to meet other needs [sc. not specified in the Act] in accordance with directions given or guidance issued by the Secretary of State", Parliament had actually conferred on the Secretary of State the powers to decide whether a particular need should be met wholly or partly from the fund, rather than the more limited power merely to decide how such payments should be made. The Court of Appeal dismissed an appeal in a case reported as *R. v Social Fund Inspector and Another ex parte Healey and Others* (1992).

3. The Separation of Powers

According to the eighteenth century French commentator Montesquieu, the doctrine of the separation of powers is that the interests of individual freedom require that the three-fold power of the State, namely the legislative, executive and judicial functions, should each be exercised by different agencies of the State. Although the strict separation of powers has never actually characterized the British constitution, there is no doubt that the Judges are frequently conscious of the fact that their own role on the constitutional stage has its limits.

As Lord Scarman said in *Duport Steels Ltd. v. Sirs* (1980), when interpreting the politically contentious provisions of the Trade Union and Labour Relations Act 1974:

"Within ... limits ... Judges ... have a genuine creative role ... But the Constitution's separation of powers, or more accurately functions, must be observed if judicial independence is not to be put at risk. For if people and Parliament come to think that the judicial power is to be confined by nothing other than the judge's sense of what is right ... confidence in the judicial system will be replaced by fear of it becoming uncertain and arbitrary in its application. Society will then be ready for Parliament to cut the power of the Judges. Their power to do justice will become more restricted by law than it need be, or is today."

Comparable and equally forthright comments can be found in the context of judicial review. In particular, it seems that judicial consciousness of the separation of powers is likely to become more acute in cases involving disputes which are closely related to the democratic process.

In *R. v. Birmingham City Council ex parte Sheptonhurst Ltd.* (1990), which was decided with a number of other similar cases, the court was concerned with the refusal of the local authorities to renew expiring sex shop licences which had been granted under the Local Government (Miscellaneous Provisions) Act 1982. The local authorities had concluded that the appropriate number of sex shops in the relevant areas was nil, even though there had been no change of circumstances since the previous decision to grant the licences. The court held that when considering an application for renewal of a sex shop licence, a local authority must have regard to the fact that a licence has previously been granted but, provided it does have such regard, a decision to refuse to renew a licence will not be perverse simply because there has been no change in the character of the relevant locality or in the use to which any premises in the vicinity are put. The court took the view that the legislature must be taken to know that a local authority is a body of changing composition and shifting opinion, whose changes and shifts reflect the views of the local electorate, and therefore what is "appropriate" may be the subject of different perceptions by different elected representatives at different times.

Judicial sympathy for local authorities in the context of those duties in cases of homelessness which were introduced by the Housing (Homeless Persons) Act 1977, was evident in *R. v. Hillingdon London Borough Council ex parte Puhlhofer* (1986). Lord Brightman said:

"My Lords, I am troubled at the prolific use of judicial review for the purposes of challenging the performance by local authorities of their functions under the Act ... Where the existence or non-existence of a fact is left to the judgment and discretion of a public body and that fact involves a broad spectrum, ranging from the obvious to the debatable to the just conceivable, it is the duty of the court to leave the decision of that fact to the public body, save in a case where it is obvious that the public body, consciously or unconsciously, are acting perversely."

Clearly cases involving homelessness involve the allocation of scarce resources. It is not surprising, therefore, that the court will be similarly reluctant to intervene where the challenge relates to the budgetary processes of a local authority. In *R. v. Greater London Council ex parte Royal Borough of Kensington and Chelsea* (1982) McNeill J. was faced with such a challenge. Whilst disinclined to grant relief on the facts of the case anyway, the judge was clearly unhappy at having been involved at all, saying that issue was one "for the political hustings, and not for the court".

The words of McNeill J. contain a clear echo of the sentiments expressed by Lord Wilberforce, in a different context, in *Anns v. London Borough of Merton* (1977), who recognized the need for

"public authorities ... to strike a balance between the claims of efficiency and thrift"

and said that

"whether they get the balance right can only be decided through the ballot box, not in the courts."

Of course, the doctrine of the legislative supremacy of Parliament ensures that statutes are normally immune from judicial review, but it is clear that even the House of Commons' endorsement of Ministerial decisions is no absolute bar to judicial review, although in such cases the courts will tread with particular care.

In *Nottinghamshire County Council v. Secretary of State for the Environment* (1986) the Secretary of State had power to differentiate between high spending and low spending local authorities when determining the annual rate support grant settlement. The settlement was then laid before, and approved by, the House of Commons. The House of Lords held that in such cases it would be improper for the courts to uphold an allegation of unreasonableness unless the Secretary of State had either misconstrued the statute which conferred the power on him, or had misled the House of Commons. Since neither of these eventualities arose in the present case, the House of Lords took the view that the responsibility for supervizing the exercise of Ministerial power fell entirely within the province of the House of Commons.

E: Predicting Judicial Outcomes

It is one thing to recount instances in which the courts, having balanced the fundamental doctrines and having directed themselves as to the distinction between appeal and review, have come down on one side or the other. It is another thing altogether to formulate a test which will accurately predict the outcome of litigation. Although there can be no doubt that Judges in each case will do what they consider to be right according to their views of constitutional propriety, there is inevitably a degree of judicial subjectivity. At this stage it is useful to look at what Harlow and Rawlings, in their book on *Law and Administration* (1984) have called "red light" theories and "green light" theories of judicial intervention, and to subdivide the field of inquiry into the macro and micro levels.

Very broadly, red light theories of judicial intervention are those which favour the traditional English view that the rights of the individual are among the highest goods known to the politico-legal system, and that State power in its many manifestations is basically an intrusion upon those rights. It follows that in many cases the law should be interpreted strictly in favour of the individual, with an essential function of the courts being to restrict encroachments on private rights by being ever ready to show a red light to public decision-makers.

By way of contrast, and equally broadly, green light theories embody the proposition that the contradistinction between 'individual rights' and 'State power' is a false one, and that the concept of 'State power' should, for these purposes, be re-defined as "the public interest". It follows from this that the conflict itself is re-defined, becoming a confrontation between narrow, sectional or individual interests on the one hand, and the public interest on the other.

Although the alignment of Judges in red light and green light terms is largely a matter of individual psychology, it seems clear that one of the basic distinctions is that adherents of the green light perspective are more likely to acknowledge the integrity and legitimacy of the political process as an instrument of social regulation, as illustrated by the decision of the House of Lords in *Nottinghamshire County Council v. Secretary of State for the Environment* (1986).

At the macro level, therefore, all Judges will have their own perceptions of the proper role of law as an instrument of social regulation. Some will be temperamentally sympathetic to red light theories, while others will incline to favour green light theories.

At the micro level, in terms of how specific cases are decided, once again the psychology of individual Judges becomes important, since they can hardly avoid having some instinctive ideas as to the justice of each case. The fact that judicial professionalism prevents cases being decided simply on that basis may reduce, but does not necessarily eliminate, the significance of the intuitive sense of justice.

In *R. v. West Dorset District Council ex parte Poupard* (1988) an applicant for housing benefit had capital assets but was living on weekly drawings from an overdrawn bank account. The question was whether the drawings were "income" such as to disqualify the applicant from receiving assistance under the Housing Benefit Regulations 1985. The local authority's Housing Review Board concluded that the drawings were income. The court held that in each case it was a question of fact whether specific sums of money were "income", and that this question was to be decided on the basis of all that the council and their Review Board knew of the sources from which an applicant for benefit was maintaining himself and paying his bills. The conclusion was that on the present facts the local authority and their Review Board had made no error of law, and had acted reasonably in reaching their decision.

On his way to reaching his decision, Macpherson J., adopting an argument advanced by counsel for the local authority, said:

> "The scheme [of Housing Benefit] is intended to help those who do not have the weekly resources to meet their bills, or their rent, and it is not intended to help comparatively better-off people (in capital terms) to venture into unsuccessful business and not to bring into account moneys which are regularly available for day-to-day spending, albeit that the use of moneys depletes their capital."

Although the Court of Appeal upheld this decision, it will nevertheless be apparent that a court with different sympathies could, with equal logic, have upheld the argument that the weekly drawings were outgo, rather than income, because each drawing increased the drawer's indebtedness to the bank.

CHAPTER 2

JUDICIAL REVIEW AND THE DOCTRINE OF *ULTRA VIRES*

A: Introduction

At its simplest the doctrine of *ultra vires* states that a legal person acts unlawfully if he purports to act beyond the scope of the powers which the law has conferred upon him. This statement is, of course, no more than a tautology: what matters is how such unlawfulness is to be identified and the nature of its consequences. Although the identification of unlawfulness is, of course, the major theme of this book, it may be useful to begin with a discrete consideration of the nature of the consequences of unlawfulness in the context of the doctrine of *ultra vires*. However, as a preliminary even to this preliminary it may also be useful to say something about the classification of decisions into judicial and administrative categories.

B: The Judicial-Administrative Distinction

Historically the judicial-administrative distinction was crucial because the courts used to take the view that certiorari was available only within the judicial category. Admittedly this led to a rather extended definition of the concept of judicial decisions, and even this was further extended by the invention of the *quasi-judicial* category, in respect of which certiorari was then said to be available.

Fortunately, in view of the uncertainty as to what would or would not be classified as being *judicial* or *quasi-judicial* on the one hand, as distinct from *administrative* on the other, certiorari is now available without reference to such classifications (see *O'Reilly v. Mackman* (1982) where Lord Diplock confirmed that this was the effect of Lord Reid's speech in *Ridge v. Baldwin* (1963)). Nevertheless, the distinction is not yet wholly redundant, because, as will become apparent from time to time in the course of this book, the courts still find comfort in the judicial-administrative distinction. Notable instances arise in relation to *delegation* and *natural justice*, which are discussed in chapters 10 and 12 respectively.

A useful starting point for identifying the nature of judicial, quasi-judicial and administrative decision-making may be found in the *Report of the Donoughmore Committee on Ministers' Powers* (1932), which formulated the following criteria.

"A true judicial decision presupposes an exisiting dispute between two or more parties, and then involves four requisites: (1) the presentation (not necessarily orally) of their case by the parties to the dispute; (2) if the dispute betwen them is a question of fact, the ascertainment of the fact by means of evidence adduced by the parties to the dispute and often with the assistance of argument by or on behalf of the parties on the evidence; (3) if the dispute between them is a question of law, the submission of legal argument by the parties; and (4) a decision which disposes of the whole matter by a finding upon the facts in dispute and an application of the law of the land to the facts so found, including where required a ruling upon any disputed question of law.

"A quasi-judicial decision equally presupposes an existing dispute between two or more parties and involves (1) and (2), but does not necessarily involve (3), and never involves (4). The place of (4) is taken by administrative action, the character of which is determined by the Minister's [*sc.* or other decision-maker's] free choice."

A classic example of a quasi-judicial decision-making process according to these criteria would be a planning appeal, where questions of fact and law would be dealt with, but where the ultimate outcome would depend largely on matters of professional and political judgment, rather than being simply the product of the application of the law to the facts.

"In the case of [an] administrative decision, there is no legal obligation upon the person charged with the duty of reaching the decision to consider and weigh submissions and arguments, or to collate any evidence or to solve any issue. The grounds upon which he acts, and the means which he takes to inform himself before acting, are left entirely to his discretion."

Although the *Donoughmore* criteria are often quoted because of their classic status, a more modern and succinct version comes from Wade:

"A judicial decision is made according to law. An administrative decision is made according to administrative policy. A judge attempts to find what is the correct solution according to legal rules and principles. An administrator attempts to find what is the most expedient and desirable solution in the public interest ... There will always be grey areas. Nevertheless the mental exercises of judge and administrator are fundamentally different. The judge's approach is objective, guided by his idea of the law. The administrator's approach is empirical, guided merely by expediency." (*Administrative Law*, 6th edition, 1988, p.46.)

In particular, it is now apparent that whenever the judicial-administrative distinction arises in the current state of the law, it is much more useful to think in terms of a spectrum of possibilities, with judicial decision-making at one end, and administrative decision-making at the other, rather than in terms of watertight compartments (see particularly *McInnes v. Onslow-Fane* (1978), discussed further at p.191).

It is now appropriate to give detailed consideration to the topic of the consequences of an *ultra vires* act.

C: The Consequences of an *Ultra Vires* Act

1. The Presumption of Legality and the Nature of Voidness
Traditionally, an *ultra vires* act was said to be either null, void, or both, with nullity and voidness each meaning the same thing for the present purposes. However, until it is quashed an *ultra vires* act may well have substantial practical effects. As Lord Denning M.R. said, in *Lovelock v. Minister of Transport* (1980):

"It seems to me to be a matter of words - of semantics - and that is all. The plain fact is that, even if ... a decision ... is 'void' or a 'nullity', it remains in being unless and until some steps are taken before the courts to have it declared void."

Furthermore there is a presumption of legality, stemming both from the basic proposition of English law that he who alleges must prove, and the presumption of regularity, which is commonly expressed in the form of the maxim *omnia praesumuntur rite esse acta.*

In *Hoffman-La Roche v. Secretary of State for Trade and Industry* (1974) the company was challenging the validity of a statutory instrument which limited the price of some of the company's drugs. The statutory instrument had been made after the Monopolies Commission had recommended a price reduction. The company alleged that the Monopolies Commission's procedure leading up to the recommendation had been unfair, and that therefore the statutory instrument was *ultra vires* and void.

When the case reached the House of Lords, Lord Diplock said:

"My Lords, I think it leads to confusion to use such terms as 'voidable',

'voidable *ab initio*', 'void' or 'a nullity' as descriptive of the status of subordinate legislation ... before its validity has been pronounced on by a court .... These are concepts developed in the private law of contract which are ill-adapted to the field of public law. *All that can usefully be said is that the presumption that subordinate legislation is intra vires prevails in the absence of rebuttal*, and that it cannot be rebutted except by a party to legal proceedings in a court of competent jurisdiction, who has *locus standi* to challenge the validity of the subordinate legislation in question." (Emphasis added.)

Although the facts of this case dealt with subordinate legislation, the principle is clearly of general application.

In *London & Clydeside Estates Ltd. v. Aberdeen District Council* (1979) the issue turned on the validity of a certificate of appropriate alternative development under the planning legislation. Lord Hailsham said:

"In the reported decisions there is much language presupposing the existence of stark categories such as ... 'void' and 'voidable' ... Such language is useful ... But ... I am not at all clear that the language itself may not be misleading in so far as it may be supposed to present a court with the necessity of fitting a particular case into one or other of mutually exclusive and starkly contrasted compartments, compartments which in some cases (e.g. 'void' and 'voidable') are borrowed from the language of contract or status, and are not easily fitted to the requirements of Administrative Law."

Generally, of course, the presumption of legality will operate against a potential challenger by raising an evidential obstacle, but it may work the other way, as illustrated by *Calder Gravel Ltd. v. Kirklees Metropolitan Borough Council* (1990).

The facts were that in 1946 a local authority resolved to grant permission to develop certain land. The actual grant of the planning permission itself was governed by paragraph 12 of the Town and Country Planning (General Interim Development) Order 1946, which provided that "the grant or refusal ... of permission to develop land shall be in writing."

Despite the provisions of the 1946 Order, however, there was no record that any written permission had ever actually been issued. Nevertheless, until 1984 everybody concerned with the land proceeded on the basis that permission to develop the land had been granted. Then the defendant council, which had become the local planning authority, argued that the absence of any record of the grant of written permission meant that, as a matter of law, there was no such permission.

On an application for a declaration that planning permission existed, the case was put on two bases. First, in the absence of any document granting planning permission, had it been proved that there was such a document which had since been lost? Secondly, and in the alternative, was the defendant council estopped by its conduct and representations from denying the existence of the permission.

Granting the application in relation to the existence of the permission, Sir Nicolas Browne-Wilkinson V-C started from the proposition that the burden of proof was on the plaintiff company. He then went on to say that, even on the balance of probabilities, the company could not discharge this burden merely by showing that for almost 40 years everybody concerned with the land had assumed that the permission existed, because this assumption had been based on the existence of the resolution to grant permission, rather than on a considered response to the question of whether any written permission had been issued.

Secondly, however, Sir Nicolas said that the absence of evidence to show that written permission had been issued did not necessarily mean that, on the evidence, it was possible to conclude that such permission had *not* been issued. Extricating himself from this apparent evidential impasse, Sir Nicolas then turned to the presumption of regularity, according to which he held that the company succeeded. The essential point was that in 1946 the local authority had had a statutory duty to issue written permission once it had passed the resolution. In the absence of evidence to show that there had been a breach of that statutory duty, the court would assume that the duty had been performed and that accordingly the written planning permission had been issued.

In these circumstances it was not necessary to determine the estoppel point.

Some statutes contain provisions which amount to express enactments of the presumption of legality. For example, s.234(2) of the Local Government Act 1972 provides:

"Any document purporting to bear the signature of the proper officer of the authority shall be deemed, until the contrary is proved, to have been duly given made or issued by the authority of the local authority. In this subsection the word 'signature' includes a facsimile of a signature by whatever process reproduced."

Bearing in mind the emphasiz which the courts place on successful challenge to an *ultra vires* act, it is worth noticing that an applicant for judicial review must overcome various procedural obstacles before he can succeed, and even then all the remedies are discretionary. These matters are pursued in more detail in chapter 3, but it must be emphasized at this stage that, where potential challengers are unable to surmount all the obstacles, the consequence will be that *ultra vires* acts will continue to have practical effects.

2. Further Aspects of Voidness

The fact that it is simplistic to speak of voidness in connexion with *ultra vires* acts can also be illustrated in a number of other ways.

First, the court may - and routinely does - quash a void act, without being troubled by the apparent illogicality of quashing something which, according to the strict view of nullity, the law does not even recognize as existing.

Secondly, there may be an appeal against a void decision. In *Calvin v. Carr* (1979), the plaintiff was part-owner of a horse. He was disciplined by stewards of the Australian Jockey Club and disqualified for one year from running horses and belonging to the Club.

His appeal to the committee of the Club failed. On appeal to the Judicial Committee of the Privy Council, it was held that there had been a breach of natural justice by the stewards, but that this had been 'cured' by the appeal to the Committee. Clearly, therefore, the original decision cannot have been wholly non-existent, otherwise there would have been nothing to be "cured". Lord Wilberforce said:

"Their Lordships' opinion would be, if it became necessary to fix on one or other of those expressions [void or voidable] that a decision made contrary to natural justice is void but that until it is so declared by a competent body or court, it may have some effect or existence in law. This condition may be better expressed by saying that the decision is invalid or vitiated. In the present context, where the question is whether an appeal lies, the impugned decision cannot be considered as totally void, in the sense of being legally non-existent. So to hold would be wholly unreal. The decision of the stewards resulted in disqualification, an effect with serious and immediate consequences ... The consequences remained in effect unless and until the stewards' decision was challenged and, if so, had sufficient existence in law to justify an appeal."

Thirdly, although voidness sounds like an absolute concept, in reality it may be relative. In *Agricultural, Horticultural, and Forestry Industry Training Board v. Aylesbury Mushrooms Ltd.* (1972) the Minister of Labour was setting up the Industry Training Board, which would raise money from employers through a levy system in order to provide training schemes. He should have consulted the Mushroom Growers' Association, but did not do so. The court held that the decision to create the Board was void as against the Mushroom Growers Association, with the result that their members did not have to pay the levy. However, as against the whole of the rest of the industry, the creation of the Board and its levying activities were effective.

In cases such as *Aylesbury Mushrooms* it might be useful to think in terms of the principles relating to severability, which are discussed further at pp.38-40. At this stage, it is simply worth noticing that in *Director of Public Prosecutions v. Hutchinson and Smith* (1990), Lord Bridge, speaking of *Aylesbury Mushrooms*, said:

"The text was not severable but the issue of severance was not canvassed in argument and I cannot help thinking that the outcome might have been different if it had been."

D: Classifying *UltraVires* Acts
Traditionally, a distinction has been drawn between *substantive ultra vires* and *procedural ultra vires*. In the case of the former, voidness has been the inevitable consequence, whereas in the case of the latter there has been some variation of consequence, according to the circumstances of the case. This classification must now be considered.

1. Substantive Ultra Vires
Substantive *ultra vires* is said to occur where the decision-maker purports to do something which he simply has no legal power to do, or in other words where there is no substance in his action. A classic situation would be where the decision-maker misadvises himself as to the extent of his legal powers, and then proceeds to act on the basis of this misunderstanding. The most frequently encountered allegations of substantive *ultra vires* involve failure to have regard to the right considerations, or acting totally unreasonably (see, further, chapter 6).

2. Procedural Ultra Vires
Procedural *ultra vires* is said to occur where the decision-maker fails to follow a procedure laid down by statute. Typical examples are failure on

the part of the decision-maker to give reasons for a decision in breach of an obligation to do so, and failure to consult someone else before he makes his decision when required to do so. (These topics are discussed in chapters 8 and 9 respectively .)

Some procedural requirements are said to be *mandatory* (or *imperative*), with the result that non-compliance will result in voidness. Others are said to be merely directory, with the result that non-compliance will not result in *voidness*. Unfortunately, classifying specific requirements in individual cases is not always straightforward.

Traditionally the leading case is *Howard v. Bodington* (1877) where Lord Penzance said:

> "In each case you must look to the subject matter; consider the importance of the provision that has been disregarded, and the relation of that provision to the general object intended to be secured by the Act ..."

More recently, however, the existence of the two categories, as such, has been doubted. In *London & Clydeside Estates Ltd. v. Aberdeen District Council* (1979) the local authority issued a certificate of appropriate alternative development, which did not comply with the statutory requirement that it should contain a statement of the applicant's rights of appeal. When the applicant did try to appeal he was out of time, and the Secretary of State refused to entertain the appeal. When the matter came before the court, the omission of the statement as to the rights of appeal was held to be fatal, with the result that the certificate was quashed. Lord Hailsham said:

> "[There is a] spectrum [at one end of which] there may be cases in which a fundamental obligation may have been ... outrageously and flagrantly ignored or defied ... At the other end ... the defect ... may be ... nugatory or trivial."

The classification of procedural requirements is further complicated by the possibility of a half-way house. As Wade puts it:

> "The same condition may be both mandatory and directory: mandatory as to substantial compliance, but directory as to precise compliance." (*Administrative Law*, 6th edition, 1988, p. 246).

In *Cullimore v. Lyme Regis Corporation* (1961) the local authority prepared a scheme of coastal protection works. The scheme indicated the land whose owners would have to contribute towards the cost. Statute provided for the amount of the contribution to be determined within six months of completion of the works. The amounts were not actually determined until twenty three months after completion. On the facts, the court held that the determinations were void, because the requirement was mandatory. However, even if it had been merely directory the local authority's argument that there had been substantial compliance could not be sustained in view of the extent of the delay.

From time to time even the Judges themselves express dissatisfaction with the traditional approach to classifying procedural requirements. In *R. v. Lambeth London Borough Council ex parte Sharp* (1987) a local planning authority wished to undertake development in a conservation area. The statutory procedure required the passing of a resolution saying that they were going to seek planning permission, followed by the giving of public notice of their intention. If, having received feedback from the public, the local planning authority still wished to proceed with the proposal, a second resolution was passed, the effect of which was that planning permission was deemed to have been granted by the Secretary of State for the Environment. The difficulty which arose in the present case was that although notices were displayed on the site in question, and published in a local newspaper, only the site notice was in the proper form. The newspaper notice did not specify the period within which objections were to be made to the local planning authority, with the result that it could be argued that this period never closed.

Woolf L.J. commented that it was almost invariably unhelpful to classify procedural requirements by reference either to the mandatory-directory distinction, or to whether they contained a provision which rendered a decision void or voidable, or to whether they contained a provision which went to jurisdiction. (See chapter 7 for a discussion of the doctrine of Jurisdictional Error). Jettisoning all these traditional angles, the judge substituted a simple two-stage approach.

First, what was the particular provision designed to achieve? In the present case, the object was clearly the opportunity to make objections, and equally clearly this requirement was of sufficient importance to justify the court giving considerable weight to any failure to comply with the requirement. But, on its own, this was not enough to dispose of the case, because the second stage was to look at the broader context surrounding the non-compliance. Here, Woolf L.J. quoted with approval the words of Parker L.J. in *Main v. Swansea City Council* (1984):

"The court must consider the consequences in the light of a concrete state of facts and a continuing chain of events. This recognizes that the court looks not only at the nature of the failure but also at such matters as the identity of the applicant for relief, the lapse of time, the effect on other parties and on the public and so on."

In other words, even where there has been a breach resulting in substantial prejudice to the applicant, there may be other supervening considerations which make it inappropriate for the court to grant a remedy.

Applying these principles in the present case, Woolf L.J. concluded that the non-compliance was fundamental, and that therefore, since there was no reason to withhold a remedy, the defect was fatal. It is worth noting that Woolf L.J. specifically acknowledged that his approach did not avoid uncertainty in individual cases, but he did point out that the more traditional approaches did not do so either, merely sounding more precise than they really were.

3. The Validity of the Substantive-Procedural Distinction

When regard is had to the fact that the concept of voidness in Administrative Law is by no means capable of being equated with simple nullity in the sense of legal non-existence, it is difficult to justify any classification of *ultra vires* acts on the basis that their consequences vary. Additionally, it can be argued that the distinction rests on some dubious conceptualizing.

The whole concept of judicial review deals with the legality of decision-making *processes*, rather than with the merits of *substantive outcomes*. Therefore, at a conceptual level, it is difficult to see why, for example, a decision which results from the decision-maker asking himself the wrong question, and therefore having regard to the wrong considerations, should be classified differently from, for example, a decision which results from the decision-maker asking somebody else the wrong question, and therefore failing to comply adequately with an obligation to consult.

It follows that any classification which depends on the void-valid distinction is likely to create at least as many problems as it solves. For this reason, the analysis presented in this book will proceed according to the most common heads of challenge, rather than to the Procrustean bed of the substantive-procedural distinction.

E: Identifying Statutory Powers

1. Generally

Since the doctrine of *ultra vires* is concerned with confining decision-makers within the limits of their powers, it is obviously a matter of the first importance to be able to identify what those powers are in any given situation.

At the most general level it may be said that the identification of powers will consist of an exercise in statutory interpretation.

However, some more detailed comment than this is clearly appropriate.

2. The "Reasonably Incidental" Principle

The classic statement of this common law principle is to be found in *Attorney-General v. Great Eastern Railway* (1880), where Lord Selborne said:

> "The doctrine [*sc.* of *ultra vires*] ought to be reasonably understood and applied and whatever may fairly be regarded as *incidental to* or *consequential upon* those things [which are authorized] ought not (unless expressly prohibited) to be held by judicial construction to be *ultra vires*." (Emphasis added.)

The case of *Webb v. O'Doherty* (1991) may be taken as an example of the principle in operation. The issue was whether or not a students' union could lawfully spend money in support of a campaign against the Gulf war. The High Court held that although there is no reason why an educational charity should not encourage students to develop political awareness and form views on political issues, it is nevertheless clear that conducting a political campaign is not a charitable activity. Furthermore, a charitable students' organization is entitled to affiliate to another body which is not itself a charity, if and only if, the purpose of the affiliation is to benefit members of the student body in their capacity as students. Therefore a students' union could not lawfully spend money in support of a campaign against the Gulf war, nor affiliate to other organisations carrying on such a campaign.

In the context of local government law the "reasonably incidental" principle has received statutory blessing in the form of s.111(1) of the Local Government Act 1972:

> "A local authority shall have power to do anything ... which is calculated to facilitate, or is conducive or incidental to, the discharge of any of their functions."

In *Attorney-General v. Smethwick Corporation* (1932) a local authority was held to be acting lawfully in establishing a stationery and book-binding works which was ancillary to its lawful activities of printing their own Committee agendas, minutes and reports, and re-binding damaged library books. It would, however, not have been lawful to have operated a commercial, trading enterprise.

On the other hand in *Attorney-General v. Fulham Corporation* (1921) a local authority had power to establish municipal wash-houses. This power dated from the time when very few working-class houses had running water. The local authority was held to be acting *ultra vires* when it extended the service by employing people actually to do the washing for the customers, and offered a collection and delivery service as well, thus providing a full-blown laundry service.

The case of *Attorney-General v. Crayford Corporation* (1962) is also not without interest. Under the Housing legislation, the local authority had a general power of management of its housing stock. The authority offered its tenants a new service, whereby the authority would arrange insurance cover for the tenants' household effects, and the premium could be collected along with the rent. One attraction of this was that the authority would receive commission from its insurance company, which would go into the public coffers.

On the question of whether the insurance service was *ultra vires*, the High Court decided in favour of the authority. The reasoning was that council tenants who suffer uninsured losses of their household effects are unlikely to have the financial resources to meet the loss without falling behind with their rent, and it is never in any landlord's interests for his tenants to fall behind with the rent. Therefore a scheme which encourages tenants to take out appropriate insurance cover is part and parcel of good management of the housing stock.

In *R. v. Richmond-upon-Thames London Borough Council ex parte McCarthy & Stone (Developments) Ltd.* (1991) the House of Lords held that although a local planning authority had no specific power or duty to provide advice to potential applicants for planning permission, s.111(1) of the 1972 Act gave implied power to do so. However, the imposition of the charge for that advice was not within s.111, because charging was not in itself calculated to facilitate, nor was it conducive nor incidental to, the discharge of the authority's functions.

The case of *Fitzpatrick v. Secretary of State for the Environment and Epping Forest District Council* (1990) involved the issue of an enforcement notice requiring compliance with the provisions of the Town and Country Planning Act. The Court of Appeal held that s.111 of the 1972 Act enables subordinate officers to be authorized to undertake administrative tasks, including the preparation of documents such as enforcement notices, on behalf of chief officers.

In *Hazell and Others v. Hammersmith and Fulham London Borough Council* (1991) the operation of s.111 came before the courts in the context of a dispute over the legality of local authority interest rate swap transactions. The local authority was incorporated by Royal Charter under s. 1(2) of the London Government Act 1963. It entered into a number of speculative financial transactions, the profitability of which depended on whether interest rates rose or fell. The transactions were conducted through a fund which was initially created by the local authority's officers without specific authorization to do so from the local authority, although such authorization was subsequently obtained.

When the District Auditor questioned the legality of the transactions, the local authority embarked on an interim strategy whereby it closed all the outstanding transactions except those where closure would cause loss to the local authority. The local authority obtained counsel's opinion to the effect that the transactions were *ultra vires*. Thereafter the only transactions which were entered into were the result of other parties exercising options.

Acting under s.19 of the Local Government Finance Act 1982, the auditor applied to the High Court for a declaration that the transactions were contrary to law and for an order for rectification of the accounts. The High Court granted both applications. The Court of Appeal agreed that the early transactions were unlawful, but upheld the legality of the transactions which were part of the interim strategy, and refused to grant an order for rectification.

On further appeal, the House of Lords restored both the declaration and the order for rectification. The House held that the Royal Charter under which the local authority had been incorporated had been granted under statutory powers, therefore the local authority could not rely on the normal presumption according to which chartered corporations possess the same contractual powers as natural persons. Furthermore, there was no express statutory authority to enter into the financial transactions, therefore in order to succeed the local authority would have to establish that the transactions were calculated to facilitate, or were conducive or incidental to, the discharge of its function of borrowing money, under s.111 of the Local Government Act 1972.

The House began this stage of the judgment by saying:

"In s.111 the word 'functions' embraces all the duties and powers of a local authority; the sum total of the activities Parliament has entrusted to it."

Nevertheless, having considered some of the more recondite areas of the legal regulation of local government finance, the House concluded that debt management was not itself a function within the meaning of s.111, and that rate swap transactions were not calculated to facilitate, nor were they conducive or incidental to, the discharge of any of the authority's functions.

Finally, the activities falling within the interim strategy could be said to be lawful only if they were calculated to facilitate, or were conducive or incidental to, the discharge of the function of borrowing money, and since the original transactions did not come within this function, it followed that the interim strategy transactions were also *ultra vires*.

In *North Tyneside Metropolitan Borough Council v. Allsop* (1992), The Court of Appeal held that the s.111 power does not extend to enabling local authorities to make enhanced severance payments to their staff over and above the sums which are specifically authorized by the relevant regulations.

2. Section 137, Local Government Act 1972

There is a long-running debate over whether local authorities should be subject to the doctrine of *ultra vires*. Some commentators argue that electoral control is sufficiently rigorous to render legal control superfluous. Others are less confident. Whatever the position ought to be, the present statutory position represents a rather uneasy compromise. Section 137(1) of the Local Government Act 1972, in its original form, said:

> "A local authority may ... incur expenditure which in their opinion is in the interests of their area or any part of it or all or some of its inhabitants ... "

provided that the amount involved in any one year did not exceed the product of a 2p rate.

The case of *Lobenstein v. Hackney London Borough Council* (1980) is a useful starting point. The background to the case was that Britain had officially boycotted the Moscow Olympics. This meant that the 'British' team was officially representing the British Olympic Association, rather than the country as such. It also meant that no government money was available to defray the team's costs. Much fund-raising took place, and Hackney London Borough Council agreed to donate £1,000. At the time of this decision it was not known whether any Hackney residents would be in the team. If they were, s.137 would clearly have been satisfied because the expenditure would have been for the benefit of some of the inhabitants.

The High Court held that the inclusion or exclusion of Hackney residents was immaterial. The expenditure was within s.137 anyway, because "civic pride" is a matter within the scope of the interests of an area.

The current form of s.137 represents amendments made by the Second Schedule to the Local Government and Housing Act 1989. Some amendment was necessitated by the replacement of domestic rates by the community charge, but the opportunity was taken to introduce other changes which effectively restrict the power conferred by the section.

The amended version of s.137 gives a local authority power to spend a limited amount of money each year on anything which, in its opinion, is in the interests of, *and will bring direct benefit to*, the whole or any part of its area, or to some or all of the inhabitants of its area.

The limit on the amount of money which can be spent under s.137 varies according to the type and population of the local authority involved. In each case the annual limit is calculated by multiplying a specified amount of money by the "relevant population of the authority's area".

The specified amount of money is £5.00 for the councils of metropolitan districts and London borough councils; £3.50 for the councils of parishes and their Welsh counterparts, namely communities; and £2.50 for the councils of counties and non-metropolitan districts. In the case of local authorities which are constituent councils for the purposes of a scheme under s.48 of the Local Government Act 1985, dealing with grants to voluntary organizations, the sum is £4.75

The method of calculating the "relevant population of the authority's area" is determined by the Secretary of State, who may also make Orders varying the sums of money specified in the Act.

In all cases there are two important qualifications. First, s.137 does not apply where the local authority has any other statutory authorization to spend money for the purpose in question. Secondly, the direct benefit which accrues must be commensurate with the amount of money to be spent.

It is worth noticing that even the new version of s.137 contains nothing to alter the principle established in *Manchester City Council v. Greater Manchester Metropolitan County Council* (1980), where the facts were that the county council, which was not a local education authority, provided financial assistance to enable children to go to fee-paying schools, and thereby escape from the comprehensive system of education provided by the city council. This was held to be lawful. Broadening this out to the level of principle, it can be said that the fact that one local authority provides a particular service does not prevent another local authority, which lacks the power to provide that service, from using s.137 money for that purpose.

In *R. v. District Auditor for Leicester ex parte Leicester City Council* (1985) the High Court held that an appropriate percentage of the local authority's total expenditure on accommodation and other overheads must be apportioned to, and included in, s.137 expenditure.

CHAPTER 3

REMEDIES

A: Introduction
This chapter will deal with the remedies which are available by way of judicial review. The next two chapters will deal respectively with the closely related topics of the procedural requirements of an application for judicial review and the distinction between public and private law.

B: The Principal Judicial Remedies in Administrative Law
The principal remedies which are exclusive to Administrative Law, and all of which are discretionary, are the prerogative orders of certiorari, prohibition, and mandamus.

Additionally, challengers in public law cases not infrequently seek the private law remedies of injunctions and declarations. Declarations merely declare what the law is, and unlike the other remedies, are not supported by any enforcement machinery. However, the kind of decision-makers to whom declarations are addressed in public law cases are unlikely to take advantage of their non-enforceability, so in reality declarations are an effective remedy.

Finally, Order 53, rule 7 of the Rules of the Supreme Court, permits a claim for damages to be made as part of an application for judicial review where the claim arises "from any matter to which the application relates".

C: The Scope of the Remedies

1. Certiorari
The history of certiorari has involved the drawing of a variety of technical distinctions, but:

> "Certiorari today lies to quash any decision of a public law body exercising public law powers" (Lewis, *Judicial Remedies in Public Law*, 1992, p.145).

The only remaining significant restriction on the availability of certiorari is that it is not available against the superior courts. The additional proposition that certiorari is not available against the Crown is of little practical significance since it clearly is available against Ministers of the Crown exercising powers vested in them, whether derived from statute or from the Royal Prerogative (see *GCHQ* (1984), discussed further at p.182). As Lewis points out (*op. cit.*, p.151), instances of the exercise of power vested in the Crown itself, such as the appointment of a Prime Minister in a hung Parliament, are likely to be non-justiciable anyway.

Where certiorari is sought, O.53, r.3(10)(a) provides that the court may grant interim relief in the form of a stay of proceedings. The meaning of "stay of proceedings" is unclear.

In *Minister of Foreign Affairs, Trade and Industry v. Vehicle and Supplies Ltd. and Another* (1991) the Privy Council indicated, by way of an *obiter dictum*, that a "stay of proceedings" is "an order which puts a stop to further proceedings in court or before a tribunal" and that it does not extend to preventing a Minister's exercise of a statutory discretion. On the other hand, in *R. v. Secretary of State for Education and Science ex parte Avon County Council* (1991), the Court of Appeal gave the phrase an extended meaning, to include any decision-making process in public law.

2. Prohibition

Prohibition is used to prevent a public body from acting unlawfully. The practical utility of this remedy is obviously limited to those relatively rare cases where challengers have prior knowledge of intended unlawfulness. In other cases, challengers will have to be satisfied with certiorari in order to quash decisions on an *ex post facto* basis. However, at the level of principle, the foregoing comments on certiorari are equally applicable to prohibition.

Additionally, there is the possibility of a conditional order, sometimes known as *prohibition quousque*, which restrains the future exercise of power until some existing unlawfulness has been remedied, as illustrated by *Re Liverpool Taxi Owners' Association* (1972), which is discussed more fully at p.189, in the context of the doctrine of legitimate expectation.

3. Mandamus

Mandamus is used to compel the performance of a public duty. The position in relation to the availability of mandamus against the Crown appears to be less clear-cut than in the cases of certiorari and prohibition (Lewis, *op. cit.*, pp. 169-170), but this is of no real practical significance, since a declaration is likely to produce the same result as mandamus. Order 53 makes no provision for interim relief by way of mandamus, but an interlocutory mandatory injunction may be available.

In *R. v. Hillingdon London Borough Council ex parte Tinn* (1988) the High Court held that mandamus was not appropriate to compel a local authority to re-purchase a property which it had previously sold to a sitting tenant, since the local authority should be free to decide for itself how to allocate its financial resources

4. Declaration

Declaratory relief is available on a very wide basis, provided, of course, that the subject-matter is justiciable. According to Woolf L.J. in *R. v. Secretary of State for Social Services ex parte Child Poverty Action Group and Others* (1989) declarations will be available wherever a real issue arises between parties who have a genuine interest in contesting the issue, and where there is a need for some relief to be granted. In *R. v. Bromley London Borough Council ex parte C and Others* (1992) the High Court concluded that the local authority's schools admissions policy was unlawful, although in view of the extent to which it had already been implemented, and the consequential chaos which would flow from quashing the policy, the court did no more than grant a declaration.

Where application is made for a declaration that certain conduct would or would not constitute a criminal offence, the court will almost always be influenced by whether or not criminal proceedings have already been instituted. In *Imperial Tobacco Ltd. v. Attorney-General* (1980), Lord Lane, with the agreement of Lords Edmund-Davies and Scarman, held that it would not be appropriate to grant a declaration where

"criminal proceedings have been properly instituted and are not vexatious or an abuse of the process of the court."

On the other hand, where criminal proceedings have not been instituted, the courts have been prepared to entertain applications for declarations as to the criminality of certain conduct in relation to abortion (*Royal College of Nursing v. Department of Health and Social Security* (1981)), the provision of contraceptive advice to girls under the age of 16 (*Gillick v. West Norfolk and Wisbech Area Health Authority* (1985)), and the distribution of a booklet containing practical advice on how to commit suicide (*Attorney-General v. Able* (1984)).

Declarations can be granted even in respect of powers vested in the Crown itself, provided of course that the subject-matter is justiciable. However, the Supreme Court Act 1981 does not bind the Crown (*R. v. Secretary of State for the Home Department ex parte Herbage* (1987)), and therefore the correct procedure would be by way of an ordinary action. Ministerial action under powers derived from statute are, of course, subject to declaratory relief obtained through the judicial review procedure in the ordinary way.

The established constitutional doctrine that the courts cannot invalidate a statute is now subject to the overriding doctrine of the supremacy of European Community law. Accordingly, a declaration that a statute is incompatible with Community law, and therefore ineffective, is now possible (*R. v. Secretary of State for Transport ex parte Factortame Ltd. (No.2)* (1991)).

Finally, it should be noted that "no interim declaration exists in English law" (Lewis, *op. cit.*, p.194).

5. Injunction

The origins of injunctive relief lie in the equitable jurisdiction of the courts. Injunctions are not available against the Crown, nor against officers of the Crown acting in their official capacity (*Factortame (No.2)* (1991)).

In private law contexts interim relief is commonly available by means of interlocutory injunctions, according to the principles established in *American Cyanamid Co. v. Ethicon Ltd.* (1975). Briefly, these principles are that there must be a real possibility that the plaintiff will succeed in the full action; the balance of convenience must favour interlocutory relief, or in other words, damages must be an inadequate remedy at the final disposal of the case, if the plaintiff wins at that stage; in finely balanced cases the court should preserve the *status quo*; regard will be had to the relative strength of the parties' cases; and any special factors must be considered. In *Cayne v. Global Natural Resources plc* (1984) May L.J. preferred to speak of "the balance of the risk of doing injustice" rather than "the balance of convenience".

Generally, therefore, a large element within the test of the balance of convenience depends on what will be the relative financial losses which each of the parties would suffer in the long term if interlocutory relief were alternatively granted or withheld. In the context of public law, however, the courts recognize that the public interest constitutes a significant element within the balance of convenience, even though it will seldom be the case that the withholding of interlocutory relief will harm the public purse.

In *Sierbien v. Westminster City Council* (1987) Otton J. decided in favour of the local authority where the proprietor of a sex shop was seeking interlocutory relief to suspend a decision refusing him a sex shop licence. Even though the proprietor would have suffered financial loss if he was denied interlocutory relief but was successful at the final stage, the court held that the public interest in the control of sex shops was of greater importance.

At the interlocutory stage in private law cases it is routine for the court to require the successful party to give an undertaking to compensate the other party by way of damages for financial loss sustained in the interim period if the final outcome differs from the interlocutory outcome. However, the court has a discretion to dispense with undertakings in damages on the part of the Crown and local authorities when they are seeking injunctions to restrain breaches of the law which would be harmful to the public or a section of the public (see, *Kirklees Metropolitan Borough Council v. Wickes Building Supplies Ltd.* (1992)).

Furthermore, an interlocutory injunction should not be issued to restrain the enforcement of an apparently authentic law unless the court is satisfied in all the circumstances of the case that the challenge to the validity of the law appears to be so firmly based as to justify an exceptional course of action (see, again, *Factortame (No.2)* (1990)).

At one time it was said that injunctive relief to restrain breaches of the criminal law would be available where the respondent had deliberately and flagrantly flouted the law (see, e.g. *Stafford Borough Council v. Elkenford* (1977) and *Stoke-on-Trent City Council v. B. & Q. Ltd.* (1984)). Since the decision of the Court of Appeal in *City of London v. Bovis Construction Ltd.* (1989), however, it is apparent that the essential foundation of the exercise of the courts' discretion to grant injunctive relief is not simply deliberate and flagrant flouting of the law, but the drawing of the inference that the unlawful activity will continue unless and until it is effectively restrained by law, and that nothing short of an injunction will be effective to achieve this end.

6. Damages

Although O.53, r.7 permits a claim for damages to be made as part of an application for judicial review, it is important to notice that the rule is purely procedural, and does not create any substantive right to damages in respect of *ultra vires* acts. In other words, where there is an application for judicial review arising out of facts which also give rise to a claim in damages, the effect of the rule is limited to obviating the need to bring separate, parallel proceedings in respect of the claim in damages.

Where the court is satisfied that an application for judicial review is being made merely to prime the pump for a claim in damages, the proper course according to the Court of Appeal in *R. v. Blandford Justices ex parte Pamment* (1991) is for the court to exercise its discretion to refuse to deal with the application for judicial review, but to allow the claim in damages to proceed as if it had been begun by writ.

D: The Discretionary Nature of the Remedies

1. Introduction
Although conceptually the situation in which the court will withhold a remedy as a matter of discretion is quite distinct from the situation in which the court will conclude that Parliament has restricted or excluded the possibility of judicial review, the practical consequences are so similar that it is appropriate in this section and the next one to seek to summarize some of the major principles governing the exercise of discretion with regard to granting or withholding remedies, as well as the principles governing restriction and exclusion.

2. The Conduct of the Applicant
The most obvious instance where the conduct of the applicant will be held against him to the point of denying relief is where he has delayed in making his application. The principles governing delay are discussed at pp.50-54.

Similarly, the applicant bears a duty of disclosure, which is discussed at pp.48-49.

3. The Practical Consequences of Granting Relief
Cases under this heading tend to fall into two categories, namely those where there there is no longer a live issue requiring a practical solution, and those where granting a remedy would be detrimental to good administration.

Taking the category where there is no longer a live issue first, in *R. v. Inner London Education Authority ex parte Ali and Another* (1990) the High Court declined to continue with proceedings where the only purpose they could serve would be to ascertain whether or not the respondent was culpable, since this was said not to be the purpose of judicial review. However, in *Lovelace v. Greenwich London Borough Council* (1991) the Court of Appeal, following the principle enunciated by the House of Lords' decision in *Ainsbury v. Millington* (1987), allowed proceedings to continue when the only immediately practical outcome was an order as to costs.

Turning secondly to those cases where granting a remedy could be argued to be detrimental to good administration, it becomes apparent that judicial attitudes have not been altogether consistent.

In *R. v. Secretary of State for Social Services ex parte Association of Metropolitan Authorities* (1986) the Secretary of State had a statutory power to make Regulations governing the scheme of Housing Benefit, which was administered by local authorities. He was required to consult the local authorities' associations. In 1982, Regulations were made and in 1984 the Secretary of State wished to amend them.

On 16 November 1984 he wrote to the local authorities' associations asking for their comments by 30 November. The Association of Metropolitan Authorities did not receive the letter until 22 November when it immediately pointed out to the Secretary of State that the practicalities of its committee system meant that it would not be able to respond until 7 December.

Meanwhile, the Secretary of State proposed to make two further amendments to the Regulations. On 4 December he wrote to the Association, mentioning one of the further proposals but not enclosing a version of the amendment. He did not even mention the other proposed amendment at all. He required a response by 12 December. On 13 December, the Association responded, but said that its comments were hasty and ill-considered.

On 18 December the Secretary of State laid the amendments before Parliament and they came into force the following day.

On a challenge by the Association, the High Court held that the Association had been entitled to be consulted, and that the consultation must be genuine, which, on the facts it had not been. However, the court did acknowledge that, in principle, the need for urgency and the exercise of political judgment could result in a short period being allowed for consultation, although clearly even these factors could not justify a total removal of real consultation. In the event, however, the court declined to give the Association a remedy, partly because it was the only local authority association to complain, and partly because, by the time the case was heard, the amended Regulations were in force and were being implemented by local authorities nationwide.

In *R. v. Bromley London Borough Council ex parte C and Others* (1992), which is also discussed at p.33, the court contented itself with a declaration in circumstances where it thought quashing a decision would be unduly harmful.

On the other hand the case of *R. v. Gateshead Justices ex parte Tesco Stores Ltd.* (1981) is instructive by way of contrast. Section 1 of the Magistrates' Courts Act 1952, provided that when an information was laid, either a justice of the peace or a clerk to the justices could issue a summons. At the time of this case there was a widespread practice of delegating to members of the clerks' staff the decision as to whether or not to issue summonses, which involved deciding whether or not the facts alleged in the information disclosed an offence. Donaldson L.J., holding that this practice was unlawful, rejected the argument that the issue of a summons is a purely administrative, or even clerical, function:

> "The requirement that a justice of the peace or the clerk to the justices acting as a justice of the peace shall take personal responsibility for the propriety of taking so serious a step as to require the attendance of a citizen before a criminal court is a constitutional safeguard of fundamental importance."

Dealing with the argument that the practice of delegation was necessary in purely practical terms, and therefore must be taken to have been impliedly authorized, Donaldson L.J. said:

> "The short answer to this is that if the practice is unlawful, expedience will not make it lawful. *Fiat justitia, ruat coelum.*"

4. The Problem of Severability

It is not uncommon for decisions, like the curate's egg in the famous *Punch* cartoon, to be good in parts. Such decisions raise the question of whether the whole decision stands or falls together, or whether the bad parts can be excised and quashed, leaving the remainder valid and effective. The criterion according to which this question is answered is often, if not particularly lucidly, known as the *test of substantial severability*.

In *Director of Public Prosecutions v. Hutchinson & Smith* (1990) the Secretary of State for Defence had a statutory power to make byelaws regulating the use of land appropriated for military purposes, provided that the byelaws did not "take away or prejudicially affect any right of common." In purported exercise of that power, the Secretary of State made the R.A.F. Greenham Common Byelaws 1985, which, despite the statutory proviso, prejudicially affected rights of common.

A magistrates' court convicted the appellants of entering R.A.F. Greenham Common, contrary to one of the byelaws. Neither of the appellants had any rights of common, but the Crown Court allowed their appeals on the basis that the byelaw was *ultra vires*. The High Court allowed an appeal by the prosecutor, on the basis that where a byelaw is drawn more widely than permitted by its enabling Act, a defendant could still be convicted of an offence contrary to the byelaw, provided that the conduct alleged to constitute the offence would still have been criminal even if the byelaw had been properly drawn.

The House of Lords allowed appeals, holding that the test of substantial severability must be applied in all cases where a court is considering a legislative instrument which is bad in part, and is seeking to determine whether the bad part can be severed, with the balance remaining and being effective. Where straightforward textual severance is possible, the test of substantial severability will be satisfied if the valid text is unaffected by, and independent of, the invalid, because then the law which the court is upholding will be the same law which the legislator enacted and not a different law.

However, where straightforward textual severance is impossible, the court cannot modify the text in order to achieve severance unless the court is satisfied that it is making no change in the substantial purpose and effect of the impugned provision. More particularly, the court must not speculate as to what the legislator might have done if he had applied his mind to the relevant limitation on his powers, but must confine its consideration to the question of whether the omission of the invalid portions results in a legislative instrument which is substantially different from that which the legislator originally produced.

On the instant facts, the House concluded the byelaw could not be cured by severance, because byelaws which preserved the rights of common would be totally different in character from the byelaws which were actually made. In Lord Bridge's words:

"Considering the Greenham byelaws as a whole it is clear that the absolute prohibition which they impose on all unauthorized access ... is no less than is required to maintain the security of an establishment operated as a military airbase and wholly enclosed by a perimeter fence. Byelaws drawn in such a way as to permit free access to all parts of the base to persons exercising rights of common and their animals would be byelaws of a totally different character."

A common source of severability problems arises in the context of conditional decisions, where the substance of the decision is lawful, but the condition is not. The question which then arises is whether it is open to the court to quash the condition, and leave the substance of the decision standing, or must quashing the condition necessarily result in the whole decision being quashed? The answer lies in *Kent County Council v. Kingsway Investments Ltd.* (1970), where the House of Lords held that the crucial question is whether the condition is fundamental to the decision. In other words, would the substance of the decision have been the same even if the decision-maker had known that the condition would be quashed?

By way of comment, it must be said that in most cases the purpose of imposing the condition will be some restriction of the rights which the individual would otherwise enjoy, and therefore the courts are likely to assume that the decision-maker did regard the condition as being fundamental, since the alternative would be to assume that the decision-maker had been seeking to impose gratuitous restrictions on the rights of the individual.

5. *Where There Is An Alternative Remedy*

The existence of an alternative remedy is sometimes said to justify the exercise of discretion against granting judicial review, but on other occasions it is treated as a factor which excludes the possibility of judicial review altogether. The topic is dealt with further at pp.41-43.

E: Provisions Apparently Restricting and Excluding Judicial Review

1. *Introduction*

This section considers various forms of statutory wording which either restrict or exclude judicial review, or at least appear to do so.

2. *Total Ouster Clauses*

Respect for the rule of law comes to the forefront of the judicial mind where there are express statutory words which appear to exclude the jurisdiction of the courts to quash a decision. The courts consistently interpret such provisions as applying only to those decisions which are *intra vires.* The argument, which is based on the simple proposition that a decision which is *ultra vires* is by definition void and therefore, legally speaking, is not a decision at all, derives from the decision of *Anisminic v. Foreign Compensation Commission* (1969), and is discussed more fully in the context of jurisdictional errors of law in chapter 7.

At this stage, however, it is worth noticing that s.14 of the Tribunals and Inquiries Act 1971 provides:

> "Any provision in an Act of Parliament passed before 1st August 1958 that any order or determination shall not be called into question in any court, or any provision in such an Act which by similar words excludes any of the powers of the High Court, shall not have effect so as to prevent the removal of the proceedings into the High Court by order of certiorari or to prejudice the powers of the High Court to make orders of mandamus."

3. *Time Limited Ouster Clauses*

A remedy in the High Court, by way of either an appeal on a point of law or a statutory application to quash, is often subject to a strict time limit. In statutes relating to land use matters this limit is typically as short as six weeks. Despite the apparently parallel logic with the *Anisminic* situation, which would require the courts to refuse to give effect to such clauses where decisions are being challenged on the basis that they have no legal existence, the courts have consistently confined themselves to enforcing such time limits strictly, and have refused to pursue the more aggressive line. The leading cases are *Smith v. East Elloe Rural District Council* (1956), *R. v. Secretary of State for the Environment ex parte Ostler* (1976), and *R. v. Secretary of State for the Environment ex parte Kent and Others* (1990).

In *Ostler* Lord Denning M.R. was particularly influenced by the consideration that void decisions do not bear the mark of their voidness until the court has so branded them, and the expiry of the appropriate time limit operates to prevent the court from embarking on the process which could have this result. However, as a matter of logic, precisely the same objection can be, but is not, raised to *Anisminic* itself.

Perhaps all that can be said by way of justifying the distinction which the courts draw between total ouster clauses and time limited ouster clauses is that the former strike at the basis of the rule of law, whereas the latter are merely examples of the general notion of limitation periods, which are so deeply ingrained in the legal system that the courts feel at ease with them.

4. Where There Is An Alternative Remedy

The existence of an alternative remedy is often said to exclude judicial review. As Lord Widgery, C.J. said in the case of *R. v. Peterkin ex parte Soni* (1972):

"Where Parliament has provided a form of appeal which is equally convenient in the sense that the appellate tribunal can deal with the injustice of which the applicant complains, this court should in my judgment as a rule allow the appellate machinery to take its course. The prerogative orders form the general residual jurisdiction of this court whereby the court supervizes the work of inferior tribunals and seeks to correct injustice where no other adequate remedy exists, but both authority and commonsense seem to me to demand that the court should not allow its jurisdiction under the prerogative orders to be used merely as an alternative form of appeal [*sic*] when other and adequate jurisdiction exists elsewhere."

Using the language of discretion (cf. p.36-38) in *R. v. Birmingham City*

Council ex parte Ferrero Ltd. (1991) Taylor L.J. said:

> "Where there is an alternative remedy, and especially where Parliament has provided a statutory appeal procedure, it is only exceptionally that judicial review should be granted. It is therefore necessary, where the exception is invoked, to look carefully at the suitability of the statutory appeal in the context of the particular case."

On the facts the Court of Appeal held that the statutory appeal procedure was geared exactly to deciding the issue in question, which was whether or not a plastic toy contained in a chocolate egg constituted a danger to children.

R. v. Poole Justices ex parte Benham (1992) is merely one of many cases where the High Court has preferred an appeal by way of case stated from a magistrates' court to an application for judicial review, because the case stated will set out the facts found by the magistrates.

On the other hand *R. v. Hillingdon London Borough Council ex parte Royco Homes Ltd.* (1974) provides a useful illustration of a common situation in which an alternative remedy may be held to be sufficiently inadequate to justify recourse to certiorari. The question was whether the company, which wished to challenge a planning decision, could proceed directly to the court, or whether it must first pursue an appeal to the Secretary of State, from whose decisions there was a statutory right of appeal. The court held that direct access to the courts was permissible in cases such as this, notwithstanding the alternative remedy, provided that the ground of challenge was simply an issue of law. In other cases, however, such as those where issues of fact, law and planning policy are all intertwined, the statutory avenue to the Secretary of State would be more appropriate, because this would enable all the issues arising out of the whole of the case to be considered together, whereas the court would be restricted to considering the legal issues in isolation.

The presumption that the existence of an alternative remedy excludes recourse to judicial review becomes irrebuttable in those cases where both the alternative remedy, and the right which it enforces, are created simultaneously. The classic case is *Barraclough v. Brown* (1897).

The undertakers who were responsible for a waterway had a statutory power to remove any boat which sank, and to sell it. If the proceeds of sale were less than the cost of removal, the same statute gave the undertakers a specific power to recover the balance in the Magistrates' Court. In the instant case the undertakers wanted to recover £3,000. This sum being very substantially more than those which normally came within the jurisdiction of the magistrates, the undertakers brought the action in the

High Court. The court held that the only remedy was in the Magistrates' Court, because the power to remove and sell the wreck, and the power to recover the cost, were both given by the same Act. It followed that undertakers seeking to avail themselves of the power of recovery must do so in accordance with the Act.

The principle in *Barraclough* must be applied strictly, however. More particularly, the contrast with *Pyx Granite v. Minister of Housing and Local Government* (1959) is instructive. The company claimed the right to quarry in the Malvern Hills under a private Act of Parliament passed in 1924. The statutory scheme of planning control introduced by the Town and Country Planning Act 1947 not only defined those situations which would constitute "development" needing planning permission, but also provided administrative machinery for doubtful cases, whereby local planning authorities could issue determinations as to whether specific proposals would constitute development. The question arose as to whether the company required planning permission, or whether they could rely on their rights under the 1924 Act rights.

The House of Lords distinguished *Barraclough* on the basis that in the instant case the right which the company was seeking to enforce existed independently of, rather than having been conferred by, the Act which provided the specific remedy. It followed that the courts could determine the question of whether their proposals constituted development, and that the company was not restricted to the machinery provided by the 1947 Act.

5. Finality Clauses

It is clear that a statutory provision to the effect that the outcome of the decision-making process shall be "final" will merely operate in relation to the facts, and will not be effective to oust the jurisdiction of the courts in respect of matters of law.

In *Re Gilmore's Application* (1957) the relevant statute provided that the decision of a medical appeal tribunal was final. Gilmore having previously lost the sight of one eye, lost the other eye in an industrial accident. The medical appeal tribunal disregarded the fact that he had had only one eye immediately before the accident, and assessed his disability at 20%. On a proper construction of the relevant regulations, it should have been 100%. The court granted Gilmore certiorari to quash the decision, on the basis that certiorari is to be taken away only by plain words, and here Parliament must have given the tribunal the privilege of finality on condition that it complied with the law. It is not in the public interest that inferior tribunals of any kind should be entitled to come to final decisions on questions of law.

6. Matters Relating to Trials on Indictment

Although s.29(3) of the Supreme Court Act 1981 excludes "matters relating to trials on indictment" from the scope of the prerogative orders, the precise scope of the exclusion is not clear. It has been held to apply to an order authorizing the vetting of a jury panel (see *R. v. Sheffield Crown Court ex parte Brownlow* (1980)), but not to a decision as to whether or not to stay an indictment, because such a decision determines whether or not a trial takes place, rather than relating to the conduct of the trial itself (see *R. v. Central Criminal Court ex parte Randle and Pottle* (1991)). A decision to grant an application for leave to prefer a voluntary bill of indictment is not subject to judicial review, but the rationale for this depends on the fact that the decision-maker in such cases is a High Court judge, rather than on s.29(3) of the 1981 Act, which, by analogy with Randle and Pottle, would not itself appear to present any obstacle (see *R. v. Manchester Crown Court ex parte Williams and Simpson* (1990)).

7. "As If Enacted" Clauses

At one time the practice of Parliamentary counsel was to say that the provisions of delegated legislation made under an Act "shall take effect as if enacted in this Act". This clearly raised the constitutional question of whether such delegated legislation became unchallengeable by virtue of the doctrine of the legislative supremacy of Parliament.

In *Institute of Patent Agents v. Lockwood* (1894) the Board of Trade had statutory power to make such rules "as they think expedient", and the rules were stated to have effect as if enacted by Parliament. The Board made rules relating to the registration of patent agents, and included provision for the payment of an annual fee by those who wished their registration to continue. People who were not registered could not call themselves patent agents.

Lockwood, who was registered, refused to pay the annual fee, arguing that if Parliament had meant to authorize the raising of taxation, it would have said so explicitly. When his registration was cancelled, he continued to call himself a patent agent, whereupon the institute brought the instant proceedings. The House of Lords held that the wording of the Act was clear, and that if it did not mean what it appeared to mean, it could not mean anything at all.

The legality, as opposed to the constitutional desirability, of Lockwood may be unexceptionable, but there remains the problem of those situations where there is inconsistency between the delegated legislation and the Act. The authorities on this point are not clear.

In *R. v. Minister of Health ex parte Davis* (1929) the statutory definition of an "improvement scheme" was "a scheme for the re-arrangement and reconstruction of the streets and houses in the area." Such schemes were made by local authorities but were subject to Ministerial confirmation. A scheme was presented for confirmation which gave the corporation of Derby power to clear an area of land, and then to sell, lease or otherwise dispose of the land.

The Court of Appeal upheld Davis' objection that this was not an improvement scheme within the meaning of the Act, and that therefore it should not be confirmed. The court was strongly influenced by the fact that if the confirmation was allowed to occur, the court would become powerless to do anything about it, because the scheme would then have effect as if it had been enacted in the Act, and concluded therefore that the proper course was to grant prohibition to prevent its confirmation.

As in *Lockwood,* the actual decision in *Davis* may be legally unexceptionable, but the dictum about the unchallengeability of a confirmed scheme was disapproved by the House of Lords in *Minister of Health v. R. ex parte Yaffe* (1931). In *Yaffe* the facts were basically similar to those in *Davis,* except that the scheme had already been confirmed. However, prior to confirmation, the Minister had deleted the offending provisions, so the scheme as confirmed was actually valid. Although it followed that there was nothing the House of Lords wanted to do about the scheme anyway, they did say, albeit *obiter,* that if the scheme had been confirmed in its original and defective form, it would not have been valid, because it would have been inconsistent with the Act, and therefore the Act itself would have had to prevail.

Fortunately, the practical consequences of the uncertainty on the authorities are only slight, since it is no longer the practice of Parliamentary counsel to use the "as if enacted" formula. However, the matter is not wholly academic, since some old examples, such as s.2(4) of the Emergency Powers Act 1920, are still in force.

CHAPTER 4

PROCEDURE

A: Introduction

In 1976 the Law Commission published a *Report on Remedies in Administrative Law,* making certain comments on the judicial remedies, and drawing attention to various inconsistencies between them. The fundamental recommendation of the report was:

> "There should be a form of procedure to be entitled an 'application for judicial review'. Under cover of the application for judicial review, a litigant should be able to obtain any of the prerogative orders, or, in appropriate circumstances, a declaration or injunction. The litigant would have to specify in his application ... which particular remedy or remedies he was seeking, but if he later desired to apply for a remedy for which he had not initially asked, he would be able, with leave of the court, to amend his application."

Although the report is now largely a matter of legal history, it formed the basis of the revision of O.53 which was introduced in 1977, taking effect from the beginning of 1978. Some doubts subsequently arose as to the efficacy of the new form of O.53, since it is in the nature of the Rules of the Supreme Court that they can deal only with matters of procedure, whereas it could be argued that some of the amendments to O.53 purport to deal with matters of substance. In an attempt to cover this point, s.31 of the Supreme Court Act 1981 was enacted. Section 31 is in substantially the same form as O.53, although the detailed differences in relation to time limits have caused some difficulty (see the case of *Caswell,* discussed fully at pp. 50-52): both are reproduced at pp.221 *et seq.*

Order 53 provides that the applications for certiorari, prohibition and mandamus *shall* be made by way of application for judicial review, and that applications for injunctions and declaration may be so made. Following the House of Lords' decision in *O'Reilly v. Mackman* (1982), a substantial body of law has developed around this apparently simple proposition (see chapter 5 for a full discussion). At this stage, however, it is appropriate to consider the main procedural aspects of applications for judicial review.

The procedural essence of judicial review is that it contains three elements which are intended to protect decision-makers against a plethora of challenges. These protective elements are the *need for leave to apply* to make an application; the imposition of a *short time limit* within which application must be made; and the need for *locus standi*. These will now be discussed in turn.

B: Applications for Leave to Apply

The need for leave to apply for judicial review must be contrasted with the position in relation to ordinary actions commenced by writ or summons, where the onus is on the defendant to apply for the action to be struck out if he feels that it is vexatious or frivolous, or that no cause of action exists.

The initial application for leave will be made *ex parte*, and will usually be dealt with as a paper application based on appropriate affidavit evidence presented by the applicant, but the applicant may request a hearing (see, O.53(2) and (3)). Where the court adjourns an application to enable the respondent to appear, the respondent should brief counsel fully, in order to help the court clarify the issues. However, at that stage a respondent should not normally be expected to file evidence, nor would discovery be appropriate (see *R. v. Oxford ex parte Levey* (1987)).

The High Court has indicated that an application to set aside leave to apply should normally be heard by the judge who granted the leave initially. Nevertheless, there may be circumstances, including cases where several Judges have each granted leave to apply against a single respondent who then wishes to challenge the grants by reference to a common argument, where this will be inappropriate. In any case, the jurisdiction to set aside leave to apply should be exercised sparingly, although a judge would be lacking in his duty if he failed to set aside leave to apply in a case where, on the material then before him, he was satisfied that the substantive application had no reasonable prospect of success (see *R. v. Secretary of State for the Home Department ex parte Begum and Others* (1989)).

In *R. v. District Auditor No. 10 District ex parte Judge* (1989) the High Court gave the following examples of circumstances which would justify the setting aside of leave: fundamentally misconceived proceedings; fraud or non-disclosure of a material fact on the part of the applicant; and a misconception of law.

The topics of setting aside leave to apply and avenues of renewal and appeal are also dealt with at pp. 5-6.

It is important to note that there is a duty of good faith on the part of the applicant. In *R. v. Kensington Income Tax Commissioners ex parte Polignac* (1917) prohibition was withheld where the applicant had concealed material facts. Similarly, in *R. v. Secretary of State for the*

Home Department ex parte Mannan (1984) an applicant for judicial review failed to disclose that representations had been made on his behalf to the Minister of State, and that a Member of Parliament had made inquiries on his behalf. Nolan J. emphasized that it was of the greatest importance that all the facts were disclosed and the applicant's counsel agreed that the application could not continue. Even inadvertent mis-statements can lead to the withholding of relief. As Hodgson J. said in *R. v. North East Thames Regional Health Authority ex parte De Groot* (1988):

"It is of fundamental importance that there should not only be complete candour but great care as well in the completion of [the form initiating the application] and the evidence supporting it."

Relief may be withheld even where the lack of candour can be traced to the applicant's lawyers rather than to the applicant personally. As Ralph Gibson L.J. said in *R. v. Secretary of State for the Home Department ex parte Ketowoglo* (1992):

"It should be clearly understood by all concerned ... that the court [will] not readily ... permit an applicant to disclaim responsibility for what was done in his name and on his behalf by his representatives."

The applicant's obligation of disclosure is counterbalanced by the court's high expectations of respondents. This has two elements. First, in *R. v. Civil Service Appeal Board ex parte Cunningham* (1991) Lord Donaldson M.R., despite doubts expressed at first instance by Otton J., returned to a theme he had introduced in *R. v. Lancashire County Council ex parte Huddleston* (1986):

"In [*Huddleston*] I expressed the view that we had now reached the position in the development of judicial review at which public bodies and the courts should be regarded as being in partnership in a common endeavour to maintain the highest standards of public administration, including, I would add, the administration of justice. It followed from this that if leave to apply for judicial review was granted by the court, the court was entitled to expect that the respondent would give the court sufficient informaion to enable it to do justice, and that in some cases this would involve giving reasons or fuller reasons for a decision than the complainant himself would have been entitled to. Parker L.J. and Sir George Waller did not share my unease at the limited disclosure made by the council in that case, but I do not understand them to have disagreed with the principle." (The topic of giving reasons generally is discussed in chapter 8.)

Secondly, in *R. v. Secretary of State for Education and Science ex parte Hardy* (1989) it was held that where a public decision-maker is aware that the legal basis of one of its decisions is being challenged, the decision should not be implemented until the courts have dealt with the challenge.

C: The Time Limit and the Question of Delay
The normal maximum time limit within which application must be made is three months, and in some situations promptness may require even more timeous application. Unfortunately, there is a variation in the wording of O.53, r.4, and s.31(6) of the 1981 Act.

O.53, r.4 provides:

"An application for judicial review shall be made promptly and in any event within 3 months from the date when grounds for the application first arose unless the Court considers that there is good reason for extending the period."

Section 31(6) provides:

"Where the High Court considers that there has been undue delay ... the court may refuse to grant (a) leave for the making of the application; or (b) any relief sought on the application, if it considers that the granting of the relief sought would be likely to cause substantial hardship to, or substantially prejudice the rights of, any person, or would be detrimental to good administration."

The leading case on the relationship between O.53 and s.31 is *R. v. Dairy Produce Quota Tribunal for England & Wales ex parte Caswell and Caswell* (1990). The facts were that in 1985 the Caswells were disappointed by a decision of the tribunal, but they were unaware of any potential remedy and therefore they took no steps to challenge the decision. However, in 1987, having received further advice, they obtained leave to apply for judicial review. At the substantive hearing of their application, the Caswells argued that the tribunal had erred in law, and they further argued that granting relief would not be prejudicial to good administration, even though they conceded that they had been guilty of undue delay. The judge held that the tribunal had erred in law, but in the exercise of his discretion he refused to grant the appellants the relief which they sought.

The Court of Appeal agreed with this result, saying that the heart of the problem was that each provision is stated to operate without prejudice to the other. Proceeding to try to unravel the difficulty, and to produce what it considered to be the least unsatisfactory solution, the court distinguished between an *ex parte* hearing of an application for leave to apply for judicial review on the one hand, and an *inter partes* hearing of the substantive application on the other.

Taking the application for leave first, the court said that at an *ex parte* hearing, the judge must refuse leave if the application is not made promptly, or within three months at the latest, unless the applicant shows good reason for the delay, in which case the judge may grant an extension of time. If the judge does grant an extension of time and therefore proceeds to deal with the application for leave, it will strictly speaking still be within his power to refuse leave where he is of the view that the granting of relief would be likely to cause substantial hardship or be detrimental to good administration. However, in practice, once good reason for the delay has been shown, the judge will normally grant leave *ex parte*, and reserve the question of substantial hardship or detriment to good administration to be argued at the hearing of the substantive application.

When the substantive application is heard following an extension of time, it will still be open to the court to refuse relief on the ground of substantial hardship or detriment to good administration. However, at this stage it will not still be open to the applicant to argue that there has been no undue delay, because failure to apply promptly, or within three months at the latest, carries with it the inevitable consequence of undue delay, even where the applicant has shown good reason for the grant of an extension of time.

Although the court refused to define, or even to give helpful examples of, "detriment to good administration", it did indicate that mere inconvenience is not enough. More positively, there must be at least evidence from which detriment can be inferred, and it is legitimate to look not only at the particular instance which is before the court, but also at the effect of the particular instance on other potential applicants and at the consequences of their applications if they were to be successful.

The House of Lords dismissed an appeal, but attempted further explanation of the law relating to delay.

First, the relationship between s.31 of the 1981 Act and O.53, r.4, is that the former specifies particular grounds for refusing to grant either leave or substantive relief as the case may be, without limiting, in the words of r.4(3) "the time within which an application for judicial review may be made".

Secondly, for the purposes of s.31(6) and (7) of the Act, the words "an application for judicial review" include an application for leave to apply for judicial review.

Thirdly, the effect of O.53, r.4 is that any application must be made promptly and in any event within three months, except that where the court is satisfied that there is good reason for delay, an extension of time may be granted.

Fourthly, however, the grant of an extension of time does not mean that the delay ceases to be undue, and does not therefore prevent the refusal of substantive relief in the exercise of the court's discretion under s. 31(6), to which the court is bound to give effect independently of any rule of court.

Fifthly, although the fact that the importance of finality may vary between one context and another means that it would not be wise to formulate any precise definition of "detriment to good administration", s.31(6) recognizes an interest in good admininistration which is independent of hardship or prejudice to the rights of third parties, and good administration requires, *inter alia*, a regular flow of consistent decisions, made and published with reasonable dispatch, so that citizens may know where they stand and how they can order their affairs.

Sixthly, the harm suffered by the applicant is relevant to the exercise of discretion under s. 31(6). Finally, in the instant case it was relevant that if the applicants succeeded the result would be the re-opening of a decision to allocate a finite quota among various recipients over a number of years, and this would plainly be detrimental to the interests of good administration.

In *R. v. Swale Borough Council & Another ex parte Royal Society for the Protection of Birds* (1990) the High Court held that it is open to a court hearing a substantive application for judicial review to conclude that there has been undue delay in making the application, even though leave to make the application was granted following a consideration of the issue of the promptness of the application, and that the question of undue delay is to be approached more objectively than the earlier question of promptness.

In *R. v. Secretary of State for Transport ex parte Presvac Engineering Ltd. and Another* (1992) the court said that where an applicant is seeking an extension of time on the basis that the public interest requires the matter to be heard out of time, the onus of proof is on the applicant who is seeking the indulgence of the court.

Delay on the part of the legal aid authorities was held to justify allowing an extension of time in *R. v. Stratford-on-Avon District Council ex parte Jackson* (1985), where the court provided a detailed analysis of the relationship between O.53 and s.31. However, in the light of *Caswell*, this judgment is now principally of historical interest.

R. v. Secretary of State for Education and Science ex parte Threapleton (1988) was more complex. The facts of the case centred on the details of the statutory procedure to be followed when schools are being closed. A local education authority formulated a proposed scheme for the reorganization of secondary education and then submitted the scheme to the Secretary of State for Education and Science for his approval. The scheme was approved by the local education authority on March 5, 1987, and by the Secretary of State on 12 January 1988.

The applicant then applied for judicial review. Essentially, three issues arose. The first one involved the adequacy of the report which had been considered by the local education authority. The second issue was whether the Secretary of State had had regard to his own policy when he approved the scheme. The third issue was whether the court should, in its discretion, withhold any relief which the applicant might show would otherwise be appropriate. In this connexion, the lapse of time between the local authority's decision and the Secretary of State's confirmation of it had clearly resulted in the expiry of the normal time limit for an application for judicial review of the local authority's decision.

On the facts of the case, the court decided against the applicant in relation to both the question of the report's adequacy, and the Secretary of State's application of policy. It followed that the question of the availability of remedies did not arise. Nevertheless, the court said that if the applicant had succeeded on the substantive grounds of the application, the issue of delay would not have been fatal. There were two factors which contributed to this conclusion.

First, the legal basis of the applicant's case had been significantly strengthened by a decision of the Court of Appeal in another case some four months after the local education authority's decision, which meant that the case had been brought - and heard - promptly, it would have been even more likely to fail. Clearly, the court did not like the idea that an applicant who acts promptly should be in a weaker position than one who delays.

Secondly, in cases of this kind, it would normally be advantageous to allow the Secretary of State's decision to be given, prior to making an application for judicial review, even though the practicalities of the time-scale mean that the normal limitation period will have expired in relation to the local authority's decision. This was justified on the basis that by waiting until the whole process has been completed, it is possible that a defect at an earlier stage may be remedied at a later stage; and even if this is not the case, at least the court will have an opportunity to look at the decision-making process as a whole, rather than in a piecemeal fashion.

Two points arising from *Threapleton* have subsequently been developed by the courts.

First, in *R. v. Association of Futures Brokers and Dealers Limited and Another ex parte Mordens Limited* (1991) it was held that judicial reluctance to grant judicial review before the conclusion of a process undertaken by a succession of decision-makers will also apply to a decision-making process undertaken by a single decision-maker, and therefore it is only in the most exceptional circumstances that the court will grant judicial review of a decision taken during the course of a hearing before that hearing has been concluded.

Secondly, in *R. v. Secretary of State for Transport ex parte Presvac Engineering Ltd. and Another* (1992), the court said, albeit *obiter*, that it was impossible to uphold an argument that time did not start to run against a potential applicant until he was in a position to formulate his application with reasonable confidence, based upon admissible and sensible evidence, because this would involve re-writing the rule. The distinction between *Threapleton* and *Presvac* seems to be therefore that it in the earlier case it was a subsequent development of law which strengthened the applicant's position, whereas in the later case it was a question of being aware of, and assembling, the factual basis of the case.

In *R. v. Chichester Justices and Another ex parte Chichester District Council* (1991) the High Court acknowledged the need for caution on the part of a local authority when spending public money. It follows that where a local authority makes an application for judicial review towards the end of the normal maximum three month time limit, the court should be mindful of the time necessary for the taking of counsel's opinion and obtaining committee authorization for the making of the application. Therefore the court should be slow to hold the local authority guilty of undue delay, especially where the local authority has made it known at an earlier date that it considers the decision which it seeks to challenge to be wrong, and that it proposes to take some action in respect of it.

D: *Locus Standi*

Order 53 provides that in order to have the standing which is necessary to mount a challenge by way of an application for judicial review, the applicant must have a "sufficient interest" in the subject-matter of the application. "Sufficient interest" is not specifically defined, but before the reform of O.53 in 1977 a substantial body of case-law had developed in relation to *locus standi*, with different criteria being applied in respect of each of the remedies.

It is not apparent from either O.53 or s.31 whether the new terminology is intended to indicate that there is a single test for identifying *locus standi*. Nevertheless, it can clearly be argued that the introduction of a test described by a single form of words was intended to reflect the introduction into the law of a single test, at least to the extent of abolishing the old technicalities which had varied according to the remedy which was being sought. In *R. v. Inland Revenue Commissioners ex parte National Federation of Self-Employed and Small Businesses Ltd.* (1981), which is also sometimes known as the *Fleet Street Casuals Case*, Lords Diplock, Scarman and Roskill (and Lord Fraser with some uncertainty) indicated that this was in fact the position.

Admittedly some case-law appears to derogate from this principle, but the appearance is probably deceptive. For example, in *R. v. Felixstowe Justices ex parte Leigh* (1987) it was held that a journalist could have *locus standi* for the purposes of obtaining a declaration that a policy of not disclosing the names of the magistrates who heard certain types of case was unlawful, while at the same time lacking *locus standi* for the purposes of obtaining an order of mandamus compelling the chairman of the bench to disclose the names of the magistrates in a specific case. The real point of the case, however, is that the journalist's purposes were adequately served by the declaration, and he had no need to know the individual identities in the specific case. In other words, the outcome would have been the same if he had sought two declarations: one would have been granted, and the other withheld, with the differentiation being due to the differing extent of the journalist's interest rather than the nature of the relief he was seeking.

In passing, it is worth noticing that local authorities have *locus standi* to bring any legal proceedings, including applications for judicial review, which they consider to be "expedient for the promotion or protection of the interests of the inhabitants of their area" (see, generally, s.222, Local Government Act 1972; and, more particularly, *Times Newspapers Ltd. & Others v. Derbyshire County Council* (1992), which is discussed further at p.80, in the context of raising issues of public law by way of defence).

The fundamental nature of *locus standi* was the subject of comment in *R. v. Secretary of State for Social Services and Another ex parte Child Poverty Action Group and Others* (1989). The substantive issue in the case arose out of delays in dealing with claims for certain types of benefit.

The delays were caused by staff shortages, and the applicants, one of whom was a major charity, argued that the Secretary of State was in breach of his obligation, under ss.97 and 98 of the Social Security Act 1986, to appoint adjudication officers and to refer cases to them forthwith. The parties agreed that the argument should concentrate on the substantive issue, and that accordingly no issue would be taken as to whether or not the Child Poverty Action Group had *locus standi*.

Both the High Court and the Court of Appeal determined the substantive issue in favour of the Secretary of State, therefore the *locus standi* point was not crucial to the outcome. Nevertheless, the Court of Appeal did make clear its view that the requirement of *locus standi* goes to the jurisdiction of the court, and it follows therefore that the parties cannot simply agree between themselves that *locus standi* will not be put in issue, since this could have the effect of conferring upon the court a jurisdiction which it may not properly have. On the facts, however, the court was willing to accord *locus standi* to the Child Poverty Action Group.

In *R. v. Poole Borough Council ex parte Beebee and Others* (1991), the essence of a condition attached to a planning permission for residential development was that the British Herpetological Society would be given one full season's notice before development began, in order to permit them to collect and relocate rare species of reptiles. The society had been working on the land for many years. An application for judicial review was made in relation to the question of whether the local authority was obliged to undertake an environmental impact assessment. Although the application failed on its merits, the society was held to have *locus standi,* because of its long association with, including its financial input into, the site, and because it was named in the condition attached to the planning permission.

The relationship between *locus standi* and the discretionary nature of the remedies in judicial review arose in *Presvac* (see p.54). Applying what the court referred to as the normal principle in the context of an application for leave to apply for judicial review, that the court should approach the issue of *locus standi* by placing the emphasiz on the subject-matter of the alleged misfeasance rather than on the possible differential effects of that misfeasance upon various people, the court went on to say that when an application for judicial review has progressed to the ultimate stage after an *inter partes* investigation in depth, and the court is reviewing the question of sufficiency of interest, it is probably a semantic distinction without a difference to seek to separate the issue of *locus standi* from the exercise of the court's discretion to grant or withold relief.

It is tempting to conclude that, generally speaking, the modern judicial attitude is such that the requirement of *locus standi* is seldom going to present an obstacle to granting relief. In *R. v. Independent Broadcasting Authority ex parte Whitehouse* (1985) the holder of a television licence was said to have sufficient interest to enable her to challenge a decision of the Independent Broadcasting Authority, even though, of course, the fee income from television licences is directed exclusively to the British Broadcasting Corporation. Similarly, in *R. v. Her Majesty's Treasury ex parte Smedley* (1985), a tax-payer was said to have a sufficient interest to challenge the legality of certain governmental expenditure. Cases such as these lead Wade to say that the *Fleet Street Casuals Case*

> "may be said to crystallize the elements of a generous and public-oriented doctrine of standing which had previously been sporadic and unco-ordinated." (*Administrative Law*, 6th edition, 1988, p.701).

However, despite cases such as *Whitehouse* and *Smedley*, the law has not yet reached the stage where establishing *locus standi* is simply an empty formality. In *R. v. Secretary of State for the Environment ex parte Rose Theatre Trust* (1990) Schiemann J. decided that a company which had been formed to pursue a campaign to save an important archaeological site from redevelopment did not have *locus standi* to challenge a decision of the Secretary of State. In more general terms, the judge formulated a number of useful propositions.

First, a court hearing a substantive application ought to consider the question of *locus standi*, rather than treating the question as being entirely a threshold matter to be finally determined at the "leave" stage.

Secondly, the question of whether an applicant has *locus standi* is not purely a matter within the discretion of the court.

Thirdly, it would deprive the phrase "sufficient interest" of all meaning if every member of the public could complain of every breach of statutory duty by every statutory decision-maker, but on the other hand a direct financial or legal interest is not required.

Fourthly, when examining an alleged failure to perform a statutory duty, it is useful to see whether the statute confers upon the applicant the right to have the duty performed.

Fifthly, the mere assertion of a sufficient interest on the part of the applicant is not enough, and, more particularly, the fact that a large number of people join together and assert that they have a sufficient interest does not create such an interest if the people, taken individually, do not have such interests.

Sixthly, a company does not acquire a sufficient interest merely because its memorandum of association contains a power to pursue a particular object.

Schiemann J. specifically acknowledged that the effect of his ruling might be to leave an unlawful decision in effective existence.

In *R. v. Legal Aid Board ex parte Bateman* (1992), the High Court acknowledged that there is a general public interest in the administration of justice, including the working of the Legal Aid Board, and that therefore the Board is subject to judicial review. However, where the Board had refused application for authority to apply to a judge to review taxation of a solicitor's costs, the client whose case was concerned was held not to have sufficient interest to seek judicial review of that refusal. The court accepted that in order to be 'sufficient' an interest need not be financial, but took the view that it must nevertheless be tangible, in the sense that it must affect the applicant's personal interest, life or environment, and mere gratitude or concern was not enough.

E: Protecting Public Rights - The Concept of the Relator Action

The foregoing discussion of *locus standi* has been based on cases which have all involved claims that the individual rights of the challenger have been infringed. Where an individual is alleging infringement of a public right, *Boyce v. Paddington Borough Council* (1903) established the rule that an individual can seek an *injunction* or a *declaration* if, and only if, either the infringement of the public right has also infringed some private right of his own, or there is some other way in which he has suffered some particular harm over and above that suffered by the public at large.

In any other case, the individual's only option is to ask the Attorney-General, as protector of the public interest, to lend his name to the action. Such an action is known as a relator action. For all practical purposes the action is the individual's. He has the conduct of the case and is responsible for costs in the same way as any other litigant would be, although as far as costs are concerned, one of the factors which the Attorney-General will take into account before allowing his name to be used is whether the relator is actually good for the costs. This is usually covered by the relator's solicitor providing a certificate.

Briefly, therefore, relator actions constitute a kind of hybrid position, whereby private law remedies have been adopted into the body of public law.

The Attorney-General has a discretion as to whether or not he agrees to lend his name. In *Gouriet v. Union of Post Office Workers* (1977) the House of Lords established that the exercise of this discretion is not reviewable by the courts. Political accountability is, of course, another matter.

As a matter of logic, the long-term status of relator actions in the light of the doctrine in *O'Reilly v. Mackman* (1982) is not altogether clear, but the matter is considered again at p.85. The doctrine in *O'Reilly v. Mackman* itself is discussed at length in chapter 5.

F: Where the Wrong Procedure is Used

1. Order 53, r.9(5)

Order 53, r.9(5), contains what is, in effect, a one way filter. If a case which ought to be brought by way of an ordinary action is in fact brought by way of an application for judicial review, the court may order that it should be allowed to continue as if it had been brought by way of an ordinary action, although of course it need not do so. On the other hand, if a matter which ought to be brought by way of an application for judicial review is actually brought by way of an ordinary action, the court cannot order that it should be allowed to continue. The reason for the distinction is obvious if regard is had to the protective elements embodied in O.53. An applicant who has jumped through hoops unnecessarily need not be penalized, but an applicant who has avoided the hoops altogether should not be allowed to proceed.

In *R. v. Reading Justices and Others ex parte South West Meat Limited* (1992) the justices had granted the Board a search warrant in respect of a company's premises. The police executed the warrant. The company was granted leave to apply for judicial review in which they sought certiorari to quash the warrant, together with other relief. At a hearing before Pill J. the Board was ordered to lodge certain affidavits within fifty-six days. On the fifty-fifth day, the Board gave notice that it would apply for an order that the proceedings should thereafter continue as if they had been begun by writ.

The court held that the application, the nature of which was unattractive and appeared to be novel, amounted to a pre-emptive strike designed either to prevent the substantive hearing from taking place, by effectively setting aside the leave which had already been granted, or alternatively to pre-determine the result of that hearing, and therefore it would be dismissed.

2. The Possibility of Severing Mixed Proceedings

It may be that a case involves issues of public law and of private law, as in *Davy v. Spelthorne Borough Council* (1983). Reduced to their essentials, the facts were that the plaintiff began an ordinary action alleging not only that an agreement between himself and the local authority was *ultra vires*, but also that the local authority was liable to him in damages for negligence in respect of certain advice it had given him.

The Court of Appeal held that, on the facts, the two matters could be disentangled from each other, and that therefore the allegation that the agreement was *ultra vires* should not be allowed to proceed, because it should have been brought by way of an application for judicial review. However, the claim for damages could proceed. On further appeal to the House of Lords, where the only issue was whether the claim for damages should be allowed to continue, it was held that although the claim for damages would involve some consideration of public law issues, this would be merely peripheral to the main issue, and therefore the claim should be allowed to proceed.

It is clear from *Davy* that, in appropriate cases, it would be open to the court to hold that a claim in damages must proceed by way of application for judicial review, where it is peripheral to a public law issue, or that public and private law issues are so inextricably interwined that they should all be dealt with by way of an application for judicial review, if the facts justify the invocation of the protective elements of O.53.

G: Miscellaneous Matters

Order 53, r.8 permits discovery of documents, interrogatories, and cross-examination of deponents on the contents of their affidavits. In practice, however, the court can be less than enthusiastic about allowing these possibilities.

For example, in *R. v. Derbyshire County Council ex parte Noble* (1990), which is discussed more fully at p.74 in the context of employment cases in public and private Law, the Court of Appeal observed that the case disclosed a conflict of evidence as to the facts, and that this meant that it was not a suitable matter to be decided by the O.53 procedure. Curiously, however, the court did not say why cross-examination would not have been been appropriate.

In *R. v. London Borough of Waltham Forest and Others ex parte Waltham Forest Ratepayers' Action Group* (1988) the Court of Appeal, dealing with an application to join particular individual councillors as respondents to an application for judicial review of a decision taken by a local authority, said that the duty of the court is to identify the real grievance of the applicants and to see how that grievance, assuming it to be established, can best be remedied in terms of speed and economy. On an application to quash a decision of a local authority to make a rate, it is therefore inappropriate that the individual councillors who voted for the making of the rate should be joined as respondents, and in particular it is improper to seek to join the individual councillors merely for the purpose of obtaining discovery from them or an order for costs against them.

CHAPTER 5

THE DISTINCTION BETWEEN PUBLIC LAW AND PRIVATE LAW

A: Introduction

The previous chapter introduced the doctrine that to a very large extent judicial review is the exclusive procedure for challenging matters involving public law. This law develops the point by considering the meaning of *public law* in this context. The seminal case on the distinction between public and private law is undoubtedly *O'Reilly v. Mackman* (1982), but it is interesting to note two previous straws in the judicial wind, namely *Barrs and Others v. Bethell* (1982) and *Re Tillmire Common, Heslington* (1982).

In *Barrs* three ratepayers of Camden London Borough Council issued a writ against certain councillors and the council itself, alleging that certain expenditure was unlawful, and seeking declarations together with ancillary orders . All the remedies being sought were discretionary. The Attorney-General had said he did not think this was a suitable case for him to lend his name to a relator action.

In the High Court Warner J. held that a litigant who has a sufficient interest for an application for judicial review does not necessarily also have a sufficient interest for the purposes of bringing an ordinary action. Additionally, in the present context, the audit provisions of the Local Government Act 1972 provided specialized procedures for challenging expenditure, quite apart from the possibility of a relator action. Finally, the discretionary nature of the remedies did not provide the defendants with the same degree of protection which they would derive from the plaintiffs' having to apply for leave to apply for judicial review, because a refusal of leave to apply protects defendants against the possibility of being subject to a remedy, the burden of having to defend proceedings, and the risk of being liable in costs. The conclusion, therefore was that the action should not be allowed to proceed in its instant form, but should be adjourned to allow the plaintiffs to renew their application to the Attorney-General for permission to bring a relator action.

In *Re Tillmire Common, Heslington* (1982), the plaintiffs were landowners who claimed that their land should not continue to be registered under the system introduced by the Commons Registration Act 1965. They began ordinary proceedings for a declaration in the Chancery Division of the High Court, to which proceedings under the 1965 Act were assigned. Dillon J. held that where the High Court is being asked to quash a decision of an inferior tribunal for an error of law, the proceedings should be brought in the Queen's Bench Division by way of an application for judicial review. The instant proceedings were stayed on the basis that they were an abuse of the process of the court.

Before coming to the leading cases it must be said that it is not always easy to detect a coherent doctrine underlying the courts' decisions in relation to the distinction between public law and private law. However, it may be helpful to make three observations.

First, where the relationship between the decision-maker and the challenger is contractual, the court will almost invariably characterize the situation as being governed by private law, although even in these cases the court sometimes finds it possible to identify some additional element of public law, which makes judicial review appropriate.

Secondly, in borderline cases the courts may be less generous to an applicant where the choice is between judicial review and some other remedy on the one hand (see, e.g., *Roy v. Kensington & Chelsea and Westminster Family Practitioners' Committee* (1992), p.63), and more generous where the choice is between judicial review or no remedy at all on the other (see, e.g., *R. v. Wear Valley District Council ex parte Binks* (1985), discussed at p.65, and *R. v. Secretary of State for the Home Department ex parte Benwell* (1984), discussed at p.75).

Thirdly, and again within the realm of judicial instinct, the courts may well be strongly influenced by their perception of whether the protective elements of the judicial review process are appropriate to the decision-making function in question.

B: The Doctrine in *O'Reilly v. Mackman* Generally

In the leading case of *O'Reilly v, Mackman* (1982) a number of prisoners wished to allege unfairness in the conduct of certain disciplinary proceedings which had been brought against them. Being well out of time for judicial review, they contented themselves with an ordinary action in which they sought declaratory relief.

The House of Lords held that the action was an abuse of the process of the court, because it represented an attempt to circumvent the procedural protection which O.53 conferred on public decision-makers. As a general principle, the House said that although O.53 provided that injunctions and declarations may be sought by way of an application for judicial review, where an issue of public law was involved this was the only way in which they could be sought. This principle was acknowledged to be capable of being subject to exceptions (e.g. where the parties consented to another procedure, or where an issue of public law arose peripherally to what was essentially a private law matter, or in such other circumstances as the courts may work out on a case-by-case basis) but the generality of the principle is clear.

In passing it must be noticed that the parties' capacity to agree that a public law issue should be dealt with other than by way of an application for judicial review does not operate the other way round. In *University College London v. Kent* (1992) the Court of Appeal said it was for the court to decide whether or not there was an issue of public law, and in cases which genuinely involved matters of private law only, the parties could not simply agree between themselves to confer upon the court jurisdiction in judicial review.

O'Reilly obviously makes the distinction between public law and private law into a matter of the first importance. The difficulty is that English Law, largely under the influence of the Diceyan concept of the rule of law, has tended to regard this distinction as either dangerous, or at the very least, unimportant.

The process of clarifying the distinction on a case-by-case basis began immediately after the decision in *O'Reilly v. Mackman* when the House gave judgment in *Cocks v. Thanet District Council* (1982). The facts involved a dispute arising out of the provisions which were then contained in the Housing (Homeless Persons) Act 1977. The scheme of the legislation is that, faced with an applicant who claims to be homeless, the housing authority has to ask certain questions, and, depending on the answers, one of various duties to the applicant may arise.

The House of Lords held that the decision-making process was a matter of public law, and therefore challenges to its legality could be made only by way of an application for judicial review. However, if the decision-making process resulted in a duty arising in favour of the applicant, the enforcement of that duty was a matter of private law. In other words, the fact that the duty was owed by a public body was irrelevant for the present purposes.

In *Roy v. Kensington & Chelsea and Westminster Family Practitioners' Committee* (1992) the Court of Appeal drew a similar distinction between the public law character of a decision-making process and the private law character of rights arising under it, although the House of Lords proceeded on a different basis. A doctor was a general medical practitioner practising under the National Health Service within the area administered by the committee. A dispute arose over the payment to which the doctor was entitled by way of a basic practice allowance under the relevant National Health Service Regulations. The amount of the payment depended on whether he was devoting a substantial amount of time to general practice under the National Health Service. He argued that periods of absence from his practice should not count against him, provided that he ensured locum cover was available. Nevertheless, the committee in the exercise of its discretion, decided to withhold a proportion of the sum which would otherwise have been due to the doctor.

The doctor brought an ordinary action against the committee. The committee applied for certain sub-paragraphs of the statement of claim to be struck out as an abuse of the process of the court, on the basis that those aspects of the challenge should have been made by way of an application for judicial review. His Honour Judge White, sitting as a judge of the Queen's Bench Division of the High Court, granted the committee's application, on the basis that the parties' reciprocal rights and duties stemmed entirely from statute and regulations, and that in deciding the extent of a doctor's entitlement to a basic practice allowance, the committee was exercising a public law function.

The Court of Appeal allowed an appeal by the doctor, holding that if the committee had failed to include the respondent's name on the medical list, his remedy would have been by way of judicial review to enforce his public law right to have his application for inclusion properly considered. However, once his name was included on the list, the doctor had a contractual right in private law to have the committee determine whether he was entitled to the full rate of basic practice allowance.

The House of Lords dismissed the committee's appeal, holding that the doctor enjoyed a bundle of private law rights, including the very important right to be paid for the work he had done, and it was irrelevant whether those rights derived from statute or contract. Subsidiary reasons for the decision were that the enforcement of the doctor's private law rights was the dominant element in the proceedings; the type of claim involved may give rise to disputed issues of fact, which would make the judicial review process less than ideal; the order sought, namely an order for the payment of money due, was not one which could be granted on judicial review; on the facts, the claim had been joined with another claim which was clearly fit to be brought in an action; and when individual rights are claimed, there should be neither need to apply for leave, nor any special time limits, nor should the relief be discretionary.

At the level of general principle, the House indicated that actions should be allowed to proceed unless they are plainly an abuse of the process of the court, and unless the procedure adopted by the moving party is ill-suited to dispose of the question at issue, there is much to be said in favour of the proposition that a court having jurisdiction should let a case be heard rather than entertain a debate concerning the form of the proceedings.

In *R. v. Wear Valley District Council ex parte Binks* (1985) Mrs. Binks operated a mobile hot-dog stall in the market place of a small town. She occupied the land by virtue of a licence granted by the local authority. Without giving her any prior warning, the local authority notified her that they had decided to revoke her licence, although subsequently the local authority did say that late-night street trading was considered undesirable, and that there was a litter problem. The chief executive had advised the local authority that it could "deal with its land as it sees fit, at its absolute discretion, in the same way as any other land owner".

The Divisional Court disagreed with the chief executive, holding that Mrs. Binks had been entitled to the benefit of natural justice (see chapter 12), which in this case meant that she should have had an opportunity to know the case against her and to make representations on her own behalf. Part of the reasoning leading to this conclusion was that the regulation of street trading involves an element of public law, although it is clear that natural justice and public law are not co-terminous (see p.183).

In *An Bord Bainne Co-operative Ltd. (Irish Dairy Board) v. Milk Marketing Board* (1984) the Dairy Board brought an ordinary action seeking damages and an injunction to restrain the Milk Marketing Board from charging different prices for milk which was to be used for making butter, according to whether the butter was to be sold to an intervention agency or directly into the United Kingdom's domestic market. The Court of Appeal held that the Dairy Board was relying on private law rights, even if the facts also involved public law rights. If the Dairy Board succeeded, the court would have no discretion as to whether or not it granted relief, although there would be a discretion as to the nature of the relief. The court concluded that judicial review is wholly inappropriate to any non-discretionary claim, and that therefore the instant proceedings had been properly brought as an ordinary action and were not an abuse of the process of the court.

In *Ettridge v. Morrell* (1986) the court was concerned with the failure of the Inner London Education Authority to perform its statutory duty of providing election candidates with school rooms in which to hold meetings. The High Court held that this was a matter of public law, and that the judicial review procedure was therefore mandatory, but the Court of Appeal reversed this, holding that the case disclosed no decision-making process in public law, and that all that was involved was the enforcement of a private right.

The background to *R. v. Kidderminster District Valuer ex parte Powell* (1992), is that police officers' pay is based on the assumption that they are living in accommodation provided free of charge by the police authority.

Accordingly, those officers who provide their own accommodation are entitled to be paid what is called a rent allowance. The matter was governed by the Police Regulations 1987 (as amended). Obviously some kind of valuation of properties had to be undertaken to enable these allowances to be calculated. In the instant case the police authority chose to use the Inland Revenue's District Valuer, although they could have used a member of their own staff or a private estate agent.

When a dispute arose as to the basis on which the District Valuer had calculated his valuation, the High Court held that the process by which the District Valuer had reached his valuation was subject to judicial review.

In addition to the common law line of authority, flowing from *O'Reilly*, s.30 of the Supreme Court 1981 provides for injunctions to be available to restrain persons from acting in certain types of substantive office of a public nature and permanent character. Section 31 provides that such injunctions shall be sought by way of application for judicial review. Section 30 is seldom used, but in *R. v. Brooker and Others ex parte Hitchin Town Football and Social Club* (1991), the High Court had no difficulty in deciding that, on the facts, trustees holding land for sporting purposes were holders of a substantive office of a public nature, and that therefore their decision-making process was subject to judicial review, although in the circumstances of the case Kennedy J. was not disposed to grant anything more than a declaration.

In *R. v. Legal Aid Board ex parte Bateman* (1992), the High Court acknowledged that there is a general public interest in the administration of justice, including the working of the Legal Aid Board, and that therefore the Board is subject to judicial review. (This case also raised a *locus standi* point which is discussed at p. 58)

In addition to the range of cases already identified, there are at least two categories of case which have made major contributions to the development of English jurisprudence on the public-private law divide, namely the regulatory body cases, and the employment cases. These will now be considered in turn.

C: The *Regulatory Body* Cases

The starting point is *R. v. Panel on Take-Overs and Mergers ex parte Datafin plc* (1987). The Panel was an unincorporated association which operated within the City of London. Its powers were neither statutory nor contractual, and it was not a government agency. Nevertheless, it produced, and monitored the operation of, a code of rules, and a finding that those rules have been contravened could have very serious consequences, including exclusion from the Stock

Exchange. Although the instant case failed on its merits, the Court of Appeal held that in principle the panel was subject to judicial review for a variety of reasons.

First, the panel's powers did not derive from agreement between itself and the parties affected by its decisions. Secondly, the government had indicated that it was willing to limit the scope of legislation in the area covered by the panel, and this was indicative of a kind of "implied devolution of power". Thirdly, the government and the Bank of England had additional powers, lying behind those of the panel. Fourthly, the applicant seemed to the court to have no right of action against the panel in either contract or tort, so if judicial review were not available the applicants would be without legal redress, and as Sir John Donaldson M.R. said, the courts must "recognize the realities of executive power" and prevent the abuse of the "enormously wide discretion which [the panel] arrogates to itself."

A similar approach was taken in *R. v. Advertising Standards Authority Ltd. ex parte The Insurance Service plc* (1990). Under a Directive issued in 1984 by the Council of Ministers of the European Economic Community, member states were obliged to "ensure that adequate and effective means exist[ed] for the control of misleading advertising". However, the Directive did "not exclude the voluntary control of misleading advertising by self-regulatory bodies."

The Advertising Standards Authority, a company limited by guarantee, included among its objects "the promotion and enforcement ... of the highest standards of advertising".

The British government implemented the Directive by making the Control of Misleading Advertisements Regulations 1988, which gave certain powers to the Director General of Fair Trading. However, the tenor of the Regulations was that the Director General would use his powers only where he was not satisfied that a complaint to the Authority had produced a satisfactory result.

In the present case, the Authority upheld a complaint concerning an advertisement issued by the applicant. The question arose as to whether the Authority was subject to judicial review in respect of the way in which it had determined the complaint. The High Court held that the Authority was subject to judicial review because it was clearly exercising a public law function which, if the Authority did not exist, would be exercised by the Director General of Fair Trading.

The case of *Law v. National Greyhound Racing Club Ltd.* (1983) falls on the other side of the line. The club was a company formed under the Companies Act. It licensed trainers, promulgated rules of racing, and appointed stewards to enforce those rules. The rules were deemed to be acepted by anyone racing at a licensed course.

When Law was suspended by the stewards for a breach of the rules, he challenged the decision in an ordinary action. When the club argued that the challenge should have been brought by way of an application for judicial review, the Court of Appeal held that the matter was governed entirely by contract (and was therefore a matter of private law, even though a large proportion of the public is interested in the proper conduct of dog racing, and therefore in the work of the club).

The principle of *Law* was applied by the High Court in *R. v. Jockey Club ex parte Massingburd-Mundy* (1990). The club, which was incorporated by Royal Charter, had extensive powers to control horse racing throughout the United Kingdom. The applicant had been approved by the club to act as a chairman of local stewards, in which capacity he had significant authority over the conduct of individual race meetings. Following a dispute arising out of a local stewards' inquiry at one race meeting, the club's disciplinary committee decided that the applicant should no longer be approved to act as a chairman of local stewards. The applicant alleged that he had been unfairly treated, but the details are not relevant for the present purpose.

The High Court dismissed an application for judicial review holding that although there is no single test which can be applied in order to determine whether the decisions of a particular body are susceptible to judicial review, in many cases it will be sufficient to show that the body derives its powers either from statute or from the exercise of the Royal Prerogative. Nevertheless, in other cases it may be necessary to examine the nature of the duties which the body is called upon to perform, and to ascertain whether those duties fall within the public domain. In the instant case it was not clear that the powers of the club were derived from the Royal Prerogative, even though the club had been incorporated by Royal Charter, but even so, an examination of the club's Charter and of some aspects of the club's work strongly suggested that, to some extent at least, the club operated in the public domain, and if the matter were free from authority, this in turn might lead to the conclusion that, to that extent, the club's decisions were susceptible to judicial review.

However, the Court of Appeal's decision in Law and the Privy Council's decision in *Calvin v. Carr* (1979) both suggested that the club was a domestic tribunal, which derived its authority over the applicant from an essentially contractual relationship, and therefore judicial review was not available to the applicant.

The court went on to say that even if some decisions of the club were susceptible to judicial review, the decision in question would not be one of them, because no public law right of the applicant had been affected, and the courts should act with restraint before interfering with the decisions of sporting bodies, however wide-ranging their powers may be.

Roch J. ventured the following observations. The fact that a body derives its existence from a Royal Charter issued under the Royal Prerogative is not decisive of the question of susceptibility to judicial review, even where disciplinary functions are involved. Other factors which are relevant include the nature and source of the power to do the act in question (e.g. whether it is a public law power or a private law power); the role fulfilled by the body (e.g. whether it holds a position of major national importance, and whether it has monopolistic or near monopolistic powers in an area in which the public generally, or a large section of the public, have an interest); the availability or otherwise of alternative effective remedies; and the extent (if any) to which the matter affects the applicant's rights *qua* subject, or in a way which is peculiar to him or to a limited class of persons.

The role of the Jockey Club came before the court again in *R. v. Jockey Club ex parte RAM Racecourses Ltd.* (1990). The club prepared a report on the future allocation of race meetings to racecourses. The report was circulated to the owners of existing racecourses, but not to the applicants, who were proposing to open a new racecourse but who were not currently racecourse owners. The applicants claimed that they nevertheless relied on the contents of the report.

In due course it became clear that the applicants would not receive the allocation of race meetings which they had expected. The applicants argued that they had had a legitimate expectation of having race meetings allocated to them, and applied for judicial review on that basis.

Dismissing the application, the court said that if the application were to succeed on the basis of legitimate expectation, the applicant would have to establish that there had been a clear and unambiguous representation; that the applicants were within a class of persons entitled to rely on the representation, even though it was not made directly to them, or that it was reasonable for them to rely on it; that the applicants did rely on the representation; that the applicants' reliance on the representation was to their detriment; and that there was no overriding interest, arising from their duties and responsibilities which entitled the respondents to change their policy to the detriment of the applicants. The burden of proving the first four elements fell on the applicants, whereas the burden of proving an appropriate overriding interest fell on the respondents.

On the facts, although the report contained a sufficiently unambiguous representation, it nevertheless lacked clarity and was internally contradictory, and therefore it was not reasonable for the applicants to rely on the representation without making further inquiries of the respondents. Additionally, the applicants were neither within a class of persons whom the respondents, actually or presumptively, intended the report to reach, nor were they members of the public, or of a section of the community, to whom the report was addressed. It followed that the applicants had failed to establish two of the necessary ingredients of their claim, and the court therefore declined to consider the other elements.

Stuart-Smith L.J. emphasized that although it was not necessary to determine the difficult question of whether the court had jurisdiction to entertain an application for judicial review in the present case, and although if the matter had been free from authority his Lordship would have held that the court did have jurisdiction, nevertheless the decision of the Divisional Court in *Massingburd-Mundy* should be followed in the present case.

Simon Brown J. emphasized that although in one sense the jurisdictional issue did not fall to be determined, the determination of that question was nevertheless logically antecedent to the determination of the question of legitimate expectation. He also said that *Massingburd-Mundy* was distinguishable from *Law* on the ground that it involved a non-renewable privilege, whereas Law involved a relationship which was essentially contractual. Furthermore, many older cases, which had proceeded on a purely private law basis, would find a natural home in applications for judicial review if they were to arise at the present time, and since the courts were concerned with a dynamic area of law which was well able to embrace new situations according to the requirements of justice, judicial review should be available in respect of those decisions of the Jockey Club which amounted to the exercise of a quasi-licensing power.

The decision of the High Court in *R. v. Football Association Ltd. ex parte Football League Ltd.* (1992) represents the re-assertion of the importance of the principle that the existence of a contract indicates a domestic relationship which is outwith the scope of judicial review. Rose J. said:

"Despite its [sc. the Association's] virtually monopolistic powers and the importance of its decisions to many members of the public who are not contractually bound to it, it is, in my judgment, a domestic body whose powers arise from and duties exist in private law only ...

"I do not find this conclusion unwelcome ... [because] ... to apply to the governing body of football ... principles honed for the control of the abuse of power by government and its creatures would involve what, in today's fashionable parlance, would be called a quantum leap. It would also, in my view, for what it is worth, be a misapplication of increasingly scarce judicial resources."

In *R. v. General Council of the Bar ex parte Percival* (1990) the applicant for judicial review was the head of a set of barristers' chambers. He became unhappy with the way in which another member of the chambers, who was the chambers' financial and general administrator, was running the chambers' financial affairs. In a worsening atmosphere, the applicant accused the administrator of dishonesty and other disreputable conduct, contrary to the Bar's Code of Conduct, and reported him to the General Council of the Bar, with a view to proceedings being taken before a Disciplinary Tribunal.

The General Council's Professional Conduct Committee decided to proceed against the administrator on a charge of breach of proper professional standards, rather than the more serious charge of professional misconduct.

The applicant sought a declaration that the Professional Conduct Committee should have preferred the more serious charge and mandamus to compel it to do so. A variety of matters arose, in respect of which the Queen's Bench Division of the High Court held that the General Council, acting through its delegate the Professional Conduct Committee, fulfilled the role of a prosecutor exercising discretion in the sifting and assessment of complaints and deciding what charges (if any) were appropriate in each case. This function had to be performed in accordance with the rules contained in the Code of Conduct, and acts or omissions in this regard could be challenged by way of judicial review. However, no strict limits should be set to the judicial review of a prosecuting body, since each case must be considered with due regard to the powers, functions and procedures of the body concerned and the manner in which it had dealt (or not dealt) with the matter in question.

More particularly, the fact that professional standards will be called into question during the course of an application for judicial review does not justify the court in exercising its discretion not to intervene. Similarly, save possibly in the most exceptional circumstances, the publicity which is unavoidably attendant on an application for judicial review cannot justify the court in declining to review something which is otherwise reviewable.

However, on the facts, the Professional Conduct Committee had acted within its broad discretion, upon correct principles and with impartiality and fairness, and therefore the application failed.

Finally, there is the decision of the High Court in *R. v. Code of Practice of the British Pharmaceutical Industry ex parte Professional Counselling Aids Ltd.* (1991). The Association of the British Pharmaceutical Industry, whose Code of Practice Committee was the respondent, was a trade association. The objective of the Code of Practice, which was administered by the committee was "to secure the acceptance and adoption of high standards of conduct in the marketing of medical products designed for use under medical supervision." The Code was drawn up after consultation with the British Medical Association and the Department of Health. Compliance with the Code was obligatory for members of the Association, and in practice it was also followed by non-members.

The respondent made a decision, which was adverse to the interests of the applicant, and against which there was no right of appeal. The applicant was not a member of the association. The question arose as to whether the respondent was subject to judicial review.

Popplewell J. held that the application failed on its merits, but at the level of principle, he felt bound, albeit reluctantly, by the *Datafin* and *Insurance Services* cases to say that the matter was within the scope of judicial review.

D: The *Employment* Cases

A substantial body of case law has accumulated around the question of whether disputes arising out of public employment are within the scope of judicial review. Although not itself concerned with the distinction between public and private law, the case of *Ridge v. Baldwin* (1963) is undoubtedly the starting point. Following his acquittal on certain criminal charges, the Chief Constable of Brighton was dismissed without a hearing. The basis of the decision to dismiss him was that, despite his acquittal, the facts which emerged at the trial showed that he was clearly not fit to be a Chief Constable.

The House of Lords held that there had been a breach of natural justice, with Lord Reid producing a three-fold classification of employees, officeholders holding office "at pleasure", and officeholders who can be dismissed only on specified grounds. According to Lord Reid, the position of each category was as follows.

Employees, who are in a master-servant relationship with their employers, are not entitled to the protection of natural justice as such. Accordingly, their remedies lie in the areas of breach of contract and/or unfair dismissal.

Officeholders who hold office at pleasure can be removed without the giving of reasons. According to Lord Reid, members of this category are not entitled to be given a hearing, because there need be no reasons for dismissal anyway. In passing, it is interesting to note that the logic of this is clearly faulty. Even though no reasons need be given, it may be that a perceived reason exists, and that without that reason the dismissal would not take place. Therefore, a hearing could result in a clarification of the facts which might lead the decision-maker to change his mind as to the dismissal.

This leaves officeholders, such as Chief Constables, who can be removed only on specified grounds. In these cases a hearing should be granted, so that the existence of the grounds can be challenged.

Lord Reid's first category appears to have been applied in the context of employment by a purely private employer in *Hill v. Parsons* (1971), where the Court of Appeal took the view that a dismissed employee's ordinary remedy was in damages, with the exceptional possibility of an injunction and/or specific performance. *Ridge v. Baldwin* was cited in argument but not in the judgments: the court seems to have regarded the non-applicability of natural justice as being so clear as to need no comment.

The Scottish case of *Malloch v. Aberdeen Corporation* (1971) provides a gloss on Lord Reid's second category. As a preliminary to considering this case it is necessary to note that in Scotland schoolteachers are holders of office at pleasure.

Malloch was dismissed, but a procedure existed under which he was entitled to three weeks' notice of the meeting at which the decision was to be considered. The House of Lords held that there was an entitlement to a hearing, because there would be no point in giving him notice of the hearing unless he was entitled to present his case.

In the *O'Reilly v. Mackman* era, the major question is, of course, whether the mere fact of being employed by a public employer is sufficient to bring disputes as to employment within the field of public law. The case law starts with *R. v. British Broadcasting Corporation ex parte Lavelle* (1983). Lavelle was employed by the BBC but she was dismissed. Her contract of employment provided a detailed procedure for such an eventuality, including rights of appeal. The High Court held that this was simply a matter of contract, and therefore of private law. The mere fact of employment by a public body was not sufficient to import the notion of public law.

In *R. v. East Berkshire Health Authority ex parte Walsh* (1984) a senior nursing officer was dismissed. The public element was slightly stronger than in *Lavelle*, because the employee was employed in accordance with nationally negotiated conditions of service, which were approved by the Secretary of State. However, the result was the same.

In *R. v. Derbyshire County Council ex parte Noble* (1990) the applicant was employed as a police surgeon by the respondent. His employment was based on a contract for services, rather than a contract of service. Following an allegation of impropriety, Noble was dismissed without a hearing. He then produced evidence which, if believed, showed that there were no grounds for his dismissal, but the respondent refused to reinstate him.

The applicant argued that there had been a breach of natural justice and that the respondent had acted unreasonably. He sought judicial review on the basis that the respondent had a statutory duty to appoint police surgeons, and that therefore there was an element of public law in his relationship with the respondent. He sought certiorari to quash the decision to terminate his employment and mandamus to compel the respondent to reinstate him.

The High Court held that there was no element of public law in the relationship between a police authority and its police surgeons, and that therefore an application for judicial review is not an appropriate method for challenging a police authority's decision not to renew the appointment of a police surgeon. The Court of Appeal dismissed an appeal, saying that although there is no universal test which can be used to determine whether a case raises issues of public law, the most generally useful approach is to look at the subject-matter of the decision in question, and then to decide whether judicial review is appropriate.

In the instant case the Court of Appeal was less sure than the High Court had been that there were no elements of public law in the relationship between the appellant and the respondent, but it agreed that the decision in respect of which complaint was made was merely in relation to the termination of a contract by the respondent, and that therefore the only rights of the appellant which were affected by that decision were his private law rights under the contract.

Judicial instinct was articulated in the case of *R. v. Chief Rabbi ex parte Wachmann* (1991). The respondent, who was the Chief Rabbi of the mainstream of Orthodox Judaism in the British Commonwealth, found that the applicant, a rabbi employed by the Jewish Congregation in Manchester, was "morally and religiously" unfit to hold rabbinical office, whereupon the applicant's congregation resolved to terminate his employment. On an application for leave to apply for judicial review, the High Court held that the spiritual functions of the Chief Rabbi lacked any real public law character, and if the court allowed the application for judicial review to be made, it was impossible to escape the conclusion that, one way or another, the court would inevitably - and totally inappropriately - be drawn into adjudicating upon matters which were intimate to a religious community.

One of Lord Reid's categories in *Ridge v. Baldwin* was before the court in *R. v. Secretary of State for the Home Department ex parte Benwell* (1984) where a prison officer was said to be a constable, and therefore to be a public office-holder, rather than an employee. As an office-holder, he could have no claim for unfair dismissal, because he was not employed, and therefore the court felt constrained to say that he could seek a remedy by way of judicial review, because otherwise he would be remediless.

The logic of *Benwell* was questioned by the Court of Appeal in *McLaren v. Secretary of State for the Home Department* (1990), where the appellant was a prison officer, who was in dispute with the Home Office. In an ordinary action, the appellant claimed declarations that the original terms of his appointment had been varied by subsequent collective agreements. He also claimed payment of certain remuneration which he alleged was due to him and which had been wrongfully withheld.

In the Chancery Division of the High Court Hoffmann J. ordered that the appellant's statement of claim be struck out, on the basis that the appellant should have proceeded by way of an application for judicial review, because his relationship with the Home Office was a matter of public law, and there was no arguable case that any private law relationship had come into existence at any material time. The Court of Appeal, in reversing this decision, made the following observations. First, the fact that a prison officer has the powers, authority, protection and privileges of a constable, does not mean that a prison officer actually is a constable, and in any event the fact that a person has such powers, authority, protection and privileges would not mean that he could not be employed under a contract of service. Secondly, in deciding whether the relationship between a public body and its employees involves a matter of public law, there are two general principles.

The first principle is that in relation to personal claims against an employer, an employee of a public body is normally in exactly the same situation as other employees, and therefore if he has a cause of action in relation to his employment, he can bring proceedings in the High Court or the County Court in the ordinary way, claiming damages, a declaration or an injunction (except in relation to the Crown). The second principle is that the fact of employment by the Crown may limit the individual's rights, but will not generally affect the enforcement of whatever rights he has. More particularly, where a person, having been appointed under either the Royal Prerogative or a statutory power, holds office under the Crown rather than enjoying an ordinary master-servant relationship, the appointment will almost invariably be terminable at will. However, this does not mean that in the event of a dispute it will be either necessary, or normally appropriate, for him to seek relief by way of an application for judicial review. Nevertheless, where some disciplinary or other body had been established either under the Royal Prerogative or by statute, and the business of that body has a sufficient public law element (which will almost invariably be the case if the employer is the Crown), rather than being entirely domestic or informal, the proceedings and determinations of the body can be an appropriate subject for judicial review.

Furthermore, if an employee of the Crown or other public body is adversely affected by a decision of his employer which affects the employers' employees generally, rather than affecting employees on an individual basis, and the employee wishes to challenge the decision on *Wednesbury* grounds, an application for judicial review would be appropriate.

However, where the public might be affected by disciplinary proceedings which are purely domestic in nature, and in respect of which, therefore, an application for judicial review would be inappropriate, an individual employee who is adversely affected by those proceedings may nevertheless, in appropriate circumstances, seek declaratory or injunctive relief to ensure that the proceedings are conducted fairly.

Finally, on the present facts, it could not be said that the appellant had no arguable case.

Before leaving the topic of public employment, it is necessary to consider *R. v. Civil Service Appeal Board ex parte Bruce* (1989). Bruce's appointment as a civil servant had been terminated. Various proceedings ensued, including an unsuccessful appeal to the Civil Service Appeal Board alleging unfairness, and the instant application for judicial review, which was based on the Board's failure to give reasons for its decisions. The High Court held that there was no contract of employment, but merely an appointment by a letter which stated that the appointment was subject to the conditions of service for civil servants and was to be held at the pleasure of the Crown. In the absence of a contract of employment, there was in principle a sufficient public law element to justify permitting an application for judicial review.. However, at a practical level disputes arising from dismissal were most appropriately dealt with by Industrial Tribunals, and therefore it was only in exceptional circumstances, which did not include the present case, that an application for judicial review should be granted.

The Court of Appeal upheld this decision.

However, *Bruce* was not followed in *R. v. Lord Chancellor's Department ex parte Nangle* (1992). A civil servant who had been disciplined was alleging that the relevant disciplinary procedures had not been followed. The Crown argued that an application for judicial review should be dismissed on the ground that the case involved matters of private law arising out of a contract of employment, or, if this was not accepted, that in any event there was an insufficient element of public law to justify judicial review.

The court agreed with the Crown that an application for judicial review was not appropriate. The court accepted that the Crown *can* enter into contracts of employment with civil servants, and that this was not inconsistent with the fact of dismissibility at will. In each case the question was whether there was an intention to create legal relations. This was to be judged objectively, as a matter of construction of the documents.

"Where the documents show that the parties enter into a relationship involving obligations, rights and entitlements which go both ways, then *prima facie* the court will hold that they intend these obligations to be enforceable and not merely voluntary."

"In such a business situation the onus is on the party asserting a lack of intention to create legal relations and the onus is a heavy one."

The court concluded that there must have been an intention to create legal relations, but that even if this was wrong and there was no contract the outcome of the case would still be the same. The availability of a remedy in public law does not flow automatically from the absence of a remedy in private law.

"[Counsel for the Crown] submits that even if there is no contract, the submission to the disciplinary proceedings is in truth a consensual one, since it arises out of the relationship of a master and a servant, employer and employee, and is part of the terms and conditions accepted by the applicant when he entered the Crown's service.

It is no answer to this submission to say that even where an applicant makes application to a tribunal (whether set up under the prerogative as in the case of the Criminal Injuries Compensation Board or the C.S.A.B. or more usually under statutory power) for redress of some kind, the applicant is consenting to the jurisdiction of the tribunal. There is an essential difference between the acceptance as part of the terms of appointment of a disciplinary code of the employer on the one hand, and an *ad hoc* submission to the tribunal such as the Criminal

Injuries Compensation Board whose jurisdiction arises *only* by virtue of the application made to it." (Original emphasis.)

E: Raising Issues of Public Law by Way of Defence

1. Introduction

One important aspect of the case-by-case working out of the principle in *O'Reilly v. Mackman* (1982) is the question of whether it is permissible to raise an issue of public law by way of defence, without applying for judicial review.

The starting point is Lord Diplock's insistence in *O'Reilly* that the purpose of the procedure by way of application for judicial review was to provide a measure of protection for public decision-makers against pettifogging challenges, and that among the factors contributing towards this protection are the short time limit within which the application must be made, and the need to obtain leave to make the substantive application. It is on this basis that seeking a declaration or an injunction by means of ordinary action, in an attempt to circumvent that protection, was characterized as an abuse of the process of the court.

The crucial question for the present purposes, therefore, is whether the position is the same where a public authority itself commences proceedings and the defendant wishes to avail himself of a defence which necessarily involves an allegation of illegality on the part of the public authority. In some cases this question has received different answers according to whether the proceedings are civil or criminal, although it is not always easy to see the relevance of this distinction.

The seminal case is *Wandsworth London Borough Council v. Winder* (1984). Winder was a tenant of the local authority. His rent was increased, he fell into arrears, and the local authority brought an action in the County Court seeking both the arrears of rent and possession of the premises. Winder claimed that the decision to increase the rent was unlawful, and that therefore he continued to have a valid tenancy in accordance with the terms in force before the purported rent increase, and that accordingly he did not owe any arrears. The question was whether the defendant could raise this argument by way of defence.

The House of Lords, emphasizing that the idea of abuse of process was central to the decision in *O'Reilly v. Mackman*, held that the defence could be raised, because it could hardly be said that a defendant was abusing the process of the court by defending himself. Lord Fraser put it thus:

"It would in my opinion be a very strange use of language to describe the respondent's behaviour in relation to this litigation as an abuse or misuse by him of the process of the court. He did not select the procedure to be adopted. He is merely seeking to defend proceedings brought against him by the appellants. In so doing, he is seeking only to exercise his ordinary right of any individual to defend an action against him on the ground that he is not liable for the whole sum claimed by the plaintiff."

Winder was, of course, a civil case, and the facts concerned a challenge to a decision which was antecedent to the decision actually to commence proceedings. On the latter point, it is useful to contrast the case of *R. v. Waverley District Council ex parte Hilden and Others* (1988). The facts of this case were complex, but the essence of the matter was that the local authority was trying to prevent the use of certain land as a gipsy camp site. A variety of proceedings ensued, including appeals to the Secretary of State under the planning legislation and prosecutions in the magistrates' and the Crown courts. The local authority came to the view that injunctions might be the most effective means of enforcing the law. Accordingly they resolved to authorize the institution of appropriate proceedings. The actual commencement of the proceedings was, however, delayed, pending further developments in relation to other aspects of the saga.

Nevertheless, in due course, the injunctive proceedings were commenced, and the point arose as to whether the defendants should be allowed to challenge the legality of the exercise of discretion to commence those proceedings.

Scott J. declined to allow the matter to be argued by way of defence, holding instead that the proper course of action was for the court to consider whether the injunction proceedings should be stayed in order to give the defendants an opportunity to apply for judicial review. In all the circumstances of the case, Scott J. decided that he would not actually stay the proceedings, because he took the view that the defendants would have had only an insignificant chance of success in proceedings for judicial review.

Two further aspects of the case are worth noticing, albeit by way of some diversion. First, the judge took the view that the reasonableness or otherwise of the decision to commence proceedings had to be judged by reference to the situation which obtained when the proceedings were actually commenced, and not when the decision was taken to authorize them. Secondly, even if there had been illegality in the exercise of discretion to commence the proceedings, the proceedings themselves would still not have been a complete nullity. The correct analysis was that there would have been valid proceedings, but that they were being maintained by an incompetent plaintiff. All that would be required, therefore, would be the substitution of a competent plaintiff, either by way of introducing someone else (such as the Attorney-General) to take that role, or by way of removing the incompetence of the instant plaintiff, by validly re-making the decision to commence proceedings.

The *Waverley* decision was approved by the Court of Appeal in *Avon County Council v. Buscott* (1988) where the local authority was seeking a summary order for possession of certain land. The defendants, who were gipsies, did not deny that they were trespassers, but did seek to challenge the reasonableness of the local authority's decision to bring the proceedings. The trial judge held that this matter could be raised only by way of an application for judicial review. The Court of Appeal upheld this. Lord Donaldson M.R. distinguished between *Winder* on the one hand and cases such as the instant one on the other:

> "Mr. Winder was seeking to raise a true defence. He was saying that he had a valid tenancy, that he did not owe any rent and, accordingly, was not liable to eviction. It was a defence on the merits. In the present case the defendants do not allege any right to occupy the land and, accordingly, do not deny that they are liable to be evicted. They do not suggest that they have any defence on the merits. What they say is quite different, namely that the Council is not entitled to enforce its rights ... When a defendant is seeking, in effect, to strike out an action on the basis of a public law right, he should, in my judgment, proceed by way of an application for judicial review, thus ensuring that the matter is dealt with speedily as a preliminary point and in a manner which gives the public authority and the public which it serves the protections enshrined in the judicial review procedure."

The same approach was taken at first instance in *Times Newspapers Ltd. & Others v. Derbyshire County Council* (1992). The local authority, using its power under s.222 of the Local Government Act 1972 to bring legal proceedings, was suing for libel. In the High Court, Morland J. held, *inter alia*, that any challenge to the legality of the exercise of the discretion under s.222 could be brought only by way of an application for judicial review. In due course, the Court of Appeal regarded this point as being less than self-evident, and suggested that the issue could possibly be raised by way of defence to the substantive action. However, as the court decided that the local authority was not entitled to sue for libel anyway, and as the question of challenging the exercise of the s.222 discretion had not been argued, the court preferred to express no decided opinion on the matter.

2. *Is There a Distinction Between Civil and Criminal Cases?*

The raising of issues of public law by way of defence has typically arisen in byelaw prosecutions where the defence has consisted of a challenge to the validity of the byelaw itself. The traditional view is that such defences are perfectly proper. For example, in *R. v. Wood* (1855) a local board of health had power to make byelaws requiring the occupier of premises to remove "dust, ashes, rubbish, filth, manure, dung and soil" from the footpath opposite their premises. It was held that a byelaw purporting to require the removal of snow was *ultra vires*, and therefore a defendant who was prosecuted for failure to remove snow should be allowed to rely on the illegality of the byelaw, and should be acquitted.

In *Director of Public Prosecutions v. Bugg* (1987) the High Court held that a magistrates' court had erred in acquitting the defendant because the validity of the byelaws, under which the prosecution was brought, had not been proved. The validity of the byelaws should be assumed unless and until the contrary is proved.

The *Wood* view is, of course, perfectly consistent with *Winder*, but more recently, an alternative view has emerged. The leading case on the alternative view is *Quietlynn Ltd. v. Plymouth City Council and Others* (1987). Various local authorities had all adopted the sex establishment licensing provisions of the Local Government (Miscellaneous Provisions) Act 1982. Quietlynn had been using premises in the area of each local authority before the day appointed for the coming into effect of the licensing provisions and wished to continue to do so thereafter. Under these circumstances, the statute entitled them to continue trading until their applications had been determined. The company therefore applied for appropriate licences, which were refused. Despite the refusal of their applications in each case, the company continued to use the premises.

All the local authorities had prosecuted the company in the magistrates' courts, where convictions were obtained in each case. Appeals to the Crown Court were allowed in two and dismissed in one.

In each case the essence of the company's argument was that the decision to refuse their applications for licences had been *ultra vires* for various reasons, with the result that the applications had never been validly determined, and therefore the company's continued trading without licences was not an offence.

The High Court held that, except in a case where a licensing decision was invalid on its face, Quietlynn's argument must fail for two reasons. First, acceptance of it would frustrate the clarity and certainty which the statutory provisions were intended to achieve. Secondly, if magistrates' courts and the Crown court were allowed to embark on inquiries as to the validity of licensing decisions in cases such as the present, there would be a danger of inconsistent decisions not only between different magistrates' courts, but also between the magistrates' courts and the Crown courts on the one hand, and the High Court on the other. The court explained away the existing exceptions to this principle, such as defences to byelaw prosecutions,by saying that these had come into being before the development of the modern law of judicial review. In modern times the correct course of action in such cases would be for the prosecution to be adjourned pending an application for judicial review.

Webster J. seems to have attached some considerable significance to the fact that *Winder* was civil, whereas the instant case was criminal. Unfortunately, he did not, however, make clear precisely why he thought the distinction was material. In view of the novelty of this decision it was somewhat startling that the House of Lords refused leave to appeal.

The *Quietlynn* approach has not been universally accepted, even in the criminal courts. In *R. v. Reading Crown Court ex parte Hutchinson* (1988) which was heard by a differently constituted court - save as to one common member - from that which decided *Quietlynn*, the High Court held that trial courts should deal with the question of the validity of a byelaw when this issue is raised, leaving the party aggrieved by the ruling, whichever way it might go, to appeal by way of case stated.

Lloyd L.J. was willing to accept that *Quietlynn* had been correctly decided on its facts, and he clearly regarded Quietlynn itself as an unmeritorious litigant. Nevertheless, he did not accept the opinion of Webster J. that the distinction between civil and criminal cases was relevant, and he could not see how, on the present facts, it could be said to be an abuse of the process of the court to challenge the validity of the byelaw by way of defence.

Mann J., the judge who was common to both cases, said that he did not repent of the decision in *Quietlynn*, but

"having heard argument in this court it seems to me that the reference to byelaws [in *Quietlynn*] would be ascribed a meaning which I, for my part, did not intend, having regard to my silence in *DPP v. Bugg*."

Whilst it may be difficult to identify either what Mann J. meant, or the meaning of what he said, what does emerge reasonably clearly is that the validity of byelaws may still be challenged by way of defence to a prosecution.

Both civil and criminal aspects arose in *R. v. South Somerset District Council ex parte DJB (Group) Ltd.* (1989), where the local authority applied to the Chancery Division of the High Court for an injunction to restrain Sunday trading and also decided to prosecute. The traders applied to the Queen's Bench Division of the High Court for judicial review to quash both decisions. Part of the case was concerned with the procedural complication that proceedings were on foot simultaneously in two Divisions of the High Court. The court resolved this by saying they should be brought together either by appointing a Chancery judge as an additional judge of the Queen's Bench Division for the purpose of hearing both cases together, or by tranferring the Chancery proceedings to the Queen's Bench Division. For the present purposes, however, the interesting point is that Woolf L.J. accepted that judicial review was appropriate for both challenges:

"It is perfectly proper, indeed necessary, to apply by way of judicial review to raise the type of point which the applicants have raised on the present applications."

He justified this on the basis of preventing a circumvention of the procedural protection built into judicial review, and on the basis of *Waverley* and *Buscott*.

Nevertheless, these comments were not well-received in *R. v. Oxford Crown Court and Another ex parte Smith* (1990), where the second respondent, as local planning authority, served a notice on the applicant under the planning legislation, requiring him to tidy up certain land. The applicant appealed against this notice to the magistrates' court, which upheld the notice. The applicant then appealed to the Crown Court where he wished to argue that, in the circumstances of the case, the notice had been *ultra vires* the second respondent, who should have taken enforcement action under other provisions of the planning legislation. The Crown Court ruled that it had no jurisdiction to deal with the *vires* argument, and upheld the notice, subject only to a minor variation.

On an application for judicial review, the High Court held that the point of planning law had been disposed of by the decision of the Court of Appeal in *Britt v. Buckinghamshire County Council* (1963), which had not been cited in the Crown Court, but which was binding on the court and which clearly indicated that the notice had been *intra vires* anyway. However, on the present facts it could not be said that raising the *vires* argument was an abuse of the process of the court within the doctrine of *O'Reilly v. Mackman*. Therefore the Crown Court had been wrong to refuse to consider the argument, even though the planning authority would still have been successful in any event, provided the court had had regard to the relevant law. On the point of principle, Simon Brown J. said:

"Occasionally, of course, to proceed with a defence otherwise than by judicial review will involve an abuse of process, as in *Quietlynn*, or perhaps if prejudicial delay would result; but that would not generally be so."

Dealing with the *dicta* in *South Somerset*, the judge quoted the appropriate passage from Woolf L.J's. judgment, before saying:

"I have great difficulty in reconciling this with the decision in *ex parte Hutchinson*. I doubt indeed whether the court in *South Somerset D.C.* heard full argument upon the necessity of raising the challenges there by way of judicial review rather than as defences to the respective proceedings. After all, judicial review was clearly one route by which the arguments could be raised, and leave must inevitably have been given beforehand. Since, therefore, Woolf L.J.'s dictum seems to me to be *obiter*; since it expressly recognizes the inconvenience of the multiplicity of proceedings resulting from that approach; and since in my judgment public bodies would generally lose little if anything through the bypassing of O.53 protections by the deployment of public law challenges as part of a true, as opposed to a *Buscott*-type, defence to civil or criminal proceedings, I have thought it right to follow *ex parte Hutchinson*."

In *R. v. Dudley Justices ex parte Blatchford* (1992), the High Court held that the decision of a local authority to apply to a magistrates' court for a warrant of commitment in respect of non-payment of community charge is not susceptible to challenge in the magistrates court itself, but may be the subject of an application for judicial review.

Finally, *Doyle v. Northumbria Probation Committee* (1991), represents a variation on the theme, to the extent that it was the decision-maker itself which was being sued and which wished to raise the issue of public law in its own defence. The facts were that the committee changed the conditions of employment of its employees in a way which was adverse to them. The employees began an ordinary action claiming damages for breach of contract. The committee applied to have the action struck out on the basis that the dispute involved matters of public law which could be raised only by way of an application for judicial review. In the High Court, Henry J. held that where a public authority is a defendant in an action which is being brought to enforce rights in private law, and it wishes to raise an issue of public law by way of defence when the plaintiff was out of time to proceed by way of an application for judicial review, it would be unfair to strike the action out. As the rights which the employees were seeking to assert in the instant case were contractual, and therefore within the realm of private law, it followed that their action should not be struck out.

The line of reasoning adopted by Henry J. may go some way to explaining the distinction, which *Hutchinson* tried to establish, between prosecutions in byelaw cases and all other prosecutions, because a prosecution will typically be brought many years after the enactment of the byelaw, with the result that an application for judicial review would be hopelessly out of time. By way of contrast, there is nothing to stop the recipient of an adverse decision directed at himself, such as the licensing refusal in *Quietlynn*, from seeking judicial review promptly. Nevertheless, in view of the importance which the common law traditionally attaches to the liberty of the subject, it is curious to see some Judges seeking to develop a doctrine which puts a defendant in criminal proceedings into a weaker position than that occupied by his counterpart in civil proceedings.

F: Relator Actions in the Light of *O'Reilly v. Mackman*

The relator procedure (see p.58) never applied to applications for the prerogative orders anyway, but only to injunctions and declarations. The fact that the House of Lords made no mention of relator actions in *O'Reilly* is therefore rather curious, since on the face of it there is now an element of doubt as to whether such actions survive in an era when the basic proposition is that challenges in matters involving public law must be brought under O.53.

However, the case of *Attorney-General ex rel. Yorkshire Derwent Trust Ltd. v. Brotherton*, which reached the House of Lords in 1990, was begun in May 1984 by way of originating summons. Admittedly this was relatively soon after *O'Reilly* and before much of the ensuing case-law had developed, but it is clear evidence of the survival of relator actions at that time. This is not altogether surprising, since the basis of the *O'Reilly* doctrine is the protection of decision-makers, and the Attorney-General's discretion may be seen to perform this function more than adequately. Additionally, bearing in mind that in *Gouriet* (see p.58) the House of Lords deferred to the Attorney-General to the extent of accepting the unreviewability of the exercise of his discretion to withhold consent to a relator action, it would be remarkable if the courts were now to hold that the whole concept of relator actions had been abolished on a *sub silentio* basis.

CHAPTER 6

THE *WEDNESBURY* PRINCIPLE: RELEVANCE AND REASONABLENESS

A: Introduction

The content of the statement of law contained in the leading case of *Associated Provincial Picture Houses Ltd. v. Wednesbury Corporation* (1947) was not new, but the words used by Lord Greene M.R. in making that statement have acquired classic status.

The facts were that the corporation had a statutory power to license Sunday entertainments. It granted a licence to the company authorizing Sunday opening of cinemas, but imposed a condition prohibiting the admission of children under the age of 15. In response to a challenge to the legality of the condition, the corporation argued that it could legitimately take the moral welfare of children into account.

The court agreed with the corporation, but the lasting importance of the case lies in the Master of the Rolls' statement of principle:

"When an executive discretion is entrusted by Parliament to a body such as the local authority in this case, what appears to be an exercise of that discretion can only be challenged in the courts in a strictly limited class of case. As I have said, it must always be remembered that *the court is not a court of appeal.* When discretion of this kind is granted, the law recognizes certain principles upon which that discretion must be exercised, but within the four corners of those principles the discretion, in my opinion, is an absolute one, and cannot be questioned in any court of law. What then are those principles? They are well understood. They are principles which the court looks to in considering any question of discretion of this kind. *The exercise of such a discretion must be a real exercise of the discretion.* If, in the statute conferring the discretion, there is found to be, expressly or by implication, matters which the authority exercising the discretion ought to have regard to, then in exercising the discretion it must have regard to those matters. Conversely, if the nature of the subject matter and the general interpretation of the Act make it clear that certain matters would not be germane to the matter in question, the authority must disregard those irrelevant collateral matters. There may have been in the cases expressions used relating to the sort of things that authorities must not do ... I am not sure myself whether the permissible grounds of attack cannot be defined under a single head. It has been perhaps a little bit confusing to find a series of grounds set out. *Bad faith, dishonesty - those, of course, stand by themselves - unreasonableness, attention given to extraneous circumstances, disregard of public policy and things like that have all been referred to*, according to the facts of individual cases, as being matters which are relevant to the question. *If they cannot all be confined under one head, they at any rate, I think, overlap to a very great extent.* For instance, we have heard in this case a great deal about the meaning of the word 'unreasonable'. It is true the discretion must be exercised reasonably. Now what does that mean? Lawyers familiar with the phraseology commonly used in relation to statutory discretions often use the word 'unreasonable' in a rather comprehensive sense. It has frequently been used, and is frequently used, as a general description of the things that must not be done. For instance, a person entrusted with a discretion must, so to speak, direct himself properly in law. He must call his own attention to the matters which he is bound to consider. He must exclude from his consideration matters which are irrelevant to what he has to consider. If he does not obey those rules, he may truly be said, and often is said, to be acting unreasonably. Similarly, *there may be something so absurd that no sensible person could ever dream that it lay within the powers of the authority.*" (Emphasis added.)

It is immediately apparent that the *Wednesbury* principle consists of two main elements: relevance and reasonableness. However, before considering each of these elements in more detail, it will be convenient to deal briefly with a number of matters relating to terminology and classification.

First, Lord Greene spoke of "bad faith" and "dishonesty" as if they were two distinct concepts. However, in *Cannock Chase District Council v. Kelly* (1978) Megaw L.J., with Sir David Cairns merged the two concepts:

"I would stress ... that bad faith, or, as it is sometimes put, 'lack of good faith', means dishonesty: not necessarily for a financial motive, but still dishonesty. It always involves a grave charge. It must not be treated as a synonym for an honest, though mistaken, taking into consideration of a factor which is in law irrelevant."

More particularly, in *R. v. Hammersmith and Fulham London Borough*

Council ex parte Lusi and Lusi (1992) the High Court said that when considering whether someone who acted in ignorance of relevant facts has acted in good faith, there is a distinction to be drawn between honest blundering and carelessness on the one hand and dishonesty on the other.

Secondly, some commentators and Judges speak of "improper purposes" or "abuse of power" as if these phrases represent distinct heads of challenge. In reality, however, any improper purposes or abuse of power will arise either through bad faith, in the sense of dishonesty, or through the decision-maker having regard to the wrong considerations, or acting unreasonably. It follows, therefore, that in either case the alternative phraseology adds nothing to the other heads of challenge, and therefore may safely be allowed to fall victim to Occam's razor.

Thirdly, in *GCHQ* (1984) Lord Diplock attempted a general restatement of the grounds for judicial review:

"One can conveniently classify under three heads the grounds upon which administrative action is subject to control by judicial review. The first ground I would call *illegality*, the second *irrationality*, and the third *procedural impropriety*. That is not to say that further development on a case by case basis may not in course of time add further grounds. I have in mind particularly the possible adoption of the principle of *proportionality* which is recognized in the administrative law of several of our fellow members of the European Economic Community." (Emphasis added.)

"By *illegality* ... I mean that the decision-maker must understand correctly the law that regulates his decision-making power and must give effect to it ... By *irrationality* I mean what can now be succinctly referred to as *Wednesbury unreasonableness* ... I have described the third head as procedural impropriety rather than as failure to observe basic rules of natural justice or failure to act with *procedural fairness* towards the person who will be affected by the decision. This is because susceptibility to judicial review under this head covers also failure by an administrative tribunal to observe procedural rules that are expressly laid down in the legislative instrument by which its jurisdiction is conferred, even though such failure does not involve any denial of natural justice."

Fourthly, it is not at all clear whether anything is gained by reformulating the *Wednesbury* principle in this way, since on the whole the revised terminology is stated to correspond to existing grounds of challenge. Admittedly, Lord Diplock's reference to *proportionality* may seem to presage the introduction of a fresh concept into English law, but this needs to be considered with a great deal of care (see p. 115 *et seq.*, in the context of *Reasonableness*).

Moreover, Lord Diplock's revision of the well-established terminology has not been universally adopted. For example, in *R. v. Devon County Council ex parte G* (1988), Lord Donaldson M.R., speaking of the term "*Wednesbury* unreasonable", said:

> "I eschew the synonym of 'irrational' because, although it is attractive as being shorter than '*Wednesbury* unreasonable' and has the imprimatur of Lord Diplock ... it is widely misunderstood by politicians, both local and national, and even more by their constituents, as casting doubt upon the mental capacity of the decision-maker, a matter which in practice is seldom if ever in issue."

On the other hand, in *R. v. Inland Revenue Commissioners ex parte Taylor (No. 2)* (1989) the phrase "unreasonable in the *Wednesbury* sense" was subject to the following comment:

> "That phraseology, though we still adhere to it out of usage if not affection, is one that properly has been replaced by the use of the word 'irrational', derived from the well-known speech of Lord Diplock in *Council of Civil Service Unions v. Minister for the Civil Service.*"

The truth of the matter is that Judges use both the terms "*Wednesbury* unreasonable" and "irrational" in such a way that it is impossible to distinguish between them.

Finally, it is interesting to note that there is nothing exclusively legal about the idea that it is crucially important to have regard to the right considerations, and to distinguish rigorously between the desirability of a result and the legitimacy of the decision-making process which precedes it. A notable extra-legal example occurs in T.S. Eliot's version of Thomas à Becket's response to the temptation of staying in order to be murdered so that he would become eligible for canonization, rather than fleeing in order to survive:

> "The last temptation is the greatest treason:
> To do the right deed for the wrong reason."
>
> *(Murder in the Cathedral.)*

B: The Principle of Relevance Generally
Merely stating the proposition that a decision-maker must have regard to
the right considerations does not provide any assistance in identifying
what those considerations will be in any particular case. Although it is
true that, in the final analysis, the right considerations can be identified
only in the context of a specific decision-making power, three matters of
general applicability may be mentioned.

First, the purpose of the statute which confers the power will always
be relevant. At the most basic level this can be illustrated by the case of
Padfield v. Minister of Agriculture, Fisheries and Food (1968). The Milk
Marketing scheme's main institutions were the Milk Marketing Board,
and a Committee of Investigation to deal with complaints about the
operation of the scheme. There were persistent complaints about unfairness
as to differential payments to farmers in different geographical areas, but
the Minister refused to exercise his statutory discretion to refer the matter
to the Committee. In the House of Lords, where the Minister was held to
be acting unlawfully, Lord Reid said:

> "It is implicit in the argument for the Minister that there are only two
> possible interpretations of this provision - either he must refer every
> complaint or he has an unfettered discretion to refuse to refer in any
> case. I do not think that that is right. Parliament must have conferred
> the discretion with the intention that it should be used to promote the
> policy and objects of the Act; the policy and objects of the Act must be
> determined by construing the Act as a whole, and construction is
> always a matter of law for the court ... If the Minister ... so uses his
> discretion as to thwart or run counter to the policy and objects of the
> Act, then our law would be very defective if persons aggrieved were
> not entitled to the protection of the court."

In *R. v. Tower Hamlets London Borough Council ex parte Chetnik
Developments Ltd.* (1988) the House of Lords was dealing with s.9(1) of
the General Rate Act 1967, under which the local authority had power to
make refunds in order to avoid injustice where there had been erroneous
overpayments of rates. The House held that, in view of the purpose of the
provision, a local authority which wished to retain erroneous overpayments
would be required to identify a relevant and sufficient reason for doing so,
such as unmeritorious conduct on the part of the ratepayer.

The case of *Pilling v. Abergele Urban District Council* (1950) is also
instructive. Under the Public Health Act 1936, the local authority had
power to license sites for moveable dwellings. They refused one

application, on the ground that the site would be harmful to amenity. The court held that this was unlawful, on the basis that only public health matters were relevant to the exercise of powers under the Public Health Act. Amenity matters were within the purview of planning law, and were therefore irrelevant in the present context.

Pilling must, however, be carefully distinguished from *Kingsley and Kingsley v. Hammersmith and Fulham London Borough Council* (1992), where the relevant regulations specified amenity and safety as the only factors to which local authorities could lawfully have regard when exercising their powers of control over advertisements. On the other hand, the statute which conferred the power to prosecute for breaches of advertisement control did not specify the factors which were relevant when exercising the discretion to prosecute. The High Court rejected a submission that the factors specified in the regulations should be implied into the statute.

Secondly, of course, it will be commonplace, for a decision to be motivated by a variety of considerations. Clearly this raises a difficulty in the present context if some of the considerations are lawful, but others are not.

For many years the case-law maintained the principle that if the court could identify a dominant consideration, and that consideration was lawful, the decision would be allowed to stand, even though other considerations, of an unlawful nature, were also present in the decision-maker's mind. Of course, quantifying the various considerations was not always easy, but in each case the courts did their best.

In *Westminster Corporation v. London & North Western Railway Co.* (1905) a power to provide a public convenience was exercised in such a way that an underpass was also provided. The House of Lords held that this was lawful. Provided a power is exercised in good faith in order to achieve a legitimate objective, it is immaterial that other objectives are also attained.

The Australian case of *Sydney Municipal Council v. Campbell* (1925) is on the other side of the line. The appellant council had two powers to acquire land by compulsion. One was for the purpose of making or extending streets, and the other was for carrying out improvements in or re-modelling any part of the city.

The appellants wished to acquire some land because its value was likely to increase. In itself this was not within their powers, so they embarked on compulsory purchase proceedings on the basis that the land was needed to extend a street. When the real motive came to light, the Austalian court restrained the local authority from pursuing the compulsory purchase procedure. The appellants then re-commenced compulsory purchase proceedings, this time alleging that the land was needed for re-modelling part of the city.

The Privy Council said that the new compulsory purchase process also failed, holding that in reality the appellants were merely trying to impose a new form on a transaction upon which they had already decided, and the need for re-modelling was not genuinely being considered.

A somewhat different test emerged in *R. v. Inner London Education Authority ex parte Westminster City Council* (1986). The education authority wanted to spend £500,000 on an advertising campaign against the Government's control of local authorities' expenditure, which would reduce its budget by £75,000,000. Westminster City Council, which was one of the local authorities which funded the education authority, claimed the expenditure was *ultra vires*. In passing it must be observed that the facts on which this case was decided arose before s.2 of the Local Government Act 1986 introduced statutory restrictions on "political" advertising by local authorities.

In the High Court Glidewell J. held that part of the motive for the expenditure was the provision of information, which was lawful under s.142(2)(a) of the Local Government Act 1972, but another - and perhaps the major - purpose was to seek to persuade members of the public to accept the education authority's views as to the undesirability of the extent of the Government's intervention in local government spending. On the facts, the outcome was that the decision was unlawful. At the level of principle it is important to notice that Glidewell J., whilst acknowledging that if the dominant reason had been legitimate the decision would not have been invalidated merely because it also achieved a subsidiary objective which would not in itself have been legitimate, summarized the key issue thus:

> "It thus becomes a question of fact for me to decide, upon the material before me, whether in reaching its decision [the decision-maker] was pursuing an unauthorized purpose, namely that of persuasion, *which has materially influenced the making of the decision."* (Emphasis added.)

In practice it may well be that this test is easier to apply than the more traditional approach, since the quantification which it requires is less precise.

Thirdly, the courts have repeatedly said that, as far as local authorities are concerned at least, there is a fiduciary duty in relation to the expenditure of public money. Thus, for example in *Roberts v. Hopwood*

(1925) (which is also discussed at p.116), Lord Atkinson said that local authorities have a duty

"to conduct the administration in a fairly businesslike manner with reasonable care, skill and caution."

Lord Sumner was more forthright, saying that the ratepayers were entitled to be protected

"from the effects on their pockets of honest stupidity or impracticable idealism."

Similarly, in *Prescott v. Birmingham Corporation* (1954) the Court of Appeal held that it was unlawful for the local authority to give public transport concessions to old-age pensioners. Following this case, however, legislation was swiftly enacted to legitimize the practice. The duty can also operate in such a way as to require a local authority to maximize income as well as minimizing expenditure. In *Bromley London Borough Council v. Greater London Council* (1982) the local authority increased the rates in order to subsidize London's public transport. Although this maximized income from one source, the House of Lords made the point that one consequence of the increase was that, under the regime of local authority finance in force at the time, the local authority would lose central government grant. Consequently the House took the view that the case involved not only fairness as between one group (the ratepayers as a whole) and another (the public transport users), but also a substantial increase in the total financial burden to be carried by the ratepayers as whole. Since this increased burden would not lead to any corresponding improvement in services, the council was acting thriftlessly and unlawfully. (This case is also discussed at p.100.)

A more complex situation arose in *R. v. Lancashire County Council ex parte Telegraph Service Stations Ltd.* (1989), where a local authority was selling a piece of land. Having provisionally accepted an offer from X, the local authority then received a higher offer from Y, but a sub-committee nevertheless resolved to proceed with the sale to X. The specific question was whether the local authority was obtaining the best price *reasonably* obtainable, as it was required to do under s.123(2) of the Local Government Act 1972. A complicating factor was that the land had been placed on the market only as a result of pressure from Y. Quashing the sub-committee's decision, McCowan J. made it clear that the local authority should have weighed the ethical and commercial factors against each other, rather than regarding the ethical factors, which they saw as being all in favour of X, as being determinative of the issue.

C: Subjective Matters as Relevant Considerations

Where decision-makers are given statutory power to do X if they are satisfied as to Y, the problem which arises is whether the courts are entitled to inquire into whether the decision-makers *should have been satisfied*, or are they bound to accept an assertion that the decision-makers were *in fact satisfied*?

The classic case is *Liversidge v. Anderson* (1941). Regulation 18B of the Defence (General) Regulations, made under the Emergency Powers (Defence) Act 1939, empowered the Home Secretary to detain, without trial, any person if the Home Secretary "had reasonable cause to believe" both that the person was "of hostile origin or associations" and also that, as a result, it was "necessary to exercise control over" them.

The majority of the House of Lords felt bound to accept the Home Secretary's assertion that he "had reasonable cause to believe" both the matters specified in the regulation. However, Lord Atkin dissented famously, saying that "if a man has X" cannot mean the same as "if a man thinks he has X", and taking the example that "if a man has a broken ankle" cannot mean "if a man thinks he has a broken ankle".

The majority view was seriously criticized by the Privy Council in *Nakkuda Ali v. Jayaratne* (1951), and eventually the House of Lords stated it to be wrong in *Inland Revenue Commissioners v. Rossminster* (1980).

The fact that "reasonable grounds to suspect" does not represent a genuinely subjective test does not mean that the formulation of such tests is beyond the wit of Parliamentary counsel. In *Norwich City Council v. Secretary of State for the Environment* (1982) the Secretary of State had power to take over the functions of local authorities in relation to the sale of council houses to sitting tenants "where it appears to [him] that tenants ... have or may have difficulty in exercising the right to buy effectively and expeditiously". The Court Appeal, acknowledging the far-reaching nature of the power, said that judicial review of the exercise of the power would be possible if the Secretary of State acted in bad faith, or by reference to irrelevant considerations, or if he misdirected himself in relation to matters of fact or law. However, Parliament had provided that the condition precedent to the lawful exercise of the discretion was simply the way in which the situation appeared to the Secretary of State, and on the instant facts there were no grounds for judicial interference.

D: Policy as a Relevant Consideration Generally

It is, of course, a matter of common observation that decision-makers in the public sector formulate and apply a wide variety of policies in order to facilitate day-to-day administration. This can, however, give rise to a problem in the *Wednesbury* context, because the decision-maker is required to have regard to all relevant considerations, and not merely to one. The challenge, therefore, is to draw a line beyond which policy becomes a blunt instrument of illegality, rather than being a useful tool of practical decision-making.

In *R. v. Port of London Authority ex parte Kynoch* (1919) Bankes L.J. said:

"There are on the one hand cases where a tribunal [sc. a decision-maker] in the honest exercise of its discretion has adopted a policy, and, without refusing to hear the applicant, intimates to him what its policy is, and that after hearing him it will in accordance with its policy decide against him, unless there is something exceptional in his case ... If the policy has been adopted for reasons which the tribunal may legitimately entertain, no objection could be taken to such a course. On the other hand there are cases where a tribunal has passed a rule, or come to a determination, not to hear any application of a particular character by whomsoever made. There is a wide distinction to be drawn between these two cases."

Similarly, in *British Oxygen v. Minister of Technology* (1970) Lord Reid said:

"The general rule is that anyone who has to exercise a statutory discretion must not 'shut his ears' to an application. There is no great difference between a policy and a rule. There may be cases where the Board should listen to argument against the policy. What it must not do is to refuse to listen at all ... a large authority may have to deal with many similar applications and then it will almost certainly have evolved a policy so precise that it could be called a rule. *There is no objection to that provided it is always ready to listen to new argument.*" (Emphasis added.)

Two questions therefore need to be considered, namely when will a policy be held to be unlawful in itself; and when will the *application of a policy* be held to be unlawful, even though the policy itself is lawful? *Stringer v. Minister of Housing and Local Government* (1971) is a classic case on the illegality of a policy. Manchester University, which owned Jodrell Bank radio telescope, purported to enter into an agreement with the local planning authority under which the latter would "discourage development [in the vicinity of the telescope] within the limits of their powers". Stringer made an application for planning permission which was rejected on the basis, *inter alia*, that the proposed development would interfere with the telescope. Stringer appealed to the Minister, who upheld the refusal of permission. The High Court then held that the purported agreement was *ultra vires* because s.29 of the Town and Country Planning Act 1971 required the planning authority to have regard to all material considerations, and the local planning authority could not validly enter into a contract which would override this duty. The court concluded that the local planning authority's decision was also void, since it was based on the void agreement. However, when the Minister dealt with the appeal, his obligation was to consider the application for planning permission *de novo*, and his decision was allowed to stand because he had had regard to all the relevant considerations, and had not been influenced by the purported agreement with the University.

The case of *Attorney-General ex rel. Tilley v. Wandsworth London Borough Council* (1981) shows that a policy may be held to be unlawful even though, in practice, the decision-maker is prepared to consider cases on an individual basis. Section 1 of the Children and Young Persons Act 1963 placed local authorities under a duty to provide advice, guidance and assistance in order to diminish the need to receive children into care under the Children Act 1948. Although the 1963 Act specifically included the provision of assistance in kind, the Wandsworth Social Services committee decided, as a matter of policy, that where a family was intentionally homeless (within the meaning of what was then the Housing (Homeless Persons) Act 1977), it would not use the power to provide assistance in kind in such a way as to provide accommodation. The committee's preferred course of action was, where necessary, to take the children of such families into care. The policy did not include any express exceptions, although the court accepted that in practice the committee was prepared to hear exceptional applications.

Holding the policy to be unlawful, Judge Mervyn Davies, Q.C., sitting as an additional judge of the Chancery Division, said:

"Assistance under the 1963 Act includes the provision of accommodation [and] it is plain that in every case where there is a family without a home for whatever reason, the local authority is obliged to consider whether the welfare of the child requires that some attempt be made to keep the family together ... the ... question ... is whether or not the existence of the resolution will disable the Social Services Committee from acting fairly when considering the future of the child of intentionally homeless parents. My view is that while the resolution stands the committee would be much influenced by the policy it lays down, and so much so as to raise doubts whether any decision reached could be said to be a fair decision. *The mere existence of the resolution means that in operating s.1 of the 1963 Act there would be differentiation between children according to the conduct of their parents."* (Emphasis added.)

In due course the Court of Appeal upheld this view.

Similarly, in *R. v. Liverpool City Council ex parte Secretary of State for Employment* (1989) the High Court repeated that there is no inflexible rule to the effect that the court will not quash a policy in advance of its implementation.

The decision of the High Court in *R. v. Halton Borough Council ex parte Poynton* (1989) is worth noticing, even if only because it is difficult if not impossible to reconcile some aspects of the judgment with the well-established principles. The facts were that the local authority refused to accept an application for a private hire vehicle driver's licence, where the applicant wished to use the licence as the basis of part-time employment. The authority's policy was, and for three years had been, that licences would be issued only to applicants who intended to use their licences as the basis of full-time work. The local authority subsequently accepted that the refusal to accept the application was unlawful, and invited the applicant to renew his application. He chose not to do so, but applied for judicial review, seeking an order of mandamus requiring the local authority to accept and determine the application without having regard to the fact that the applicant wished to use the licence for the purposes of part-time work only.

In a judgment which lacked any reference to the *Wandsworth* case, Otton J. made several points in the course of dismissing the application. First, in the absence of any decision in respect of an application for a licence, the court had no jurisdiction to order mandamus requiring the local authority to accept and determine an application according to law. Secondly, the applicant was, in reality, seeking to quash a policy which had existed for three years. This was an inappropriate use of the judicial review procedure. Thirdly, it was an additional ground for refusing relief that, if the application for a licence had been considered and refused, the applicant would have had an alternative remedy by way of appeal to the magistrates, and from them to the Crown Court. Curiously, having said that the application for judicial review failed, Otton J. went on to say:

"It must not be thought ... that this decision, or the manner in which it is arrived at, in any way predetermines the validity of such a policy, if it exists, or the application of such a policy or the merits of Mr. Poynton's application should he make it."

Each of these points requires comment. The first point may be technically sound, but in the light of the clear statement of principle in the *Wandsworth* case, it appears to be no more than a technicality, bearing in mind that Otton J. himself went on, as his second point, to say that in reality the proceedings were seeking to quash the local authority's policy, and that this was inappropriate. This ground for refusing relief might appear to be somewhat more sustainable, at least to the extent that it amounts to complaining of delay on the part of the applicant. On closer analysis, however, this would not necessarily amount to good reason for denying relief, unless it could be shown that quashing the policy would cause substantial hardship or be detrimental to good administration. The third point simply misses the thrust of the applicant's challenge, which was clearly aimed at the legality of the policy itself, rather than decisions which might be made as a result of implementing it.

The full import of the judge's final comment is less than clear. However, at best it would appear to mean that the whole of the operative part of the judgment is concerned with denying relief to the applicant at the level of the exercise of discretion, rather than because of any lack of jurisdiction to grant relief. If this interpretation does in fact accord with what Otton J. meant to say, two points come to mind. First, it is small comfort to an applicant to be told that the court could have helped him, but chose not to do so. Secondly, and more importantly, no convincing reason was given for the exercise of discretion in this way.

Bearing in mind that the *Halton* case is inconsistent with clear authority which appears not to have been cited to the court, it is probably best to conclude simply that the case was wrongly decided, at least to the extent that it conflicts with the earlier authority.

E: Party Policy as a Relevant Consideration

1. The Common Law
Where party-political factors enter the decision-making process the courts may find particular difficulty in applying the law relating to

multiple considerations (see pp.92-93). Cases in this category will, of course, involve a rather uneasy interface between the basic constitutional doctrines of the separation of powers and the rule of law.

At a general level, the courts have no difficulty in acknowledging that changes in public opinion from time to time may legitimately be reflected in changes of policy which may in turn be reflected in changing attitudes on the part of decision-makers.

In the case of *R. v. Birmingham City Council ex parte Sheptonhurst Ltd.* (1990) and other cases decided with it, (see also p.9), the local authorities refused to renew expiring sex shop licences which had previously been granted under Schedule III of the Local Government (Miscellaneous Provisions) Act 1982. The High Court held that, when considering an application for renewal of a sex shop licence, a local authority must have regard to the fact that a licence has previously been granted. However, provided it does have such regard, a decision to refuse to renew a licence will not be perverse merely because in the intervening period since the previous grant there has been no change in the character of the relevant locality or in the use to which any premises in the vicinity are put. The reasoning behind this was that Parliament must be taken to know that a local authority is a body of changing composition and shifting opinion, whose changes and shifts reflect the views of the local electorate.

Turning more specifically to the legality of party policies as relevant considerations, a useful starting point can be found in some judicial pronouncements on the status of promises contained in election manifestos. In *Secretary of State for Education and Science v. Tameside Metropolitan Borough Council* (1976) the parties were in dispute over the retention of the 11-plus examination. This case is considered in more detail at p.125, but in the present context it is sufficient to note that Lord Diplock regarded the fact that the Conservatives had campaigned on the basis of retention to be a legitimate factor in their decision-making process following their election to power. However, an election promise can be only one relevant consideration, and of course all relevant considerations must be taken into account.

In *Bromley London Borough Council v. Greater London Council* (1982) the Labour party had campaigned for the Greater London Council elections on the basis that they would, *inter alia*, cut fares on London Transport, and make the ratepayers generally bear the financial burden of the ensuing loss. The case really turned on a detailed exercise in the interpretation of the statutory provisions governing the provision of public transport in London, but the House of Lords made it plain that it was unlawful simply to implement an election promise, without considering all the factors which were relevant to the decision in question.

The manifesto theme also emerged, alongside other arguments, in *R. v. London Borough of Waltham Forest ex parte Waltham Forest Ratepayers' Action Group* (1988). The local authority resolved to increase the rate by 62% for domestic premises and by 56.8% for non-domestic premises. A number of grounds of challenge were raised in an application for judicial review, *inter alia*, to quash that decision.

First, it was argued that the decision to impose such large increases was irrational in a *Wednesbury* sense.

Secondly, it was argued that some councillors who voted for the increases had wrongly had regard to what they regarded as commitments contained in their party's manifesto and that this had led them into a breach of their fiduciary duty to the ratepayers. (The fiduciary duty of local authorities is discussed at pp.93-95.)

Thirdly, it was argued that some councillors who voted for the increase had wrongly had regard to collateral matters, and/or had improperly fettered the exercise of their discretion. This argument was based on the proposition that by accepting the Labour party whip, they had rendered themselves liable to penalties if they failed to vote in accordance with party policy. It was also argued that the councillors in question had wrongly accepted instructions from a joint Local Government Committee, comprising representatives of the Labour parties of the three Parliamentary constituencies which covered the area of the local authority.

Finally, it was argued that the local authority had failed to comply with its statutory obligation to consult industrial and commercial ratepayers.

The High Court dismissed the application on the facts of the case. However, a number of statements of principle emerged.

First, councillors who support a manifesto before their election are entitled to regard the policies contained in that manifesto as one of the most important factors in their decision-making process, but they cannot lawfully regard the manifesto as a commitment to carry out those policies regardless of any other considerations.

Secondly, although it was not surprising that persons outside the local Labour parties might think that the joint Local Government Committee was dictating to the local authority's Labour group, it was nevertheless for the applicants to prove that such dictation did in fact occur, and this they had failed to do.

Thirdly, if a councillor genuinely believes that it is desirable that the party of which he is a member should remain in power to enable it to pursue policies which he favours, this is a relevant consideration for him to take into account when deciding which way to vote on a particular proposal which has the support of the majority of the party, even though he personally is opposed to it. Furthermore, if the alternative to voting with the majority of the council is that he should resign from the party group or from the council, this is not, as a general principle, an improper fetter on his discretion, although there may be exceptions to the generality of this principle, for example in relation to decisions on applications for planning permission.

Fourthly, on the consultation issue, the fact that the views expressed by the ratepayers who were consulted did not result in a change in the proposed increases was not in itself a ground for impugning the genuineness of the consultation process.

On appeal to the Court of Appeal, the appellants' case rested on the argument that the decision was unlawful because six or seven councillors had voted for the increase on the basis of party policy, even though their personal view was that the increase was unreasonably high, and if they had abstained or voted against the increase, the resolution could not have been carried since the voting was 31 to 26.

The Court of Appeal dismissed the appeal on the facts, but indicated that there is no unlawful fetter on an individual councillor's discretion provided that he is free to remain a member of the local authority despite the withdrawal of the party whip, and provided also that he remembers that whatever degree of importance he attaches to group unity and conformity with group policy, the ultimate decision is for him alone as an individual. The court also said that it is for each councillor to make up his own mind on how to vote, giving such weight as he thinks appropriate to the views of other councillors and to the policy of the group to which he belongs. Unless he abdicates this personal responsibility, no question can arise as to the validity of his vote. Stocker L.J. said that there is nothing morally or legally culpable in a councillor voting in support of a majority which has considered and rejected his arguments, provided that he considers all the available options and concludes that the maintenance of political unanimity is of greater value to the ratepayers than insistence on his own point of view. Russell L.J. said that party loyalty, party unanimity, and party policy are all relevant considerations for the individual councillor, and his vote becomes unlawful only if he allows these considerations, or any other outside influences, to dominate him so as to exclude other considerations which are necessary for a balanced judgment. A councillor's vote could be impugned, and any resolution supported by his vote is potentially flawed, if by automatically toeing the party line a councillor deprives himself of any real discretion.

Further instructive illustrations of the law relating to the independence of members of local authorities principle can be found in two cases involving the operation of para. 39(2) of Schedule 12 of the Local Government Act 1972, which confers a second or casting vote on the chairman of a local authority meeting. Both cases involve Bradford City Council, and they share a common factual background.

For many years the political parties in Bradford had agreed to take turns in providing a candidate for the office of Lord Mayor, with the result that the election for that office was always uncontested. In 1988, a Conservative Lord Mayor held office at a time when no party had an overall majority on the council. When the Lord Mayor was being chosen, a Social and Liberal Democratic councillor had said that the candidate would have his support only on the condition that he did not act politically while he was in office. Subsequent by-elections resulted in the Conservatives holding exactly half the seats on the council, which meant, of course, that they had an effective majority if the Lord Mayor used his second or casting vote in their favour.

In *R. v. Bradford Metropolitan City Council ex parte Wilson* (1989) the High Court declined to interfere in a case where the Lord Mayor had used his second or casting vote honestly, and according to his own perception of what was best in the public interest. The court said that the purpose of the chairman's second or casting vote was to break deadlocks which would otherwise arise, because the common law did not provide such a vote. This led the court to reject a suggestion that chairmen should always use the second or casting vote in such a way as to preserve the status quo, because this would maintain the deadlock, rather than breaking it.

Similarly, in *R. v. Bradford Metropolitan City Council ex parte Corris* (1989), dealing with the use of the second or casting vote on another occasion, the Court of Appeal held that the High Court had been right to reject an application for judicial review where the casting vote had been used in favour of the implementation of the policies of the Lord Mayor's own party. The court declined to hold that the lawful exercise of the vote was fettered either by the convention of a rotating Lord Mayorship, nor by the conditional nature of the support given to the Lord Mayor by the Social and Liberal Democratic councillor, who had opposed the use of the office of Lord Mayor for political purposes.

The local authorities fared less well in *R. v. London Boroughs of Camden, Ealing and Hammersmith & Fulham ex parte Times Newspapers Ltd. & Others* (1987). Under s.7 of the Public Libraries and Museums Act 1964 the respondent local authorities had a duty

"to provide a comprehensive and efficient library service ... and for that purpose ... to provide ... such books and other materials ... as may be requisite."

The first applicants were newspaper and periodical proprietors, all of which were important examples of their type. The other applicants were residents of the respondents' areas.

The first applicants were involved in an industrial dispute as a result of which they dismissed some of their employees. With a view to giving encouragement and support to the employees, the respondents excluded certain of the first applicants' publications from their public libraries. The sole reason for the ban in the case of the second and third respondents was to provide a weapon in aid of the dismissed workers in their actions in the industrial dispute by damaging the first applicants. The first respondents shared this reason for the ban, but they also expressed the additional reason that some of the dismissed workers lived in their area.

The High Court held that the ban was inspired by the respondents' political views, and that the use of their powers under s.7 of the 1964 Act for such purposes could not have been within the contemplation of Parliament. More particularly, the ban was unlawful because it had been imposed for an ulterior purpose and in any event no rational local authority could have thought that such a ban could be legitimately imposed.

Another similar decision of the High Court is to be found in the case of *R. v. Derbyshire County Council ex parte The Times Supplements Limited and Others* (1991), where political motives were seen as being evidence of bad faith. Section 38 of the Education (No. 2) Act 1986 imposed a duty on local education authorities to advertise any vacancy in a post which was part of the complement of a school

"in a manner likely ... to bring it to the notice of persons ... who are qualified to fill the post."

Following the publication by *The Sunday Times* of articles critical of a very influential member of the respondent local education authority, and of the authority itself, the respondent decided that it would no longer advertise vacant posts in *The Times Educational Supplement*, or in any other publication owned by Mr. Rupert Murdoch, even though *The Times Educational Supplement* had greater market penetration among teachers than any other publication, and even though, prior to the publication of the articles in *The Sunday Times*, no member of the respondent authority had complained of the service provided by *The Times Educational Supplement*.

Granting an application for judicial review, the High Court held that, on the evidence, the respondent's decisions had clearly been made in bad faith and had been motivated by vindictiveness, therefore certiorari would be granted to quash the decisions, a declaration would be made that the decisions were *ultra vires* and unlawful, and an injunction would be granted restraining the respondents from acting on the decisions.

At the level of principle, the case of *R. v. Lewisham London Borough Council ex parte Shell U.K. Ltd.* (1988) is worth noticing, even though, in the local authority context within which the case arose, some of the arguments have since been covered by the provisions of ss.17 *et seq.* of the Local Government Act 1988, which prohibit local authorities from taking non-commercial considerations into account in relation to supply and works contracts.

The applicant company belonged to an international group of companies. The applicant company itself did not trade with South Africa, but other members of the group did so. The respondent local authority served an area approximately 18% of whose population was black. For a number of years the local authority had taken steps to show its opposition to the South African government's policy of apartheid, and it was the founder of a consortium of local authorities known as Joint Action Against Apartheid.

The local authority held discussions with one of the applicant company's parent companies, during which the local authority unsuccessfully invited the parent company to pursue a policy of withdrawal from South Africa. The local authority then adopted a policy of boycotting all Shell products, subject to alternative products being available on reasonable terms. Through Joint Action Against Apartheid, the local authority also encouraged other local authorities to maximize the pressure on Shell to withdraw from South Africa. Part of the local authority's justification for this action was the duty, imposed by s.71 of the Race Relations Act 1976, to

"make appropriate arrangements with a view to securing that their various functions are carried out with due regard to the need (a) to eliminate unlawful racial discrimination; and (b) to promote equality of opportunity, and good relations, between persons of different racial groups."

An application for judicial review was granted. The court held that the purpose of the boycott was not merely to satisfy public opinion locally, or to promote good race relations, but was inextricably mixed up with a desire to apply pressure on the Shell Group to withdraw from South

Africa. Not only was the local authority's intention to apply pressure on the Shell Group to withdraw from South Africa an extraneous and impermissible purpose, which had had a substantial influence on the local authority's decision, but also the local authority had acted unfairly in seeking to bring pressure on the applicant company in order to change the overall policy of the Shell group of companies towards South Africa. It followed that the local authority's decision was vitiated as a whole and the court should intervene.

The court acknowledged that there are many fields in which joint campaigns between local authorities can be justified, but in circumstances such as those of the instant case the statutory powers of a local authority cannot be employed in order to persuade other local authorities to bring pressure to bear on trading companies, and therefore in this connexion too the local authority had acted *ultra vires*.

2. Non-Commercial Matters: ss.17 et seq. of the Local Government Act 1988

As already mentioned, the *Shell* case arose before the introduction of ss.17 *et seq.* of the Local Government Act 1988. These provisions were introduced to prevent what the government perceived to be an abuse of power by local authorities (and analogous bodies listed in the Second Schedule to the Act), who might seek to impose their own political views on other people with whom they entered into contracts. Briefly, the statutory intention is to prohibit non-commercial matters from being taken into account when bodies within the scope of the Act make decisions relating to contracts for the supply of goods, materials or services, or for the execution of works.

Turning to the provisions in more detail, "non-commercial matters" are defined at some length in the Act. They include matters such as the rates of pay which a contractor pays his workforce, and the sexual and ethnic composition of that workforce; any involvement of a contractor in irrelevant fields of Government policy (for example, defence contracts); the involvement of a contractor in industrial disputes; the country of origin of supplies to, or the location in any country of, business interests of a contractor; and the political, industrial or sectarian affiliations or interests of a contractor, or his directors, partners or employees (the key terms in this provision being defined in such a way that, for example, freemasonry is plainly included).

Similarly, s.18 of the Act, provides that, broadly speaking, the duty imposed by s.71 of the Race Relations Act 1976 is also specifically excluded as a relevant factor.

Section 19(7) of the 1988 Act provides that enforcement of the provisions dealing with non-commercial considerations is by means of applications for judicial review and claims for damages by aggrieved contractors.

The decision of the High Court in *R. v. Islington London Borough Council ex parte the Building Employers' Confederation* (1989) deals with two points of principle on the interpretation of the legislation, and is therefore worthy of notice.

The court held that it would defeat the purpose of the Act to allow a local authority to avoid the prohibition on interfering in relations between contractors and their workforces by the simple device of putting obligations upon contractors, while omitting any specific requirement that the contractors should include corresponding provisions in their own contracts with their workforce.

The second point turned on the meaning of the phrase "terms and conditions of employment by contractors of their workers" in s.17(5)(a) of the 1988 Act, which is part of the definition of non-commercial matters. The court held that the provision relates only to the contractual terms and conditions as between contractors and their employees, and does not extend to the physical conditions in which those employees work.

3. Local Authorities' Committees and Schools' Governors

The theme of one decision-maker seeking unlawfully to influence others also emerged in *Brunyate and Another v. Inner London Education Authority* (1989) where the House of Lords asserted the independence of the governing body of a voluntary school, with the result that the local education authority acted unlawfully when it removed governors whom it had appointed, merely because they would not support the local education authority's policy.

By way of contrast, where the local authority has delegated matters to a committee, which is, of course, an integral part of the local authority's structure rather than being an independent entity as were the governors in *Brunyate*, the local authority is entitled to ensure that the committee implements the local authority's policy. Therefore, where some members of the committee obstruct the local authority's policy with the result that the policy cannot be implemented, the local authority is entitled to remove those councillors from the committee, and replace them with other councillors who will implement the local authority's policy. The application of this principle does not amount to a fetter on the exercise of discretion by individual councillors, because removal from a committee in these circumstances should be seen merely as a political party taking steps to ensure its own cohesion, rather than as amounting to punishment of individuals for failing to comply with party policy (see the Court of Appeal's decision in *Lovelace v. Greenwich London Borough Council* (1991)).

When undertaking the replacement process, regard would have to be had to ss.15 *et seq.* of the Local Government and Housing Act 1989, which may be summarized as imposing a requirement that local authorities should generally achieve political balance on committees and subcommittees. Broadly speaking, this requirement is satisfied if the political complexion of each committee and subcommittee reflects, as far as possible, the political complexion of the local authority itself. The requirement may be dispensed with if the local authority so agrees without dissent (s.17). In any event failure to comply with the requirement does not invalidate business transacted during the period of non-compliance (s.16(3)).

Brunyate was distinguished in *R. v. Warwickshire County Council ex parte Dill-Russell and Cheney* (1991). The facts were that the local education authority had a policy that the number of each political party's nominations to school governorships should be proportionate to the strength of that party's representation on the local education authority itself.

As a result of the implementation of Part II of the Education (No. 2) Act 1986, the quadrennial terms of office of councillors and governors were out of step with each other to the extent that the desired reflection of political representation might occur only for the last eight months of the term of each successive council. Accordingly, in pursuance of its policy, the respondent resolved that all existing local education authority governors of county and special schools should be re-appointed or replaced with effect from October 1, 1989. Various consequential decisions were then made in relation to individual governors.

The appellants argued that the respondent had breached the *Brunyate* principle by usurping the governors' independence.

The High Court dismissed an application for judicial review, holding that the respondent had acted lawfully because its intention was to preserve the existing policy that its own political complexion should be reflected in the political complexion of nominations to governorships, and that therefore the respondent's decisions in relation to individual governors did not constitute politically motivated usurpation of their independence.

The Court of Appeal upheld this decision, saying that on the instant facts there was no distinction to be drawn between the legitimate use of the power to appoint governors in a manner which reflected party weighting and a sensible use of the power to remove governors which simply sought to keep that weighting in existence. However, the court did go on to say that it would not follow that the power of removal could be lawfully exercised in all cases where a disproportionate representation came into existence, because other considerations must also be taken into account in each case, including the need for continuity on governing bodies and the requirements of procedural fairness.

Before leaving the topic of the legality of political factors in decision-making, the classic case of *Roberts v. Hopwood* (1925) must be mentioned. This case is drawn from the statutory arena of local government audit law, rather than from the common law field of judicial review, but the principle underlying the decision is equally applicable in both areas.

The council of the London Borough of Poplar was dominated by socialists who felt strongly that there should be a minimum wage for all workers, irrespective of their job. Accordingly, at a time when the cost of living was actually falling, the council agreed to pay substantial increases to its most poorly paid workers. The new pay rates took no account of comparable rates of pay for comparable work done for other employers. There was, of course, no doubt that the council had power to pay wages to its employees.

The House of Lords indicated that expenditure on a lawful object could nevertheless be unlawful if it was excessive, and that in any event 'wages' are payment for work done, so if there ceases to be a causal relationship between the work and the payment, the money which is paid over cannot be wages but must be a gratuity disguised as wages. The result was that the payments were unlawful.

F: The Principle of Reasonableness Generally

In the *Wednesbury* case itself Lord Greene M.R. clearly indicated that unreasonableness was capable of being a ground of challenge. The question therefore arises as to the relationship between relevance and reasonableness in a *Wednesbury* context. In one sense, of course, it can be said to be unreasonable to act without regard to the right considerations. It would follow from this that, in some cases at least, one concept may be seen as subsuming the other.

Nevertheless, in practice the concept of *Wednesbury* unreasonableness is better considered as being a longstop. There are two possible approaches. In the first place, a decision-maker may have regard to all the right considerations, and disregard all the wrong considerations, and yet his conclusion may still be unreasonable, in the sense of bearing no reasonable relation to the considerations which he had in mind. Alternatively, the court may conclude that whatever considerations may appear to have been taken into account, the final decision is so unreasonable in relation to those considerations that the decision-maker must, in fact, have been motivated by other considerations.

It is important to realise at the outset that the courts will be slow to find that there has been unreasonableness in this context: they will need to be satisfied that the decision-maker has acted *so unreasonably that no reasonable decision-maker could have done what he has done*, or, to adopt the words of Lord Diplock in the *GCHQ* case, that the decision

"is so outrageous in its defiance of logic or of accepted moral standards that no sensible person who had applied his mind to the question could have arrived at it."

Even though challenges on this ground may be very difficult to establish, they may nevertheless sometimes succeed. Consideration of some examples will be instructive.

In *Backhouse v. Lambeth London Borough Council* (1972) the local authority was faced with a choice of action under the Housing Finance Act 1972. The Act required local authorities either to introduce a scheme of fair rents, or to increase rents across the board by 50p per week. The local authority did not wish to pursue either alternative, so it identified one council house which was not only vacant, but was also in such poor condition that it was unlikely ever to be let. The local authority then increased the rent of this one house from £7 per week to £18,000 per week. When this increase was averaged out across the whole of the local authority's housing stock, it could be argued that rents had been increased by 50p per week. The High Court had no difficulty in holding this to be totally unreasonable.

The principle of reasonableness has been used in the law of town and country planning to quash conditions attached to planning permissions. When granting planning permission a local planning authority may attach "such conditions as they think fit". In *Hall & Co. Ltd. v. Shoreham-by-Sea Urban District Council* (1964) the local authority granted planning permission subject to a condition that the applicant should not only construct an access road, but should also give the public a right of way over it. The High Court held that the condition was totally unreasonable, because local authorities have statutory powers to create highways, which they should use where appropriate. They should not use the planning legislation to place the burden of providing public facilities on the shoulders of private developers, as the price of getting planning permission.

The case of *R. v. Hillingdon London Borough Council ex parte Royco Homes Ltd.* (1974) also illustrates the point. The local authority granted planning permission for residential development. The developer intended to sell the units to private buyers, and was therefore displeased to find that the planning permission was subject to a condition to the effect that the developer should let the properties to people on the council's housing waiting list and give them security of tenure for ten years. The High Court found the condition to be totally unreasonable.

In passing it is worth noticing that in both *Hall* and *Royco Homes* the final outcome was that the whole planning permission was quashed along with the objectionable condition, because the court refused to sever the condition. The principles governing the severability of decisions generally are dealt with at pp. 38-40.

Policy considerations resulted in unreasonableness in *Wheeler v. Leicester City Council* (1985). The respondent local authority held and administered a recreation ground under s.10 of the Open Spaces Act 1906. For many years the ground had been used by the Leicester Football Club. Approximately one quarter of the population of the local authority's area were of Asian or Afro-Caribbean origins. The local authority had a policy of boycotting South African goods and they also took the view that there should be no sporting links with South Africa.

In 1984 three members of the club were invited to join a side organized by the English Rugby Football Union which was to tour South Africa. The local authority asked the club to press the Union and the three members to call off the tour. The club's reply included a statement that the club condemned apartheid and that the three members had not only been supplied with copies of a memorandum prepared by the Anti-Apartheid movement, but had also been asked seriously to consider its contents before finally deciding whether to join the touring side. Nevertheless, when the tour took place, the three members of the club joined it. The Policy and Resources Committee of the local authority subsequently decided that the club should be suspended from using the ground for 12 months, with the situation being reviewed thereafter.

In the High Court, Forbes J. refused an application for judicial review against the local authority. The applicant also lost in the Court of Appeal, but eventually succeeded in the House of Lords, where it was held that although in exercising its statutory discretion the local authority was fully entitled to have regard to what they thought was in the best interests of race relations, the conduct of the local authority in the present case was suggestive of something more than merely powerful persuasion and was, therefore, unreasonable on *Wednesbury* principles. The House concluded that there had been a procedural impropriety because the local authority had sought to achieve their aims in an unfair manner. The House also said that a private individual or a private organization cannot be obliged to publish views dictated by a public authority and therefore the local authority had abused its powers in seeking to punish the club when the club had done no wrong.

In *R. v. London Borough of Hackney ex parte Evenbray Ltd.* (1988) the applicants for judicial review were the proprietors of an hotel situated in the area of the respondent local authority. The hotel catered mainly for businessmen and tourists, but a physically separate part of it was used to accommodate homeless persons on a bed and breakfast basis. The homeless persons were sent to the hotel, and paid for, by various local authorities, although about 90% of the homeless persons were sent there by the respondent.

The respondent then made a direction under s.19 of the Housing Act 1961, restricting to nil the number of individuals and households who could occupy the premises. This direction was based on the propositions that the hotel was a house in multiple occupation and that its lack of individual kitchen facilities made it unsuitable for such use. The applicants applied for judicial review to quash the direction, on a variety of grounds, including total unreasonableness on the part of the respondent. The High Court granted the application, holding that no reasonable local authority, having chosen to accommodate homeless persons in an hotel, could then invoke statutory powers on the basis that the hotel was not reasonably suitable for such use because it lacked kitchen facilities for the individual occupiers.

In *R. v. Lancashire County Council and Another ex parte Telegraph Service Stations Limited* (1989), which is more fully discussed at p.94, McCowan J. held that no reasonable sub-committee, having been presented with the full picture, could have arrived at the decision at which that sub-committee had actually arrived.

On the other hand, it is not unreasonable for a local authority to prosecute in the face of advice from its officers that such action will be ineffective (see *R. v. South Somerset District Council ex parte DJB (Group) Ltd.* (1989)) , which is also discussed at p. 83.

G: Uncertainty as Unreasonableness
If the meaning of a requirement is so uncertain that people cannot know whether they are complying with it, the courts may hold the requirement to be unlawful on the ground of unreasonableness.

In *Nash v. Finlay* (1901) a byelaw, which provided that "no person shall wilfully annoy passengers in the street", fell foul of this principle.

The more recent case of *R. v. Barnet London Borough Council ex parte Johnson and Jacobs* (1991), is also instructive. The local authority owned certain land which had been acquired for the purposes of a public park. Byelaws regulating the use of the park provided *inter alia* for the local authority to permit activities within the park which would otherwise have been prohibited.

A committee, which wished to use the park for a "local community annual festival, promoting local artists and community groups", applied to the local authority for permission to do so, and for financial assistance. The local authority was willing to grant the applications, subject to certain conditions. The committee challenged certain aspects of the conditions prohibiting them from doing any or all of the following: allocating exhibition space to political groups; allowing the use of any part of the park for any political activity whatsoever; permitting political parties to participate in the festival; and permitting attendance at the festival by any political party or any organization seeking to promote or oppose any political party. The relevant minutes recorded that the officers concerned were "instructed to ensure that [the policy of excluding political activities] becomes a condition of any hiring."

The local authority argued that it had no power to authorize the use of the park for political purposes, and therefore it was entitled to impose conditions to ensure that such activity did not occur. The local authority also argued that the conditions were lawful because they had been formulated with regard to the statutory purpose and were not *Wednesbury* unreasonable.

On an application for judicial review, the High Court held that the presence of political and quasi-political groups at fairs, fetes, festivals and carnivals up and down the country is commonplace, and such groups are all part of community life, therefore the local authority's argument that it had no power to permit such activities would be rejected. Furthermore, in the present case the individual conditions were unlawful because they were all open to such a variety of possible meanings as to be in effect meaningless, and to be *Wednesbury* unreasonable; to the extent that the conditions did have any meaning, they were clearly discriminatory and therefore outside the statutory purpose; and the minutes leading up to the imposition of the conditions disclosed the application of a blanket policy. However, even though the local authority had acted unlawfully, the decisions were long spent, and appropriate declarations would be difficult to frame, and therefore no relief other than delivery of the court's judgment was appropriate.

Dismissing an appeal, the Court of Appeal held that the local authority had acted unlawfully by imposing conditions which were designed to inhibit the manner in which the public made use of the park, rather than regulating public enjoyment of the park. Although in the light of this finding it was not necessary to go any further, the court wholeheartedly endorsed the views of the High Court that the conditions were so ill-defined as to be meaningless and/or incapable of reasonable compliance. However, had it been necessary to decide the point, the court would have held that the phrase "party-political activities" has a well-recognized meaning, and that s.2(3) of the Local Government Act 1986 disabled the local authority from giving financial assistance for such activities.

At this stage it must be remembered that the topic under discussion is *uncertainty*, and in this connexion the case of *Fawcett v. Buckinghamshire County Council* (1960) is worth careful consideration. The local planning authority granted planning permission for two houses on land which would not normally have been released for this purpose. The planning permission was subject to a condition that

> "the occupation of the houses shall be limited to persons whose employment or latest employment is or was employment in agriculture as defined by s.119(1) of the Town and Country Planning Act 1947, or in forestry, or in an industry mainly dependent upon agriculture, and also including the dependants of such persons as aforesaid."

Reading this carefully, it will be apparent that the condition, if valid, would permit occupation by the widow of a retired sheep-shearer from Australia, which may seem to do little to satisfy the needs of the agricultural community in Buckinghamshire. Nevertheless, the House of Lords upheld the validity of the condition. This decision may seem strange: certainly, it would have been understandable if the House of Lords had decided it the other way. Perhaps the best statement of principle from the whole of the litigation in this case comes from the Court of Appeal, where Lord Denning M.R. said:

> "A planning condition is only void for uncertainty if it can be given no meaning or no sensible or ascertainable meaning and not merely because it is ambiguous or leads to absurd results. It is the daily task of the courts to resolve ambiguities of language and to choose between them; and to construe words so as to avoid absurdities or to put up with them. And this applies to conditions in planning permissions as well as to other documents."

The closing words of this comment clearly indicate the generality of the principle.

In passing it is interesting to note that the modern practice when imposing what is generally known as *the agricultural occupancy condition* is to insert the word "locally" so that it reads "employment locally in agriculture," which leaves only the problem of how local it has to be. However, according to the Court of Appeal in *Alderson v. Secretary of State for the Environment and Another* (1984), the word "locally" does have an ascertainable meaning, which can be identified in each case when considered within a specific factual context.

At this stage it is worth emphasizing the extreme difficulty of establishing that a decision-maker had acted unreasonably. A classic case is *Brinklow v. Secretary of State for the Environment* (1976), where a local authority made a compulsory purchase order in respect of certain land which it proposed to develop for housing. The financial aspect of the proposed development was that the cost of the houses would be five times the market rate. The court acknowledged that the cost was high, but declined to say that it was so high that no reasonable local authority could have decided to incur it.

H: Proportionality and Unreasonableness

A potentially important question arises from Lord Diplock's mention, in the *GCHQ* case, of *proportionality* as a distinctively European concept, and its possible introduction into English law.

Essentially, the idea of proportionality, stemming from Aristotle's principle of distributive justice, simply means that social burdens should be distributed in a fair manner, with fairness being determined according to the capacity of members of society to bear the burdens in question. However, the concept as such has never been expressly incorporated into English law, although various decisions have indicated that a lack of proportionality in the more vernacular sense of fairness can result in illegality.

The real issue which arises in the present context is the relationship between proportionality and *Wednesbury* unreasonableness, since something which is disproportionate is likely to be totally unreasonable. A number of cases may be considered in this connexion.

In *R. v. Barnsley Metropolitan Borough Council ex parte Hook* (1976) a committee of the local authority upheld the revocation of a market trader's licence, following a complaint that he had urinated in the street. Although the Court of Appeal's decision to quash the revocation was largely concerned with an allegation of bias, it is clear that both Lord

Denning M.R. and Sir John Pennycuick regarded the punishment as being wholly disproportionate to the misconduct.

The case of *Roberts v. Hopwood* (1925), which was discussed at pp. 93–94, can also be seen as an example of disproportionality, since there was no proportionately causal relationship between the amount of the work done and the amount of the money paid.

Other cases in which proportionality has been instrumental in the reasoning, without being identified by name, include *R. v. Brent London Borough Council ex parte Assegai* (1987). The facts were that Dr. Assegai, who was described as "a large and colourful character", was a member of the local Labour Party. A disagreement occurred at a private meeting, and Dr. Assegai made some disparaging remarks about two Labour councillors. A scene ensued and the police were called. One consequence of this incident was that the local authority banned Dr. Assegai from visiting any property owned by the local authority. Woolf L.J., holding the ban to be unlawful, said the local authority's action was

> "wholly out of proportion to what Dr. Assegai had done. Where the response is out of proportion with the cause to this extent, this provides a very clear indication of unreasonableness in a *Wednesbury* sense."

Although the court in *Assegai* did not refer to any principles of Community law, clearly the principle of proportionality could have been relied upon explicitly. However, it seems that there is no need for the introduction of proportionality as such into English law.

The leading case is *R. v. Secretary of State for the Home Department ex parte Brind and Others* (1991), which involved the legality of certain directives issued by the Secretary of State in relation to television reporting of events in Northern Ireland. The High Court held that where a decision was neither perverse nor absurd, and was one which could have been made by a reasonable decision-maker properly taking into account the relevant law, English law had not yet developed to the point where the decision could be held to be unlawful merely because it was not in proportion to the benefit to be obtained or the mischief to be avoided. When the case reached the Court of Appeal, Lord Donaldson M.R., upholding the decision of the High Court, specifically developed a theme which Watkins L.J. had introduced in the High Court:

> "Acceptance of 'proportionality' as a separate ground for seeking judicial review rather than a facet of 'irrationality' could easily and speedily lead to courts forgetting the supervisory nature of their jurisdiction

and substituting their view of what was appropriate for that of the authority whose duty it was to reach that decision. I therefore propose to consider the submission that the directives were disproportionate to the needs of the situation as being an aspect of the submission that the directives were 'perverse' or, as I would put it, '*Wednesbury* unreasonable' or, as Lord Diplock would have put it, 'irrational'."

The House of Lords agreed. Lord Lowry said:

"There is *no* authority for saying that proportionality in the sense in which the appellants have used it is part of the English common law and a great deal of authority the other way" [original emphasiz].

He continued:

"This, so far as I am concerned, is not a cause for regret for several reasons:-
"1. The decision-makers, very often elected, are those to whom Parliament has entrusted the discretion and to interfere with that discretion beyond the limits as hitherto defined would itself be an abuse of the judges' supervisory jurisdiction.
"2. The Judges are not, generally speaking, equipped by training or experience, or furnished with the requisite knowledge and advice, to decide the answer to an administrative problem where the scales are evenly balanced, but they have a much better chance of reaching the right answer where the question is put in a *Wednesbury* form. The same applies if the judges' decision is appealed.
"3. Stability and relative certainty would be jeopardized if the new doctrine held sway, because there is nearly always something to be said against any administrative decision and parties who felt aggrieved would be even more likely than at present to try their luck with a judicial review application both at first instance and on appeal.
"4. The increase in applications for judicial review of administrative action (inevitable if the threshold of unreasonableness is lowered) will lead to the expenditure of time and money by litigants, not to speak of the prolongation of uncertainty for all concerned with the decision in question, and the taking up of court time which could otherwise be devoted to other matters. The losers in this respect will be members of the public, for whom the courts provide a service."

Lord Lowry concluded his speech with the following comment:

"It finally occurs to me that there can be very little room for Judges to operate an independent judicial review proportionality doctrine in the space which is left between the conventional judicial review doctrine and the admittedly forbidden appellate approach. To introduce an intermediate area of deliberation for the court seems scarcely a practical idea, quite apart from the other disadvantages by which, in my opinion, such a course would be attended."

CHAPTER 7

JURISDICTIONAL ERROR

A: Introduction

The previous chapter discussed the *Wednesbury* principle of relevance and reasonableness. This principle covers cases where decision-makers have legitimately embarked upon the decision-making process, but have nevertheless fallen into unlawfulness either by taking account of irrelevant considerations, by ignoring relevant considerations, or by acting totally unreasonably. Although decision-makers in these cases are acting unlawfully, there is a sense in which they may be said to be making an error within their jurisdiction, because they do at least have the power to make the decision: the illegality stems from the way in which they exercise that power.

This chapter deals with a problem which may be seen as being logically antecedent to, but much less commonly argued than, the *Wednesbury* problem, namely the situation which arises when the decision-maker makes an error which goes to the root of his power to make the decision at all, and as a result of which there is no legal foundation for his decision-making process. In such cases the decision-maker may be said to have made a *jurisdictional error*. Admittedly, in the course of this chapter it will become apparent that, in some situations, it can be argued that any error of law goes to the decision-maker's jurisdiction, and that therefore the dichotomy between jurisdictional and non-jurisdictional errors is fundamentally false. Be that as it may, the idea of the distinction forms a useful starting point for thinking about certain cases, especially those where Parliament appears to have excluded the jurisdiction of the courts.

The distinction between the two categories of error was indicated in *R. v. Lincolnshire Justices ex parte Brett* (1926), where Atkin L.J. said that jurisdictional questions are to be contrasted with "the main question" or "the actual matter committed to [the decision-maker]." This comment helps to explain some alternative terminological possibilities which may be encountered, principal among which are *preliminary* or *threshold* or *collateral* error - i.e. the error is in relation to a preliminary matter, or one which deals with the threshold which must be crossed before the decision-maker can be said to have power to deal with the real question, or is collateral to the real question. These variations are purely terminological and have no substantive significance.

Unfortunately, identifying the kind of error which the courts regard as jurisdictional is by no means a straightforward matter in every case. In particular it may be necessary to distinguish between matters of *fact* and matters of *law*; and between decisions made by courts and those made by other decision-makers.

Before progressing any further, however, it may be useful to consider a classic example of jurisdictional error.

In *White and Collins v. Minister of Health* (1939) a local authority exercised a power to make a compulsory purchase order in respect of certain land. The power was stated not to be exercisable if the land in question formed part of a park or garden.

A compulsory purchase order was made and was confirmed by the Minister of Health. When the owners of the land challenged the compulsory purchase order on the basis that the land formed part of a park, the High Court refused to interfere with the local authority's finding of fact that the land was not part of a park.

However, the Court of Appeal quashed the compulsory purchase order on the ground that the jurisdiction to make the order was conditional on the land not forming part of a park. Since the land in question did, in fact, form part of a park, it followed that there was no jurisdiction to make the order.

Sometimes the jurisdictional nature of this kind of error can be more clearly identified if the other questions facing the decision-maker are also articulated. Suppose, for example, the land is required for the provision of new housing. In order to justify making the compulsory purchase order, the decision-maker would have to make decisions in relation to a number of matters, including the capacity and condition of the existing housing stock in the area; future population trends; and whether other land, which was equally or more suitable, could be acquired by agreement, thus avoiding the necessity to dispossess anyone by compulsion. These are all aspects of - to borrow the terminology of Atkin L.J. in *Brett* - the "main question" or the "actual matter committed to [the decision-maker]."

Historically the courts have sometimes regarded the distinction between matters of fact and matters of law as being devoid of significance for the present purposes. In *R. v. Shoreditch Assessment Committee ex parte Morgan* (1910) Farwell L.J. said:

"It is a contradiction in terms to create a tribunal with limited jurisdiction and unlimited power to determine such limit at its own will and pleasure - such a tribunal would be autocratic, not limited - and it is immaterial whether the decision of the inferior tribunal on the question of the existence or non-existence of its own jurisdiction is founded on law or fact."

Despite the generality of these words, however, it is important to notice that the modern approach of the courts is that the distinction between matters of fact and matters of law is significant. This means, of course, that some means of drawing the distinction would be useful. Unfortunately, the courts have been unable to offer definitive guidance as to the nature of the distinction, but the following extract from the judgment of Denning L.J., in *British Launderers' Research Association v. Central Middlesex Assessment Committee and Borough of Hendon Rating Authority* (1949), provides as good a basic framework as any:

"It is important to distinguish between primary facts and the conclusions from them. Primary facts are facts which are observed by witnesses and proved by oral testimony or facts proved by the production of a thing itself, such as original documents. Their determination is essentially a question of fact for the tribunal of fact, and the only question of law that can arise on them is whether there was any evidence to support the finding. The conclusions from primary facts are, however, inferences deduced by a process of reasoning from them. If, and in so far as, those conclusions can as well be drawn by a layman (properly instructed on the law) as a lawyer, they are conclusions of fact for the tribunal of fact: and the only questions of law which can arise on them are whether there was a proper direction in point of law; and *whether the conclusion is one which could reasonably be drawn from the primary facts*: see *Bracegirdle v. Oxley* [1947]. If, and in so far, however, as the correct conclusion to be drawn from primary facts requires, for its correctness, determination by a trained lawyer - as for instance, because it involves the interpretation of documents or because the law on the point cannot properly be understood or applied except by a trained lawyer - the conclusion is a conclusion of law." (Emphasis added.)

Conceptually speaking, the distinction between a factual dispute (for example, who hit whom first) and a legal dispute (for example, what has to be established before a plea of self-defence can succeed) is clear enough. Practically speaking, however, it can be extremely difficult to identify the dividing line between law and fact.

In *Brutus v. Cozens* (1972) the issue was whether it was "insulting behaviour", for the purposes of the Public Order Act 1936, to disrupt the

Wimbledon tennis championships by staging an anti-Apartheid demonstration. The House of Lords decided that the finding of the magistrates that the conduct was not insulting was a matter of fact, and that therefore it could not be impugned on appeal. "Insulting" was seen as being an ordinary enough word, and, according to Lord Reid:

> "The meaning of an ordinary word of the English language is not a question of law."

However, in *Edwards v. Bairstow* (1955) the House of Lords decided that the meaning of "adventure in the nature of trade" for the purposes of income tax legislation was a question of law. The Revenue had assessed the taxpayers to income tax on profit made from the purchase and sale of certain machinery, on the basis that the transaction was an "adventure in the nature of trade", but the taxpayers succeeded on appeal to the General Commissioners. On further appeals by the Revenue, both the High Court and the Court of Appeal held that the matter was one of fact, and that therefore the General Commissioners' finding could not be overturned.

In the House of Lords, however, Lord Radcliffe, holding that the question was a matter of law, said:

> "The law does not supply a precise definition of the word 'trade' ... In effect it lays down the limits within which it would be permissible to say that a 'trade' ... does or does not exist. But the field so marked out is a wide one and there are many combinations of circumstances in which it could not be said to be wrong to arrive at a conclusion one way or the other. If the facts of any particular case are fairly capable of being so described, it seems to me that it necessarily follows that the determination ... that a 'trade' does nor does not exist is not 'erroneous in point of law' ... All these cases in which the facts warrant a determination either way can be described as questions of degree and therefore as questions of fact."

On the other hand:

> "If the Case [i.e. as stated by the General Commissioners] contains anything *ex facie* which is bad law and which bears on the determination, it is, obviously, erroneous in point of law. But without any such misconception appearing *ex facie* it may be that the facts found are such that *no person acting judicially and properly instructed as to the relevant law could have come to the determination under appeal.* In

these circumstances, too, the court must intervene. It has no option but to assume that there has been some misconception of the law, and that this has been responsible for the determination. So, there, too, there has been an error in point of law. I do not think it much matters whether this state of affairs is described as one in which there is no evidence to support the determination, or as one in which the evidence in inconsistent with, and contradictory of, the determination, or as one in which the true and only reasonable conclusion contradicts the determination. Rightly understood, each phrase propounds the same test. For my part, I prefer the last of the three." (Emphasis added.)

On the central question in the instant case, Lord Radcliffe asked:

"What detail does [this purchase and sale] lack that prevents it from being an adventure in the nature of trade, or what element is present in it that makes it capable of being aptly described as anything else?"

Comparing *Brutus* with *Edwards*, however, it is difficult to see any distinction in principle between having to decide whether the factual conduct of demonstrating amounts to "insulting behaviour" for the purposes of one statute, and having to decide whether the factual conduct of buying and selling amounts to "an adventure in the nature of trade" for the purposes of another statute.

It is not altogether surprising, therefore that academic commentators tend to unite in scepticism as to whether the law/fact distinction has any practical utility as a basis for predicting judicial outcomes. Thus Craig says:

"The case law on judicial review provides little in the way of guidance on the question of whether a certain issue is one of law or fact." (*Administrative Law*, 2nd edition, 1989, p.313.)

Wade is even more forthright:

"The truth is ... that there can hardly be a subject on which the courts act with such total lack of consistency as the difference between fact and law ... It may be that Judges instinctively agree with an American comment*:

'No two terms of legal science have rendered better service than 'law' and 'fact' ... They are the creations of centuries. What judge has not found refuge in them? The man who could succeed in defining them would be a public enemy' *Leon Green, *Judge and Jury*, p.270" (*Administrative Law* (6th edition), 1988, p.940).

However, if regard is had to both the *British Launderers* case and *Edwards* v. *Bairstow*, it becomes apparent that one version of the judicial approach to the instant question is very similar to the concept of *Wednesbury* unreasonableness (which is discussed at length in chapter 6). Provided the decision is one which a reasonable decision-maker could have made *in the light of the primary facts and on a correct understanding of the law*, the court will not interfere. Even here, of course, there is a practical difficulty in predicting the precise stage at which the courts will say that the decision-maker has overstepped the mark.

B: Errors of Fact

It will be commonplace for a statute to provide, in effect, that if a certain factual state exists, then the decision-maker may exercise his powers. The jurisdictional fact which must exist may, of course, consist of various elements. For example in *White & Collins* (which is discussed at p.120) there were two elements: the property to be acquired must have been land, and that land must not have formed part of a park.

R. v. Fulham, Hammersmith & Kensington Rent Tribunal ex parte Zerek (1951) contains one of the leading statements of principle justifying judicial intervention where there has been a jurisdictional error of fact. The facts were that an Act of 1946 governed furnished lettings and an Act of 1949 governed unfurnished lettings. On a reference to the Rent Tribunal under the 1949 Act, the landlord argued that the 1946 Act was the relevant one, because the tenant had signed a document stating that the property was furnished.

The tenant argued to the contrary, saying that he had entered into an agreement on an unfurnished basis, but that the landlord had refused to allow him to take possession unless he signed a document to the effect that the property was furnished.

The tribunal decided that the document which the tenant had signed was a sham, and that therefore the 1949 Act was the relevant one. Having assumed jurisdiction under the 1949 Act, the tribunal proceeded to reduce the rent. The landlord applied for certiorari, on the basis that the tribunal had had no jurisdiction under the 1949 Act. On the facts, the landlord failed, because the High Court took the view that all the evidence was in favour of the tenant. However, the real interest of the case lies in the following statements of principle. Lord Parker C.J. said:

"If a certain state of facts has to exist before an inferior tribunal have jurisdiction, they can inquire into the facts in order to decide whether or not they have jurisdiction, but cannot give themselves jurisdiction by a wrong decision upon them; and this court may, by means of proceedings for certiorari, inquire into the correctness of the decision. The decision as to the facts is regarded as collateral because, though the existence of jurisdiction depends upon it, it is not the main question which the tribunal have to decide."

Similarly, Devlin J. said:

"[The tribunal] cannot ... give itself jurisdiction merely by its affirmation of the fact ... If their jurisdiction depends upon the existence of a state of facts, they must inform themselves about them, and if the facts are in dispute reach some conclusion on the merits of the dispute. *If they reach a wrong conclusion, the rights of the parties are not affected. For, if the tribunal wrongly assumes jurisdiction, the party who apparently obtains an order from it in reality takes nothing.*" (Emphasis added.)

"The court is not, as I conceive it, finally determining the validity of the tribunal's order as between the parties themselves ... but is merely deciding whether there has been a plain excess of jurisdiction or not. Where the question of jurisdiction turns solely on a disputed point of law, it is obviously convenient that the court should determine it then and there. *But where the dispute turns on a question of fact, about which there is a conflict of evidence, the court will generally decline to interfere.*" (Emphasis added.)

The *Wednesbury* principle may be useful when seeking to decide whether there has been an error of fact, in the sense that the court may conclude that either the decision-maker failed to have regard to the right considerations or that no reasonable decision-maker could have made that finding of fact. The classic case is *Secretary of State for Education and Science v. Tameside Metropolitan Borough Council* (1976).

The legal background to the case lay in s.68 of the Education Act 1944, which provided that the Secretary of State could give such directions to the local education authority "as appear[ed] to him to be expedient", provided he was

"satisfied, either on complaint by any person or otherwise, that any local education authority ... have acted or are proposing to act unreasonably with respect to the exercise of any power conferred or the performance of any duty imposed by or under this Act."

The factual background to the case was that in May 1976 the Conservatives gained control of the local education authority from Labour. Whilst Labour had been in control, they had intended to introduce comprehensive education, and to abandon all selective secondary education with effect from September 1976. These proposals had been one of the issues in the election campaign.

In June 1976 the local education authority, by then under Conservative control, submitted to the Secretary of State plans which involved the retention of a form of selection for the September intake into secondary education. In previous years, of course, the selection process would have been undertaken much earlier, but in view of Labour's plans to drop selection, nothing had been done in respect of the 1976 intake.

The Secretary of State took the view that the local education authority was acting unreasonably, within the meaning of s.68, on the basis that such a late reversion to selection would cause chaos in the schools. Accordingly, the Secretary of State issued a direction requiring the Labour plans for comprehensive education to be implemented. The High Court granted mandamus to enforce this, but the Court of Appeal, holding that selection procedures could be carried out in time, allowed an appeal by the local education authority.

The House of Lords upheld the Court of Appeal. Speaking of s.68 of the 1944 Act, Lord Wilberforce said:

"Sections in this form may, no doubt, exclude judicial review on what is or has become a matter of pure judgment. But I do not think that they go further than that. *If a judgment requires, before it can be made, the existence of some facts, then, although the evaluation of those facts is for the Secretary of State alone, the court must inquire whether those facts exist, and have been taken into account, whether the judgment has been made upon a proper self-direction as to those facts, whether the judgment has not been made upon other facts which ought not to have been taken into account. If these requirements are not met, then the exercise of judgment, however bona fide it may be, becomes capable of challenge.*" (Emphasis added.)

Thus, on the facts, it was the Secretary of State who had acted unlawfully in accusing the local education authority of unreasonableness, when in fact there were no grounds for the accusation.

This type of judicial attitude gives rise to what is sometimes known as the "no evidence" rule. In other words, where there is no evidence to support a decision, the decision will be quashed, because to make a decision without the necessary supporting evidence indicates that the decision-maker has made an error of law.

In *Fairmount Investments Ltd. v. Secretary of State for the Environment* (1976) a public inquiry was held into whether certain houses should be compulsorily purchased as part of the implementation of a slum clearance scheme. The local authority's case emphasized that the foundations of the houses in the area had previously been subject to settlement, but did not indicate that the houses owned by the objector in question were subject to continuing settlement. No reference was made at the public inquiry to the houses' foundations, nor was the settlement identified as being so serious as to prevent economic rehabilitation of the houses. After the inquiry, and in accordance with the usual practice, the Inspector visited the site, and then concluded, *inter alia*, that the foundations were unsound and that the rehabilitation of the houses would not be an economically viable proposition.

Although the compulsory purchase order was confirmed, the House of Lords ultimately held that the confirmation must be quashed because there was no evidence on which the decision could have been based. It is worth noticing that the courts take a fairly strict view of what is meant by "evidence" in this context.

In *Coleen Properties Ltd. v. Minister of Housing and Local Government* (1971) the effect of the relevant provisions of the Housing Act 1957 was that where there was a slum clearance scheme, properties which were adjacent to the slum properties, but which were not themselves slums, could be included if this was necessary for the sensible redevelopment of the site.

At the public inquiry the local authority's advocate said that his authority thought that a particular non-slum property should be included, but no witness for the authority said so. The property in question was ultimately included, but the court held that there was no evidence to support the inclusion.

Similarly, in *R. v. Housing Benefit Review Board of the Royal Borough of Kensington & Chelsea ex parte Robertson* (1988) the question, which arose in the context of entitlement to Housing Benefit, was whether a woman who was serving a sentence of imprisonment was *temporarily* absent from the premises which she had been occupying as her home. She was legally represented before the local authority's Housing Review Board, but she did not attend personally, nor was any evidence given on her behalf. The Board decided the matter against her.

The High Court held inter alia that what advocates say is not evidence, and therefore there was no evidence on which the Board could have concluded, even if it had wished to do so, that the prisoner intended to return to the premises, and that therefore it could not be said that her absence was temporary.

In passing, and by way of explanation of the apparent harshness of decisions such as these, it must be remembered that, unlike witnesses, advocates are never on oath, nor are they subject to cross-examination.

A final question remains in relation to jurisdictional errors of fact: which errors are jurisdictional and which are not? In answering this question it may be difficult to avoid the conclusion that this is one of those areas which the courts prefer to keep fluid, in order to justify whatever decision seems to them to be appropriate in each case, but nevertheless some answer must be attempted.

Wade (*op. cit.*, p.288) concludes that findings of fact are more likely to be treated as jurisdictional, and therefore more likely to be reviewable, in an administrative context than in a judicial one. The explanation for this appears to be that administrative decision-making will typically involve the exercise of discretion, and the courts' inherent respect for the rule of law is such that the greater the element of discretion which the decision-maker possesses, the more likely it is that findings in respect of any prescribed factual matters will be held to be jurisdictional, and therefore to be subject to judicial review.

Finally, the judicial review procedure, which in practice tends to rely heavily on affidavit evidence, is not particularly well adapted to handling disputed issues of fact, so it would not be altogether surprising if the courts were to decide borderline cases in favour of non-reviewability.

C: Errors of Law

The old doctrine that decisions of inferior courts and tribunals were liable to be quashed by certiorari if there was an error of law on the face of the record was resurrected in *R. v. Northumberland Compensation Appeal Tribunal ex parte Shaw* (1952) after a long period of disuse. This doctrine had always been anomalous because the remedy, which is otherwise exclusively connected with the doctrine of *ultra vires*, was available even though the error was considered to be *within jurisdiction*. In other words, the error was not seen as being jurisdictional, and therefore there was no need for the illegality to be analysed in terms of the doctrine of *ultra vires*.

The decision in *Shaw* served a useful purpose at the time by giving the courts an additional power to control the proliferation of statutory decision-makers which emerged as an integral part of post-war social reconstruction. Since then, however, the law has moved on, and as the remainder of this chapter will show, at least some, if not all, errors of law on the part of inferior courts and tribunals are now regarded as being jurisdictional. Whether this means that the doctrine of error of law on the face of the record can now safely be relegated to the obscurity whence it came is the subject of comment at the end of this chapter (see p.137).

Before reaching that stage, however, it is necessary to try to formulate a test which will enable jurisdictional errors of law to be identified. The short answer is that it will depend on the nature of the decision-maker, but a longer version of this answer must now be considered.

The leading case is *Anisminic v. Foreign Compensation Commission* (1969). The Foreign Compensation Commission had been created by the Foreign Compensation Act 1950 in order to deal with claims made by British subjects against foreign governments. Where there were several claims against a foreign government, that government would pay a lump sum to the British government. The Foreign Compensation Commission would then process claims and make payments, using the money provided by the foreign government. The significant factor was s.4(4) of the 1950 Act:

"The determination by the commission of any application made to them under this Act shall not be called in question in any court of law."

In the aftermath of the international difficulties involving Egypt and the Suez canal in the 1950's, the British and Egyptian governments made a treaty under which the latter paid £27,500,000, out of which compensation was to be paid to British claimants. The Foreign Compensation (Egypt) (Determination and Registration of Claims) Order 1962 was then made, under which a claim was to be treated as being established on proof of certain matters. Among the matters specified were that the dispossessed owner and his successor in title were British. The phrase "successor in title" was not defined, which was unfortunate because two clearly distinct meanings are possible. The first meaning covers a transferee of property (e.g. a purchaser) where the original owner still exists , whereas the second meaning covers a transferee of property (e.g. a beneficiary under a will) who acquires title when the original owner ceases to exist.

The facts of the case were that Anisminic, a British company, had owned property in Egypt. The property was sequestrated by the Egyptian Government in 1956. In 1957, Anisminic agreed with the Egyptian Government that T.E.D.O. (an Egyptian state organization) should buy the property for £500,000. The actual value of the property was over £4,000,000, and accordingly Anisminic reserved the right to claim compensation against anyone else except the Egyptian Government. Anisminic subsequently claimed against the Foreign Compensation Commission, which rejected the claim on the basis that T.E.D.O. was Anisminic's successor in title, and it was clearly not British, therefore one of the qualifying conditions specified in the Order in Council was not fulfilled.

The question then arose as to whether Anisminic was barred from seeking judicial review by the wording of the Act which provided that determinations of the Foreign Compensation Commission could not be called in question in any court.

The House of Lords found in favour of Anisminic on the basis that the nationality of the successor in title was relevant only where the original owner had ceased to exist. It followed that the Foreign Compensation Commission, in asking itself the wrong question, had done something which it had no power to do. In other words, the Foreign Compensation Commission had acted outside its jurisdiction, which meant that the so-called determination was *ultra vires* and void. Therefore the statutory provision precluding the challenge of determinations had no relevance because on the correct legal analysis there was no determination to be challenged.

Lord Reid said:

"I have come without hesitation to the conclusion that in this case we are not prevented from inquiring whether the order of the Commission was a nullity. It has sometimes been said that it is only where a tribunal acts without jurisdiction that its decision is a nullity. But in such cases the word 'jurisdiction' has been used in a very wide sense, and I have come to the conclusion that it is better not to use the term except in the narrow and original sense of the tribunal being entitled to enter on the enquiry in question. But there are many cases where, although the tribunal had jurisdiction to enter on the enquiry, it has done or failed to do something in the course of the enquiry which is of such a nature that its decision is a nullity. It may have given its decision in bad faith. It may have made a decision which it had no power to make. It may have failed in the course of the enquiry to comply with the requirements of natural justice. It may in perfect good faith have misconstrued the provisions giving it the power to act so that it failed to deal with the question remitted to it and decided some question which was not remitted to it. It may have refused to take into account something which it was required to take into account. Or it may have based its decision on some matter which, under the provisions setting it up, it had no right to take into account. I do not intend this list to be exhaustive. But if it decides a question remitted to it for decision without committing any of these errors it is as much entitled to decide that question wrongly as it is to decide it rightly."

In order to approach an understanding of the present state of the law, it is necessary to consider subsequent judicial interpretation and application of the *Anisminic* decision as a whole, and of Lord Reid's speech in particular.

In *Pearlman v. Keepers of Harrow School* (1979) the original issue was whether the installation of gas central heating was a "structural alteration" for the purposes of the Leasehold Reform Act 1967. Disputes over such matters were dealt with by the County Court, and the statute stated the decision of the County Court judge was to be "final and conclusive". This clearly precluded the possibility of an appeal in the ordinary way.

In the instant case the County Court ruled against the tenant, and the question of the effect of the preclusive clause in relation to judicial review therefore arose. The tenant's application for leave to apply for judicial review was refused, whereupon he appealed to the Court of Appeal. The Court of Appeal, by a majority, held that the clause did not have a preclusive effect in this case, because the judge had erred in law, and therefore he was acting without jurisdiction.

Lord Denning M.R. said that after *Anisminic* the distinction between jurisdictional and non-jurisdictional errors of law should be discarded:

"The way to get things right is to hold thus: no court or tribunal has any jurisdiction to make an error of law on which the decision of the case depends. If it makes such an error, it goes outside its jurisdiction and certiorari will lie to correct it."

While Eveleigh L.J. agreed, Geoffrey Lane L.J. did not, saying:

"I am, I fear, unable to see how [the judge's] determination, assuming it to be an erroneous determination, can properly be said to be a determination which he was not entitled to make. The judge is considering the words in the Schedule which he ought to consider. He is not embarking on some unauthorized or extraneous or irrelevant exercise. All he has done is to come to what appears to this court to be a wrong conclusion on a difficult question. It seems to me that, if this judge is acting outside his jurisdiction, so then is every judge who comes to a wrong decision on a point of law."

Although he was in the minority in *Pearlman*, Geoffrey Lane L.J. saw his approach approved by the Privy Council in *South East Asia Firebricks v. Non-Metallic etc. Union* (1980), where it was held that a statutory provision which apparently excludes the court's power to quash a decision, does not prevent the court from deciding that a particular decision is a nullity, and the proceeding to quash it.

The line of authority develops through *Re Racal Communications Ltd.* (1980), which some series of reports refer to as *Re A Company*. The Director of Public Prosecutions applied to the High Court for authority to inspect a company's books in connexion with certain criminal proceedings. The apparent difficulty was that the relevant statute provided that the High Court's decision "shall not be appealable". Nevertheless, the Court of Appeal regarded itself as having power to review the decision. In due course, the House of Lords emphatically rejected this, on the basis that the High Court exercises a supervisory jurisdiction over other bodies, and is not itself liable to review. This being so, and Parliament having enacted a clause which precluded any appeal, the High Court's decision was unchallengeable, even if it was unlawful.

The key to the decision of the House of Lords may be found in certain *dicta* of Lord Diplock. Unfortunately the clarity of the *dicta* is more than somewhat marred by an inordinate fondness for compound negatives:

"Parliament can, of course, if it so desires, confer upon administrative tribunals or authorities power to decide questions of law as well as questions of fact or administrative policy; but this requires clear words, for the presumption is that where a decision-making power is conferred on a tribunal or authority that is not a court of law, Parliament did not intend to do so. The breakthrough made by *Anisminic* .. was that, *as respects administrative tribunals and authorities*, the old distinction made between errors of law that went to jurisdiction and errors of law that did not, was for practical, purposes abolished.

"But there is no similar presumption that where a decision-making power is conferred by statute upon *a court of law*, Parliament did not intend to confer upon it power to decide questions of law as well as questions of fact. Whether it did or not and, in the case of inferior courts, what limits are imposed on the kinds of questions of law they are empowered to decide, depends upon the construction of the statute, unencumbered by any such presumption.

"Upon any application for judicial review of a decision of an inferior court in a matter which involves, as so many do, interrelated questions of law, fact and degree the superior court conducting the review should not be astute to hold that Parliament did not intend the inferior court to have jurisdiction to decide for itself the meaning of ordinary words used in the statute to define the question which it has to decide. This, in my view, is the error into which the majority of the Court of Appeal fell in *Pearlman*." (Emphasis added.)

In the Divisional Court case of *R. v. Surrey Coroner ex parte Campbell* (1982) Watkins L.J. emphasized that in *Re Racal* Lord Diplock had said:

"In *Anisminic* this House was concerned only with decisions of administrative tribunals."

He went on to say:

"In our judgment the *Anisminic* principle was not intended to be applied to a court .... in our view ... the principle is limited to tribunals established by statute, and probably to those tribunals from whose decisions, under the relevant statute, there is no right of appeal."

In *O'Reilly v. Mackman* (1982) Lord Diplock himself returned to the theme, saying:

"The landmark decision ... [in *Anisminic*] ... liberated English public law from the fetters that the courts had theretofore imposed on themselves so far as determinations of inferior courts and statutory tribunals were concerned, by drawing esoteric distinctions between errors of law committed by such tribunals that went to their jurisdiction, and errors of law committed by them within their jurisdiction. The breakthrough that *Anisminic* made was the recognition by the majority of this House that if a tribunal whose jurisdiction was limited by statute or subordinate legislation mistook the law applicable to the facts as it had found them, it must have asked itself the wrong question, i.e. one into which it was not empowered to inquire and so had no jurisdiction to determine. Its purported 'determination', not being a 'determination' within the meaning of the empowering legislation, was accordingly a nullity."

One difficulty arising from this passage is whether Lord Diplock was using the word "tribunal", at its second and third appearances, in the broad sense of "any body which decides issues", or in contradistinction to "court". In the Divisional Court case of *R. v. Greater Manchester Coroner ex parte Tal* (1984) Robert Goff L.J. thought the broader sense had been intended:

> "It is ... now plain that, in his observation in [*Re Racal*], relied on by the court in *Campbell*, Lord Diplock did not intend to say that the *Anisminic* principle did not extend to inferior courts as well as to tribunals."

He went on to describe Lord Diplock's statement of the principle in *O'Reilly v. Mackman* (which came between *Re Racal* and *Campbell*) as being "authoritative", and drew attention to the fact that, in *Re Racal* itself, Lord Salmon had bracketed together "decisions made by commissioners, tribunals [and] inferior courts."

However, Robert Goff L.J. went on to indicate that the distinction between inferior courts and other inferior decision-makers is not wholly without significance for the present purposes:

> "We wish to add that, although we think it right to conclude on the authority of Lord Diplock's statement of the law in *O'Reilly v. Mackman* that, as a matter of principle, the *Anisminic* principle applies to inferior courts as well as inferior tribunals, nevertheless we do not wish to be understood as expressing any opinion that the principle will apply with full force in the case of every inferior court."

In passing, it may be noted that one potentially complicating aspect of *Tal* is that Robert Goff L.J. said:

> "Since *Anisminic*, the requirement that an error of law *within the jurisdiction* must appear on the face of the record is now obsolete" (Emphasis added.)

This comment seems to blur the essential drift of his judgment which is that such errors necessarily take the decision-maker *outside his jurisdiction*, and is perhaps best regarded as a slip of the judicial tongue.

As a provisional summary, therefore, it can be said that in the case of the High Court and those courts above the High Court, errors of law are not treated as being jurisdictional, because the essential constitutional function of these courts is to make rulings as to law, and therefore even if they get the law wrong they are still acting within their jurisdiction.

At lower levels the identity of the decision-maker becomes a major determining factor. Errors of law are less likely to be classified as being jurisdictional if made by inferior courts, and more likely to be so classified if made by other decision- makers. However some attempt must be made to clarify the element of imprecision in this statement.

As far as magistrates' courts are concerned, in *Tal* Robert Goff L.J. said that the case of *Edwards* (1979) appeared to indicate that there was an exception to the *Anisminic* presumption where magistrates are acting in committal proceedings. In other words, errors of law made by magistrates when committing defendants to the Crown Court are jurisdictional.

More recently, in *R. v. Miall* (1992), the Court of Appeal has come to precisely the same conclusion, albeit without reference to *Edwards*. A committal for trial at the Crown Court was held to be a nullity because there was no legal basis for it. The court therefore quashed the committal, rather than the conviction which the Crown Court subsequently imposed. Procedurally, this was achieved by the court briefly reconstituting itself as a Divisional Court, and then reverting to its true role. The court was at pains to emphasize that the distinction betwen quashing the committal and quashing the conviction was not simply academic, because the result of the route which was adopted was that further proceedings in respect of the same matter could be taken against the defendant, whereas quashing the conviction would have been an end of the matter.

In *Neill v. North Antrim Magistrates' Court* (1992), Lord Mustill, giving the judgment of a unanimous House of Lords, held that judicial review would lie to quash a committal for trial where there had been a material irregularity resulting in real prejudice. The House was, however, very careful to say that relief would not be granted as a matter of course, and that cases where the allegation was merely that the evidence relied upon at the committal stage was merely insufficient (as distinct from inadmissible) would need to be given particularly anxious consideration.

As far as other inferior decision-makers are concerned, the question will always ultimately be one of statutory interpretation. In *R. v. Registrar of Companies ex parte Central Bank of India* (1986) the relevant statute provided that a certificate issued by the registrar should be "conclusive evidence" of certain matters. In the course of a long and complex judgment all three Judges seem to have agreed that the effect of the provision was at least to prevent the admission of any evidence to indicate that the registrar had erred in law. Additionally, Slade and Dillon L.JJ. thought that the provision amounted to a rebuttal of the presumption that errors of law made by the registrar are jurisdictional. However, Slade L.J. was particularly influenced by the argument that the purpose of the provision was to promote certainty by allowing everyone to rely on the legal efficacy of such certificates. This argument allowed him to assert that, despite the decision in the instant case, a decision of the registrar could be reviewable in a case where the certificate was clearly bad on its face.

The underpinning of the doctrine of jurisdictional error in terms of constitutional theory is clear enough in relation to tribunals and similar decision-makers. At the strictly theoretical level, the position is less clear in relation to inferior courts, since it is part and parcel of the function of any court to determine issues of law. In the case of inferior courts, however, there may be some doubt as to whether the practical reality in terms of legal expertise can always be said to reflect the theoretical proposition.

Clearly the superior courts are not without their doubts as to the ability of the magistrates' courts when it comes to dealing with anything other than the most routine matters of law. In *R. v. Chichester Justices ex parte Chichester District Council* (1991) the High Court said that it is unwise for magistrates to refuse to commit a defendant for trial for reasons turning on the correct interpretation of legislation such as the Town and Country Planning legislation, unless it is abundantly clear that the interpretation advanced on behalf of the defendant is correct. If the point is arguable, the better course is for the magistrates to commit the defendant for trial, thus leaving such matters of statutory interpretation to be resolved by the Crown Court judge, with the assistance of full argument from counsel.

In conclusion, therefore, there appear to be some elements of uncertainty within the doctrine of jurisdictional error, although problems seem to arise relatively infrequently in practice. This may be largely due to the fact that many of the cases which could be presented in reliance on the doctrine are more easily and naturally presented in terms of the principle of *Wednesbury* relevance, with the greatest potency of the doctrine as currently understood being in relation to those cases where a statutory provision purports to oust the jurisdiction of the courts.

Perhaps the best summary of the position comes from Wade:

"All that can be said with certainty at the present stage is that there is a medley of contradictory opinions in the appellate courts and the conflict between the rival interpretations of *Anisminic* is unresolved.

"What can perhaps be said, nevertheless, is that the main current of judicial opinion is running in favour of holding all error of law to be reviewable. This may be achieved either by adopting the Denning-Diplock analysis ... or else by simply ignoring all the esoteric argument about jurisdiction and holding that error of law is inherently something that it is the business of the court to remedy." (*Op. cit.,* p.302.)

D: A Postscript on the Doctrine of Error of Law on the Face of the Record

The current state of the law in relation to jurisdictional errors of law leaves something of a question mark over the doctrine of error of law on the face of the record, which was outlined at pp.128-129.

If all errors of law made by tribunals and similar decision-makers are, by definition, *ultra vires*, it follows that the doctrine of error of law on the face of the record is now redundant. On the other hand, it could be argued that the doctrine could still play a useful role in the exceptional kind of case represented by the *Central Bank of India* case. Indeed, in that case, Slade L.J. specifically said that a certificate might be reviewable if it were bad on its face. This creates a problem.

The ratio of the case is based upon the need for certainty on the part of those relying on the certificates, and the obvious fact that this will be undermined by the existence of any power to quash. The counter-argument, that certainty will not in fact be undermined if quashing is limited to those cases where the defect is clear on the face of the certificate, may be convincing at first blush, but in reality it almost certainly underestimates the creativity of lawyers to develop ideas of what is or is not "clear".

CHAPTER 8

GIVING REASONS FOR DECISIONS

A: Introduction

Bearing in mind the fact that judicial review is concerned with the legality of the decision-making process, it may seem obvious that decision-makers should be obliged to state the reasons for their decisions, because in the absence of reasons being given, the operation of the presumption of legality makes it very difficult indeed to bring a successful challenge.

Unfortunately, the basic *Wednesbury* proposition that the court can intervene where the decision-maker has had regard to the wrong considerations does not address the even more basic question of whether there is any obligation to state the reasons on which a decision is based. Three principal questions arise, namely when does the law impose a requirement for the giving of reasons; if there is such a requirement in a given case, what must the decision-maker do in order to comply with the requirement; and in each case what are the consequences of failing to give reasons? Finally some miscellaneous matters must be considered.

B: The Statutory Position

Individual statutes may impose a requirement to give reasons for decisions, and many do so. For example, as a general proposition it can be said that under successive Town and Country Planning Acts there has been an obligation on decision-makers, be they local planning authorities or Secretaries of State, to give reasons when making decisions which are adverse to the applicant. Precise details can be found in various sections of the Acts.

However, quite apart from individual statutory provisions, s.10 of the Tribunals & Inquiries Act 1992 contains one very wide-ranging provision. Section 10 imposes an obligation to give reasons on those tribunals listed in Schedule I to the Act, provided that a request for a statement of reasons is given on or before the giving or notification of the decision. Detailed procedural rules for individual tribunals may, of course, dispense with the requirement for a request. The scope of s.10 can be indicated by listing some of the decision-makers to which it applies:

> The Lands Tribunal; Mental Health Review Tribunals; Betting Levy Appeal Tribunal; Controller of Plant Variety Rights; Plant Varieties and Seeds Tribunal; Industrial Tribunals; Rent Assessment Committees; Local Valuation Courts; Immigration Adjudicators; Immigration

Appeal Tribunal; Value Added Tax Tribunals; Director General of Fair Trading; Social Security Appeal Tribunals.

In *R. v. Civil Service Appeal Board ex parte Cunningham* (1991) Otton J. said that where the predecessor of the 1992 Act did not put a given decision-maker under an obligation to give reasons, it did not follow that that obligation could not be derived from other sources.

C: The Position at Common Law

The position under statute being simply a matter of statutory interpretation in each case, it is more fruitful in general terms to examine the position at Common Law, to see what rights (if any) exist in the absence of a relevant statutory provision.

In 1932 the *Report of the Donoughmore Committee on Ministers' Powers* stated that the right to reasons was "the third principle of natural justice" (the right to a hearing and the rule against bias being the other two - see chapter 12).

However, there is no doubt that this was, and is, an inaccurate account of the law. In *Riceslip Parish v. Henden Parish* (1698), when dealing with a dispute between two parishes over liability to support a pauper, Holt C.J. said:

> "Where the justices of the peace give a special reason for their settlement, and the conclusion which they make in point of law will not warrant the premises, there we will rectify their judgment; *but if they had given no reason at all, then we would not have travelled into the fact.*" (Emphasis added.)

Similarly, in more modern times, in *R. v. Gaming Board ex parte Benaim and Khaida* (1970) the Gaming Act 1968 required an applicant for a gaming licence to obtain a certificate of consent from the Gaming Board as a preliminary to applying for the licence itself. The Act specified the matters, such as the character and financial standing of applicants, to which the Board must have regard, but was silent as to the giving of reasons. The Court of Appeal held that the Board was not obliged to state its reasons for refusing an application for a certificate. Lord Denning M.R., who seemed to find significance in the fact that magistrates are not bound to give reasons, concluded that the Board should enjoy a similar dispensation:

> "After all, the only thing they have to give is their *opinion* as to the

capability and diligence of the applicant. If they were asked by the applicant to give their reasons, they could answer quite sufficiently: 'In our opinion, you are not likely to be capable of or diligent in the respects required of you." (Original emphasiz.)

The *Gaming Board* case clearly raises the question of the reviewability of subjective matters: see p.95 for further discussion of this topic.)

There is, however, some indication that the courts may be willing to move away from this position and impose an obligation to give reasons. In *R. v. Civil Service Appeal Board ex parte Cunningham* (1991) the applicant for judicial review had worked in the prison service for 23 years. He had no right of access to an Industrial Tribunal, but he was subject to the Civil Service Pay and Conditions of Service Code, which provided, inter alia, that "the conditions applying to civil servants will not be less favourable than those applying to other employees."

Following an allegation that the applicant had assaulted a prisoner, he was not prosecuted but disciplinary charges were brought against him, resulting in a recommendation that he should be dismissed. Despite an appeal to the Civil Service Appeal Board, which found that his dismissal would be unfair and recommended his reinstatement, the Home Office decided that the recommendation for dismissal should stand, and remitted the case to the Board for assessment of compensation on the basis of unfair dismissal. The applicant was earning £16,900 p.a. Without giving any reasons for its decision, the Board assessed compensation at £6,500.

In the High Court Otton J. granted an application for judicial review, holding that if the applicant's case had been heard by an Industrial Tribunal, he would have been entitled to be given reasons; and therefore, although English administrative law does not contain any general requirement that reasons for decisions should be given, and without wishing to establish any precedent whatsoever, reasons should be given in the present case, because the statement in the Code indicating that civil servants would not be treated less favourably than other employees, created a legitimate expectation that reasons would be given.

Dismissing an appeal, the Court of Appeal held that, in addition to the ground of legitimate expectation on which Otton J. had based his decision, the granting of judicial review was also justified on the broader ground that fairness requires a tribunal such as the Board to give sufficient reasons for its decisions to enable the parties to know not only the issues to which it had directed its mind, but also that it had acted lawfully.

The extent, if any, to which this decision will be developed generally is open to conjecture.

D: Where there is an Obligation to give Reasons, What Must be Done in Order to Comply with It?

It will be apparent that in purely practical terms a decision may be made for one reason which is unsupportable in law (or even for no identifiable reason). In such cases, the person responsible for recording the decision might be tempted to present the matter in a more legally acceptable light. This fact of administrative life underlies the classic piece of doggerel:

"When the meeting is over, they go for their dinner,
But their secretary stays getting thinner and thinner,
Racking his brains as he tries to report
What he thinks that they think that they ought to have thought."

It also explains why the courts will not always accept reasons at face value: they may say that the reasons presented to them are inadequate.

It is important, of course, never to forget the *presumption of legality* (see pp.17-19), as a result of which it is incumbent on the challenger to persuade the court of the inadequacy of the decision-maker's reasons. Clearly, the degree of persuasion which is necessary will vary according to the court's instinctive reaction to the facts of the particular case. More particularly, the courts will be strongly influenced by their perceptions of why reasons are required in the first place, since this will provide a benchmark against which the adequacy of any individual reasons may be assessed.

In *Iveagh v. Minister of Housing and Local Government* (1963) Megaw J. said that the purpose of requiring reasons to be given was to enable the parties to know

"whether the Minister's decision has or has not been reached as a result of the application of correct principles of law and the correct construction of the relevant enactment."

This leads directly to *Re Poyser & Mills' Arbitration* (1963), where the landlord of an agricultural holding served a notice to quit on his tenant, alleging the latter to be in breach of a covenant in the tenancy agreement, but without specifying what the breach actually was. The relevant statute required reasons to be given. Holding the notice to be bad, Megaw J. said:

"Parliament having provided that reasons shall be given ... [means] that proper, adequate reasons must be given: the reasons that are set out, whether they are right or wrong, must be reasons which not only will be intelligible, but also can reasonably be said to deal with the substantial points that have been raised ...[but] ... I do not want it to be thought for a moment that I am saying that any minor or trivial error, or a failure to give reasons in relation to every particular point that has been raised at the hearing, would be sufficient to invoke the jurisdiction of this court."

Similarly, in *Westminster Bank Ltd. v. Minister of Housing and Local Government* (1970) planning permission for an extension to a building was refused on the basis that the extension would unduly prejudice a future highway improvement scheme. This refusal did not create any obligation to pay compensation to the owner, whereas the alternative procedure of creating an Improvement Line, would have done so. The court quashed the decision, holding that where there are two routes to a decision, one of which involves paying compensation and the other does not, the balance of public and private interests requires that the route requiring compensation shall be taken. (For the extent of a local authority's fiduciary duty in relation to public money, see pp.93-95). On the question of the adequacy of the Minister's reasons for dismissing the owner's appeal against the refusal of planning permission, Donaldson J. said:

"It is not an obligation to give sufficient reasons, *which is a totally different conception going directly to the merits of the decision* ... the reasons need not be set out with the complexity which so often flows from a determined search for the ultimate in precision, but rather that so far as possible they shall be couched in language which is really intelligible to those who have been spared a lawyer's training". (Emphasis added.)

Despite the courts' general support for the proposition that a requirement to give reasons can be met only by the provision of adequate reasons, they do recognize that in some cases there is a limit to the extent to which a decision-maker can explain his reasons. In *Guppys (Bridport) Ltd. v. Sandhoe* (1975) the problem was whether the rental value of premises should be ascertained by reference to the rents paid for comparable premises, or by reference to a joint consideration of the premises' capital value, and a notional return on that capital. The rent officer and the rent assessment committee both adopted the first approach, whilst the landlord preferred the second. The landlord argued that the decision-maker should state the reasons why one approach was being adopted rather than the other. Rejecting this, Lord Widgery C.J. said:

"Such explanations are not possible. They are matters of judgment, impression and sometimes even instinct, and it is quite impossible to give detailed reasons to explain how the system of decision has worked."

In *Givaudan v. Minister of Housing and Local Government* (1966) an inspector's report from a public inquiry into a refusal of planning permission was submitted to the Minister, who then issued a decision-letter accepting the Inspector's conclusion and recommendation and dismissing the appeal. The decision-letter summarized most of the inspector's report, but omitted one crucial matter. The High Court quashed the Minister's decision, on the basis that it was impossible to be certain which conclusions of the Inspector were accepted by the Minister, with the result that there was substantial doubt as to what he had (or had not) taken into acount.

Similarly, in *French Kier Developments v. Secretary of State for the Environment* (1977), an inspector recommended that a planning appeal should be allowed. Although the Secretary of State accepted the findings of fact, and did not suggest that the inspector had misdirected himself on planning policy, he dismissed the appeal because he disagreed with the weight the inspector had attached to various matters. Willis J. said that the Secretary of State's reasons were

"so vague, inadequate and unintelligible as to leave anyone reading the [decision] letter quite unable to understand why, when so much of the factual conclusions were accepted by the Secretary of State, the Inspector's recommendation was rejected."

Finally, it is worth noticing that a simple recitation of reasons will not be sufficient if there are no grounds on which those reasons could be based. It is appropriate at this stage to recall the *Tameside* case, which is discussed more fully at pp.125-126, and the cases decided under the "no evidence" rule, which is discussed at pp.127-128.

E: The Effect of Failing to give Reasons Where there is a Statutory Requirement To Do So

The leading case is *Brayhead (Ascot) Ltd. v. Berkshire County Council* (1964), where planning permission was granted subject to conditions. No reasons were given for the conditions, despite a statutory obligation to do so. When the planning permission was implemented, without the conditions being observed, the local planning authority took enforcement action.

The question arose, therefore, as to whether the absence of reasons invalidated the conditions. The High Court held that the requirement as to the giving of reasons was mandatory in the sense that the court would grant mandamus to compel the local planning authority to say what the reasons were, but that their absence did not invalidate the conditions.

Even mandamus may be withheld if the court is satisfied that the identity of the respondent is such that a declaration will be sufficient (see, e.g., *R. v. Civil Service Appeal Board ex parte Cunningham* (1991), discussed more fully at p.141).

F: The Effect of Failing to give Reasons Where there is No Statutory Requirement To Do So

Where there is no statutory requirement to give reasons for a decision, it may seem that *ex hypothesi* the courts are impotent, since the presumption of legality (see *Hoffman-La Roche*, which is discussed at p.17), makes it difficult to impute illegality to a decision-maker who fails to state his reasons when under no obligation to do so. In practice, however, the courts have been a little more inventive than this, taking the view that in the final analysis the crucial question is whether or not the case discloses evidence of unlawfulness.

A useful starting point is the Privy Council case of *Minister of National Revenue v. Wright's Canadian Ropes Ltd.* (1947). The relevant statute gave the Minister power to

"disallow any expense which he in his discretion may determine to be in excess of what is reasonable or normal for the business carried on by the taxpayer"

and gave the taxpayer a right of appeal.

When it was shown that the facts which were proved to have been before the Minister, and which were subsequently placed before the court, could not have justified the decision, the Privy Council refused to make an assumption in favour of the Minister, even though it was proved that the Minister had had other material before him, including a report from an Inspector of Taxes. This material had not been disclosed in the legal proceedings. Lord Greene M.R., giving the judgment of the Privy Council, said:

"If [the Minister] had in fact had such material [as would have justified his decision] it would, in their Lordship's opinion, have been impossible to suppose that he would not have informed the respondents of at least the substance of it when the matter was originally brought before him so as to give the respondents a fair opportunity of meeting the case against them. The contrary supposition would involve that the appellant had come to a decision adverse to the respondents on material of which, so far as he knew, the respondents were completely ignorant, and knowledge of which he deliberately withheld from them."

The case is also noteworthy for the inference which the court drew from the existence of a statutory right of appeal. Lord Greene M.R. said:

"Their Lordships find nothing in the language of the Act or in the general law which would compel the Minister to state his reasons ... But this does not necessarily mean that the Minister by keeping silence can defeat the taxpayer's appeal. To hold otherwise would mean that the Minister could in every case, or, at least, the great majority of cases, render the right of appeal given by the statute completely nugatory. The court is, in their Lordship's opinion, always entitled to examine the facts which are shown by evidence to have been before the Minister when he made his determination. If those facts are in the opinion of the court insufficient in law to support it, the determination cannot stand. In such a case the determination can only have been an arbitrary one."

The Privy Council concluded that the proper inference was that the Minister's decision was arbitrary, and therefore unlawful.

The leading House of Lords' authority is *Padfield v. Minister of Agriculture, Fisheries and Food* (1968), which is also discussed at p.91). Lord Reid said:

"It was argued that the Minister is not bound to give reasons for refusing to refer a complaint to the committee, that if he gives no reasons his decisions cannot be questioned, and that it would be very unfortunate if giving reasons were to put him in a worse position. But I do not agree that a decision cannot be questioned if no reasons are given. If it is the Minister's duty not to act so as to frustrate the policy and objects of the Act, and if it were to appear from all the circumstances ... that that has been the effect of the Minister's refusal, then it appears to me that the court must be entitled to act."

Even more forthrightly, Lord Upjohn said:

"If he does not give any reasons for his decision it may be, if

circumstances warrant it, that a court may be at liberty to come to the
conclusion that he had no good reason for reaching that conclusion."

These *dicta*, powerful though they are, must be kept in proportion, and
must not be taken as a surreptitous introduction of a general requirement
to give reasons. In *R. v. Secretary of State for Trade and Industry ex parte
Lonrho plc* (1989) the House of Lords was at pains to emphasize that an
absence of reasons in a case where they are not legally required cannot,
in itself, be evidence of illegality, although if there is other evidence of
illegality, the absence of reasons may be supportive of it.

There is also the possibility that the court may consider an absence of
express reasons as indicating the unlawful implementation of policy. In
*R. v. Secretary of State for the Environment ex parte Halton Borough
Council* (1984) the County Council proposed to establish a gipsy caravan
site on certain land in the area of the Borough Council. The Borough
Council objected, which meant that the matter came before the Secretary
of State under s. 8 of the Caravan Sites Act 1968. The Secretary of State
had already issued a Circular to the effect that he would not intervene in
disputes of this kind unless they raised issues of more than merely local
significance. He directed the County Council to proceed. The Borough
Council succeeded in an application for judicial review. The Secretary
of State conceded that he had not made a decision on the merits, but
argued that he could call-in the matter at a later stage.

Taylor J., holding that the *Padfield* principle was relevant, quoted the
passage from Lord Reid's judgment which is abstracted above. He then
went on to quote Lord Reid further:

"It is quite clear from the Act in question that the Minister is intended
to have *some* duty in the matter. It is conceded that he must properly
consider the complaint. He cannot simply say (albeit honestly)

'I think that in general the investigation of complaints has a
disruptive effect on the scheme and leads to more trouble than (on
balance) it is worth; I shall therefore never refer anything to the
committee of investigation.'

To allow him to do so would be to give him power to set aside for his
period as Minister the obvious intention of Parliament, namely, that an
independent committee set up for the purpose should investigate
grievances and that their report should be available to Parliament. This
was clearly never intended by the Act. Nor was it intended that he

could silently thwart its intention by failing to carry out its purposes. I do not regard a Minister's failure or refusal to give any reasons as a sufficient exclusion of the court's surveillance." [Original emphasiz.]

Carrying on with his judgment in his own words, Taylor J. said:

"If he gives [no reasons] then, in the circumstances of this case, the proper inference may be that there is no reason beyond a blanket policy of not becoming involved."

Furthermore, when an application for judicial review is on foot, there is authority for the proposition a decision-maker should then disclose his reasons (see *R. v. Lancashire County Council ex parte Huddleston* (1986), discussed in the context of *R. v. Civil Service Appeal Board ex parte Cunningham* (1991) at p.49). However, in *Huddleston* the court did make the point that the respondent's duty of disclosure did not extend to justifying applicants using the grant of leave to apply as a licence to go on fishing expeditions in search of previously unperceived grounds of challenge.

The obligation to give reasons when an application for judicial review is on foot seems to arise from the central importance of the decision-maker's reasoning when dealing with an application for judicial review. It follows, therefore, that the obligation does not extend to legal proceedings generally.

In *Cannock Chase District Council v. Kelly* (1978) a council tenant, who at that time had no security of tenure at all, argued that the local authority had had no grounds for serving a notice to quit. For the present purposes, the significance of the case lies in the following comment:

"A local authority cannot be required to state its reasons ... or to assume an evidential burden at a trial, merely by reason of a defence which says, in effect, 'You have no good reasons'."

The courts also recognize a limited exception based on public policy. In *Inland Revenue Commissioners v. Rossminster* (1980) the House of Lords was considering s.20C(3) of the Taxes Management Act, which contained a power for the Commissioners to obtain a warrant to enter premises and seize documents. The House held that an officer applying for a warrant must have reasonable cause to believe that incriminating documents would be found, but that public interest immunity relieved him from having to state the reasons for that belief. Lord Diplock said:

"Since no reasons have been given by the decision-maker and no unfavourable inference can be drawn from this *fact because there is obvious justification for his failure to do so*, the presumption that he acted *intra vires* can only be displaced by evidence of facts which cannot be reconciled with there having been reasonable cause for his belief that the documents might be required as evidence or alternatively which cannot be reconciled with his having held such belief at all." (Emphasis added.)

As might be expected, however, the courts are cautious when invited to sanction extensions of this exception. In *R. v. Inland Revenue Commissioners and Another ex parte Coombs & Co.* (1991) an Inspector of Taxes, acting under s.20 of the Taxes Management Act 1970, gave notice to a firm of stockbrokers, requiring them to produce certain documents for the purposes of an enquiry into the tax liability of a third party, but giving no reasons for the giving of the notice The notice was indorsed by one of the General Commissioners.

On the stockbrokers' application for judicial review, the Inland Revenue Commissioners, who had made no application to cross-examine the affidavit evidence, contended that they were not obliged to give reasons and that no adverse inference could be drawn from their failure to do so. They further contended that the onus was on the recipient of the notice to produce evidence which would satisfy the court that the Inspector could not reasonably have formed the opinion that the notice should be given. Schiemann J. dismissed the application, but the stockbrokers succeeded in the Court of Appeal.

The court held that there were three potentially relevant areas of public interest, namely the ascertainment of an individual's liability to pay tax, the protection of the public from unjustified disclosure of information, and the safeguarding of the administration of justice. In cases where there was an impending prosecution, the interests of safeguarding the administration of justice could justify the Inland Revenue Commissioners in withholding their reasons, but in the present case there was no impending prosecution, and the effect of the Inland Revenue Commissioners' failure to give reasons was to prevent the court from performing its proper function of deciding whether the Inspector could reasonably have formed the opinion in question. The court concluded, therefore, that reasons should have been given.

At the level of principle, Taylor L.J. said that although the Commissioners' respect for confidentiality must itself be respected, the court is entitled to look at their affidavits and ask whether, without breaching confidentiality, they could have been more forthcoming, provided that the notice to produce the evidence was more than a mere fishing exercise. Addressing the question of the weight of the evidence, Taylor L.J. said that the stockbrokers' evidence was neither supported nor rebutted by the Commissioners' silence, and therefore it retained whatever weight it had on its own merits.

However, the House of Lords allowed an appeal by the Inland Revenue, holding that the failure to give evidence was credibly explained on the basis of a general duty of confidentiality, and that therefore the failure did not show that the Inspector's decision was unreasonable.

G: The Council of Europe's View

In 1977 the Committee of Ministers of the Council of Europe adopted a resolution (no. 77/31), entitled *On the Protection of the Individual in Relation to the Acts of Administrative Authorities.* The resolution recommends that the law and administrative practice of member states should be guided by five principles which were set out in an annex to the resolution.

The gist of the fourth principle is that an administrative act which adversely affects a person's rights, liberties or interests, must be reasoned. The reasons need not necessarily be given automatically, nor at the time of the decision: availability on subsequent request may be sufficient.

Although the resolution is clearly not part of English law, it could be used as persuasive authority in support of an argument for the giving of reasons in a particular case.

CHAPTER 9

CONSULTATION

A: Introduction

A requirement of consultation before a decision is made will usually arise either by statute or by delegated legislation. Sometimes, however, a requirement may arise from an established pattern of consultation in circumstances which give rise to a legitimate expectation that the pattern will continue, as happened in the *GCHQ* case (see p.182).

Viewed from one perspective, the law relating to consultation is simply part of the *Wednesbury* principle, because a requirement that the decision-maker must consult someone else, will make sense only if he must take their views into account as being relevant considerations. Nevertheless, for purposes of analysis and exposition, it is convenient to consider this area of law discretely.

Whenever the law imposes a requirement of consultation, two questions arise: what does *consultation* mean, and what are the consequences of a failure to consult?

B: The Meaning of *Consultation*

One of the leading cases on the meaning of *consultation* is *Fletcher v. Minister of Town and Country Planning* (1947). Under the New Towns Act 1946 the Minister had to consult interested local authorities before he could make a New Town Order. In the instant case, on 26 July 1946 the Minister addressed a conference of six local authorites who were affected by the proposal to create the new town of Hemel Hempstead. He explained the project and invited comments and questions. The following day he published a Draft Order, to which there were objections.

On 19 November he attended a private meeting with the local authorities, in order to explain why he favoured the project. He made no speech but he did invite questions. However, he made it clear that a note of the meeting which was being taken was not to be used in any subsequent proceedings, and he excluded any discussion of the topics of water and sewerage.

A public inquiry was held in early December, following which the Order was confirmed. On an application to quash the Order it was argued, *inter alia*, that consultation should involve an exchange of views; that it should have happened before the Draft Order was made; and that the meeting of 19 November did not count, because of the restrictions imposed on it by the Minister.

The court held that, on the facts, the two meetings were linked and that, taken together, they did constitute consultation. Moreover, it was sufficient that the consultation preceded the final confirmation of the Order. At the level of principle, the court declined to define consultation, but did indicate that the substance of events mattered more than their form.

A somewhat similar situation arose in relation to the designation of Crawley New Town, giving rise to the case of *Rollo v. Minister of Town and Country Planning* (1948), where the Court of Appeal said that the Minister must give the local authority sufficient information to enable them to tender advice, together with a sufficient opportunity to do so. More particularly, Bucknill L.J. approved what the judge at first instance had said, namely:

"The Minister with receptive mind must by such consultation seek and welcome the aid and advice which those with local knowledge may be in a position to proffer."

C: The Adequacy of Consultation

The case-law on the adequacy of consultation shows that defective consultation can give rise to three possible legal outcomes. The resulting decision may be quashed as a whole; it may be valid against those who are consulted and void as against those who are not; or it may be upheld notwithstanding the defect.

In *Lee v. Department of Education and Science* (1968) the Secretary of State had power to make Orders amending the Articles of Government of certain schools. He proposed to make an Order changing a grammar school into a comprehensive school. A scheme to this effect was first proposed on 31 August 1967. In a letter dated 14 September, the Secretary of State informed the governors of the school that he proposed to exercise his powers and invited representations by 12 noon on 18 September. The governors challenged this on the basis that there must be a real, and not merely an illusory, opportunity for them to make their views known. The High Court held that the time-scale allowed was wholly unreasonable and that a period of four weeks would have been appropriate.

The leading authority in which a decision was treated as being valid against those who were consulted, whilst being void against those who were not consulted, is the *Aylesbury Mushrooms* case, which is discussed fully at p.21.

In *Coney v. Choyce* (1975) a decision was upheld despite defective consultation. As part of the process of re-organization of Roman Catholic secondary education, wide publicity was given to certain proposals. However, in the case of two schools there was partial non-compliance with the statutory requirements of consultation, to the extent that notices were not displayed at or near the schools' main entrances.

The Secretary of State decided that enough had been done to publicize the proposals and proceeded with the scheme. On a challenge by some of the parents concerned, the High Court held that the object was to consult a representative number of the people affected by the proposals. In this case there had been no substantial prejudice, and a mere irregularity did not invalidate the Secretary of State's approval of the scheme.

It is, of course, always worth remembering that the remedies in judicial review are discretionary. In *R. v. Secretary of State for Social Services ex parte Association of Metropolitan Authorities* (1986) the Secretary of State had a statutory power to make Regulations governing the scheme of Housing Benefit, which was administered by local authorities. He was required to consult the local authorities' associations. In 1982, Regulations were made and in 1984 the Secretary of State wished to amend them.

On 16 November 1984 he wrote to the local authorities' associations asking for their comments by 30 November. The Association of Metropolitan Authorities did not receive the letter until 22 November when it immediately pointed out to the Secretary of State that the practicalities of its committee system meant that it would not be able to respond until 7 December.

Meanwhile, the Secretary of State proposed to make two further amendments to the Regulations. On 4 December he wrote to the Association, mentioning one of the further proposals (but not enclosing a version of the amendment), and not mentioning the other proposed amendment at all. He required a response by 12 December. On 13 December the Association responded, but said that its comments were hasty and ill-considered.

On 18 December the Secretary of State laid the amendments before Parliament, and they came into force the following day. On a challenge by the Association, the High Court held that the Association had been entitled to be consulted, and that the consultation must be genuine, which, on the facts it had not been. However, the court did acknowledge that, in principle, the need for urgency and the exercise of political judgment could result in a short period being allowed for consultation, although clearly even these factors could not justify a total removal of real consultation. In the event, however, the court declined to give the Association a remedy, partly because it was the only local authority association to complain, and partly because, by the time the case was heard, the amended Regulations were in force and were being implemented by local authorities nationwide.

D: Voluntary Consultation

The cases considered above have all arisen where there was an obligation to consult. However, the case of *R. v. Governors of Haberdasher Aske's Hatcham Schools ex parte Inner London Education Authority* (1989) establishes that where a decision-maker voluntarily pursues a consultative process, without being legally obliged to do so, the consultations must be undertaken in a fair and proper manner, just as they would have to be if they were obligatory.

Additionally, as mentioned at the beginning of this chapter, the *GCHQ* case shows that a pattern of consultation which begins on a voluntary basis may create a legitimate expectation, and thus become obligatory.

E: Consultation and the Relevance of the Statutory Purpose

In accordance with first principles, a requirement of consultation will not be allowed to frustrate the legislative purpose: see, by analogy, *Padfield*, discussed fully at p.91.

The leading case is the Privy Council's decision in *Port Louis Corporation v. Attorney-General of Mauritius* (1965).

The Governor of Mauritius had statutory power to alter local government boundaries. Consultation with the local authorities concerned was required, but there were no provisions as to the machinery of consultation There was a proposal to enlarge Port Louis by taking in some surrounding villages. The detailed timescale of the facts giving rise to the case was as follows:

2 May: the Minister of Local Government wrote to the Town Clerk of Port Louis, enclosing a map and detailed proposals, and asking for his authority's views by 13 May.

11 May: eleven out of the total of sixteen councillors resigned. The remainder did not constitute a quorum, and therefore no views could be given.

11 June: six additional councillors were appointed by an enactment specifically created for the purpose.

18 June: the Minister asked for a reply to his letter.

8 July: the local authority wrote back, asking for detailed replies to 54 points before it would be in a position "to start giving the proposal the thorough study which it calls for."

10 July: the Minister asked for a reply by 18 July.

11 July: the Minister replied to the letter of 8 July saying that the points raised by the local authority would be considered. The local authority then insisted on being given the information it had requested.

13 August: the local authority were informed that the Governor had decided to change the boundaries and the following day this was formally done.

The local authority alleged that the boundary change was *ultra vires*. The Privy Council held that it was sufficient if the local authority knew of the proposals and had had an adequate opportunity to respond. It would be unreasonable for the law to allow the Governor to be frustrated in the way the local authority had tried to frustrate him.

F: Consultation and Delegation

The next chapter deals with the law relating to *delegation*. However, at this point it is convenient to identify a crucial danger area in practice, namely the thin dividing line between *lawful consultation* and *unlawful delegation*. The following cases illustrate the point.

In *Lavender & Son Ltd. v. Minister of Housing and Local Government* (1970) it was the policy of the Minister to refuse to grant planning permission for mineral working on land which the Minister of Agriculture wished to see retained for agricultural use. In the High Court, Willis J. quashed a decision made in pursuance of this policy, on the basis that the Minister of Housing and Local Government had effectively abdicated his own discretion by delegating the decision to the Minister of Agriculture.

On the other hand, in *Kent County Council v. Secretary of State for the Environment and Another* (1977), where the Secretary of State for the Environment, having sought and accepted the advice of the Secretary of State for Energy, had granted planning permission for certain development, the court was willing to hold that what had occurred was legitimate consultation, rather than illegitimate delegation. Clearly, there are evidential difficulties in situations such as this, and equally clearly the decision-maker may welcome the presumption of legality (see pp.17 *et seq.*). In purely practical terms, however, much will often depend on the precise way in which the decision-making process is recorded.

CHAPTER 10

DELEGATION

A: Introduction

The *Wednesbury* principle deals with the issues of relevance and reasonableness. However, an even more basic aspect of the principle is that the decision-maker must make his own decision. Unfortunately this area of public law has been unhelpfully cross-fertilized by the introduction of the maxim *delegatus non potest delegare*, which simply means that someone to whom a function is delegated cannot further delegate that function. The origin and rightful resting-place of the maxim lies in the area of private law relating to agency, where a principal may be bound by the acts of his agent, without necessarily being similarly bound by the acts of his agent's agent.

An initial difficulty in applying the *delegatus* maxim in public law is that it is not always easy to see any initial act of delegation in the ordinary sense of the word, but only a statutory conferring of a power. The only way in which an act of delegation can be identified in such circumstances is by adopting the view that Parliament, in conferring a statutory power to make decisions, is choosing not to make the decisions itself, but to delegate their making to the decision-maker. The element of artificiality in this analysis will be readily apparent.

The best way, therefore, to approach the *delegatus* maxim in public law, is to say:

"An element which is essential to the lawful exercise of power is that it should be exercised by the authority upon whom it is conferred, and by no-one else." (Wade, *Administrative Law*, 6th edition, 1988, p. 357.)

However, Wade also emphasizes that this principle is no more than a *presumption of statutory interpretation*, and that it is certainly not a principle of law. It follows from this that the starting point in each case must be the statute in question, because this presumption - in common with all other presumptions of statutory interpretation - may be either rebutted or reinforced by the plain words of the statute. An example of reinforcement may be found in the Fugitive Offenders Act 1881, s.6 of which states:

"A Secretary of State ... may, if he thinks it just, by warrant *under his hand* order [a] fugitive to be returned to the part of Her Majesty's dominions from which he is a fugitive." (Emphasis added.)

Section 15 of the Public Order Act 1986 contains an example of limited rebuttal by express provision, to the extent that a chief constable may delegate, as far as Assistant Chief Constable level but no further, the power to give directions in respect of public processions and assemblies.

A more widely significant (albeit still limited) example of rebuttal by express provision is contained in s.101 of the Local Government Act 1972, which is considered in more detail at pp.164 *et seq*.

However, in the usual case where the statute which confers the power is silent as to whether performance can be delegated, it becomes important to be able to predict how the courts will exercise their discretion to characterize a specific act of delegation as either lawful or unlawful. Before considering this matter more closely, however, it is appropriate to consider one doctrine by which the courts have sometimes sought to avoid the problem rather than to solve it, namely the *alter ego* doctrine.

B: The *Alter Ego* Doctrine

According to the *alter ego* doctrine the acts of a senior official within the context of public administration can be regarded as the acts of the titular head of the relevant department or organization, on the basis that the official is the "other self" (or *alter ego*) of the titular head.

In *Carltona Ltd. v. Commissioners of Works (*1943) the company owned a factory which was requisitioned by the Commissioners of Works. The order requisitioning the factory was challenged on a number of grounds, but the court accepted that the Assistant Secretary who was in charge of the matter was the proper decision-maker. Lord Greene M.R. said:

> "In the administration of government ... the functions which are given to Ministers ... are ... so multifarious that no Minister could ever personally attend to them ... [so] ... the powers given to Ministers are normally exercised ... by responsible officials ... Public business could not be carried on if that were not the case."

In *Point of Ayr Collieries Ltd. v. Lloyd-George* (1943), where the facts were substantially similar to *Carltona*, Lord Greene M.R. returned to the delegation theme with the very tentative cosmetic suggestion that in important cases the Minister himself should sign the piece of paper, but he was still at pains to emphasize that such personal action was not a necessary pre-condition to legal effectiveness.

The precise limits below which the *alter ego* doctrine can be used have never been identified, but two cases are instructive.

In *Nelms v. Roe* (1969) the Road Traffic Act 1960 specified that certain notices were to be signed by or on behalf of the Commissioner of Police for the Metropolis. In fact they were signed by an Inspector. The court held that authority to sign was impliedly delegated to a Superintendent, and there was further implied authority to delegate the matter further to the Inspector. But Lord Parker, C.J. was not prepared to treat the Superintendent as the Commissioner's *alter ego*:

> "It is not, I think, sufficient to say that it is a principle which is applicable whenever it is difficult or impracticable for a person to act himself, in other words that whenever he has to act through others the principle applies."

The case of *R. v. Secretary of State for the Home Department ex parte Oladehinde and Another* (1990) concerned the division of functions between immigration officers, who are concerned with regulating entry into the United Kingdom, and the Secretary of State for the Home Department, who is concerned with regulating the continuing right to remain. The facts of the case were that the Secretary of State authorized certain immigration officers, holding posts at not less than a certain grade, to make provisional decisions as to deportation.

The appellants had been given leave to enter the United Kingdom, but one of them breached a condition which prevented him from seeking employment and the other one overstayed his leave. In each case, an immigration inspector issued a notice of intention to deport under s.3(5)(a) of the Immigration Act 1971. The inspectors had been authorized by the Secretary of State to act on his behalf.

Following appeals to an immigration adjudicator and to the Immigration Appeal Tribunal, the Divisional Court granted an application for judicial review, holding that the purported authorization of the inspectors to perform this function was unlawful on the bases that it was both outside the *Carltona* principle, and contrary to the policy of the statute.

The Court of Appeal allowed an appeal, holding that the Secretary of State's devolution of power was within the common law constitutional power of a Minister of the Crown to devolve the performance of his functions to responsible officials, provided that in any specific case the immigration inspector concerned had had no previous involvement with the immigrant.

The Court of Appeal also indicated that in cases falling outside the limited right of appeal conferred by s.5(1) of the Immigration Act 1988, the only remedy available to challenge a notice of intention to deport pursuant to s.3(5) of the Immigration Act 1971 is an application for judicial review, and an application for leave to apply should not be delayed while an abortive appeal is mounted, in case the delay is held to be a ground for refusing leave to apply. (The topic of delay generally is discussed at pp.50 *et seq.*)

Dismissing appeals against this decision, the House of Lords held that there was no reason why, relying on the *Carltona* principle, the Home Secretary should not authorize members of the immigration service to take decisions, provided that the authorization does not conflict with, or embarrass them in, the discharge of their specific statutory duties, and that the decisions they are authorized to make are suitable to their grading and experience. On the facts, the present cases related to the existence rather than the exercise of the power concerned, and therefore did not fall within the right of appeal conferred by s.5(1) of the Immigration Act 1988, but were properly to be dealt with by way of application for judicial review.

C: Delegation in Practice

1. Generally

Even if the *alter ego* doctrine does not apply *eo nomine* to all cases of practical difficulty, the courts clearly recognize that the practicalities of day-to-day administration may require an assumption that when conferring a statutory power, Parliament also impliedly conferred a power of delegation.

The leading case is *Local Government Board v. Arlidge* (1914) where a public local inquiry was held into the question of whether a house was unfit for human habitation. In accordance with the usual practice, the inquiry was conducted by an inspector, who submitted a report to the Board, which then made the final decision. Responding to a ground of challenge that the Board itself had not inquired into the matter, Viscount Haldane L.C. said:

"The Minister at the head of the Board is directly responsible to Parliament like other Ministers. He is responsible, not only for what he himself does, but for all that is done in his Department. The volume of work entrusted to him is very great and he cannot do the great bulk of it himself. He is expected to obtain his materials vicariously through his officials, and he has discharged his duty if he sees that they obtain these materials for him properly. To try to extend his duty beyond this and to insist that he and other members of the Board should do everything personally would be to impair his efficiency. *Unlike a judge in a court he is not only at liberty but is compelled to rely on the assistance of his staff.*" (Emphasis added.)

Viscount Haldane's comment contrasting the position of Judges and administrators leads neatly to a consideration of the present relevance of the administrative/judicial classification.

In *Barnard v. National Dock Labour Board* (1953) the Order creating the National Board expressly delegated certain disciplinary functions to Local Boards. The court concluded that it was unlawful for a Local Board to sub-delegate their disciplinary functions to its secretary, who was the port manager. The result was that certain disciplinary action taken by the port manager was a nullity. Denning L.J., having rejected the argument that the disciplinary function was administrative in character, said:

"No *judicial* tribunal can delegate its functions unless it is enabled to do so expressly or by necessary implication." (Emphasis added.)

It is important to note that this may be misleading if it is taken to mean that *administrative* functions can always be delegated even in the absence of authority to do so, either expressly or by necessary implication. The correct analysis of the cases leads to the conclusion that there is a presumption that all delegation is unlawful unless there is express authorization or necessary implication, and that the courts will be more ready to find there to be necessary implication in administrative cases, so that in these cases the presumption will be more easily rebutted.

In *Jeffs v. New Zealand Dairy Production and Marketing Board* (1966) the relevant statute authorized the Board to appoint committees who would then advise the Board. This represented a departure from earlier statutes which had authorized the delegation of almost any functions to committees. The Board appointed a committee to "investigate ... and report back to the Board" on a question of zoning certain produce, which was a matter with significant commercial ramifications.

There was no requirement that the committee should take evidence, but in fact the committee did hold a public inquiry before submitting a report and making a recommendation to the Board. The report stated that submissions had been made but did not provide details of the evidence that had been received. The Board, which had no information other than the committee's report, proceeded to accept the recommendation.

The Privy Council held that the Board was exercising a judicial function and that therefore it had to act on evidence. Furthermore, the

Board could not lawfully delegate the considering of the evidence entirely to the committee, so the Board had acted unlawfully in making the decision without considering the evidence.

In *R. v. Gateshead Justices ex parte Tesco Stores Ltd.* (1981) s.1 of the Magistrates' Courts Act 1952 provided that when an information was laid, either a justice of the peace or a justices' clerk could issue a summons. At the time of this case there was a widespread practice of delegating to members of justices' clerks' staff the decision as to whether or not to issue summonses. The essence of this decision, which in reality is almost entirely routine, involves deciding whether or not the facts alleged in the information disclose an offence. Donaldson L.J., holding that this practice was unlawful, rejected the argument that the issue of a summons is a purely administrative, or even clerical, function:

> "The requirement that a justice of the peace or the clerk to the justices acting as a justice of the peace shall take personal responsibility for the propriety of taking so serious a step as to require the attendance of a citizen before a criminal court is a constitutional safeguard of fundamental importance."

Dealing also with the argument that the practice of delegation was necessary in purely practical terms, and therefore must be taken to have been impliedly authorized, Donaldson L.J. said:

> "The short answer to this is that if the practice is unlawful, expedience will not make it lawful. *Fiat justitia, ruat coelum.*"

In *Hill v. Anderton* (1982) the House of Lords agreed with the approach of Donaldson L.J. in the *Gateshead* case.

The decision in *Selvarajan v. Race Relations Board* (1976) was on the administrative side of the administrative-judicial distinction. One of the Board's conciliation officers investigated a complaint and recommended a finding that unlawful discrimination had not occurred. This recommendation was considered by a committee of seven members, of whom only the chairman and two others had seen all the papers in the case. Lord Denning M.R. said:

> "The most troublesome point is that several members of the Board did not have all the papers. Four of them had only a summary ... and a recommendation ... It may reasonably be inferred that these four were not in a position to form an opinion of their own. They must have gone

by the opinion of the other three members .... If this had been a judicial body, I do not think this would be right. Every member of a judicial body must have access to all the evidence and papers in the case, he must have heard all the arguments, and he must come to his own conclusion. The maxim *delegatus non potest delegare* applies strictly to judicial functions. But it is different with a body which is exercising administrative functions or which is making an investigation or conducting preliminary inquiries, especially when it is a numerous body."

Lord Denning M.R. went on to distinguish *Jeffs*:

"On the construction of the statute [in *Jeffs*], the Board had no power to delegate its functions ... But in the present case the Board undoubtedly had power to delegate its functions."

The administrative-judicial distinction is not necessarily the only point of reference which the courts will use, as indicated by *R. v. Director of Public Prosecutions ex parte Association of First Division Civil Servants* (1988). The facts arose in the context of the Prosecution of Offences Act 1985, which created the Crown Prosecution Service. The Director of Public Prosecutions devised a system of screening cases. Members of staff who were not legally qualified would read files in order to see that they were complete, and to decide whether there was sufficient evidence and whether a prosecution was in the public interest. If the screener decided that all was in order, the case would proceed, whereas problem cases would be referred to a legally qualified Crown Prosecutor. One result of this procedure was that summary matters which seemed to the screener to be in order, and in respect of which the defendant pleaded guilty by post, would have gone through the system without being considered by a lawyer at any stage.

The High Court, having considered the 1985 Act in some detail, granted a declaration:

"[The Director] may not lawfully delegate to any person not being a Crown Prosecutor, the decision whether in any criminal proceedings (i) the evidence is sufficient to proceed and/or (ii) the prosecution is in the public interest".

The declaration did not extend to prohibiting delegation of the function of checking that the file is complete, which appears to be more of a clerical function rather than one requiring the application of legal judgment.

The court not only emphasized that cases which may be insignificant in the context of the Crown Prosecution Service's overall workload could nevertheless be matters of great concern to the defendants, but also pointed out that the report of the Royal Commission which preceded the Act had placed considerable emphasiz on the need for every prosecution to be subject to independent legal scrutiny.

Where the decision which is being challenged is legislative in character, the courts are likely to be particularly strict in holding delegation to be unlawful. In *Jackson, Stansfield & Sons v. Butterworth* (1948) the Minister of Works had power to license building works under the Defence (General) Regulations 1939. In the case of works costing under £100, he purported to delegate this function to local authorities. Holding this to be unlawful, Scott L.J. said:

> "The delegation ... was not within the authority of the Minister of Works ... The method chosen was convenient and desirable, but the power so to legislate was, unfortunately, not there."

In accordance with the first principles of judicial review, where there has been unlawful delegation it will be irrelevant that the decision would probably have been the same anyway.

In *Allingham v. Minister of Agriculture, Fisheries and Food* (1948) the Minister delegated to a County War Agricultural Committee the power to control agriculture. The Committee decided that 8 acres should be devoted to sugar beet, but left it to their executive officer to decide precisely which 8 acres it should be. The officer consulted a local sub-committee and then served a notice specifying a field.

Lord Goddard C.J. accepted that if the decision had been reported to the County Committee in the form of a recommendation, it might well have been adopted, but held nevertheless that the way it had actually been done amounted to unlawful delegation by the County Committee to their officer. It followed that the officer's notice was a nullity, and a farmer could not be properly convicted of failure to comply with it.

2. Section 101, Local Government Act 1972

The most significant statutory provision expressly authorizing delegation is s.101, Local Government Act 1972, subsections (1) and (2) of which provide:

> "(1) Subject to any express provision contained in this Act or any Act

passed after this Act, a local authority may arrange for the discharge of any of their functions -
    (a)   by a committee, a sub-committee or an officer
          of the authority; or
    (b)   by any other local authority.

(2) Where by virtue of this section any functions of a local authority may be discharged by a committee of theirs, then, unless the local authority otherwise direct, the committee may arrange for the discharge of any of those functions by a sub-committee or an officer of the authority and where by virtue of this section any functions of a local authority may be discharged by a sub-committee of the authority, then, unless the local authority or the committee otherwise direct, the sub-committee may arrange for the discharge of any of those functions by an officer of the authority."

For some years this apparently straightforward provision caused no difficulty, and in particular it was used as the legal basis for the practice of taking chairman's action on matters of urgent business arising between scheduled meetings. However, in *R. v. Secretary of State for the Environment ex parte Hillingdon London Borough Council* (1986) the High Court, in a decision which was subsequently upheld by the Court of Appeal, applied a restrictive interpretation to s.101, holding that a single member of a local authority did not fall within the terms of the section. It followed that planning enforcement notices, the issuing of which had been authorized by the chairman of the planning committee, were unlawful and void.

Conscious of the practical difficulties which this decision would cause, Woolf J. accepted the suggestion of counsel for the recipient of the enforcement notices, to the effect that in future local authorities should delegate such decisions to an officer, subject to a proviso that he should consult the chairman of the appropriate committee before taking action. Unfortunately, as a consideration of the principle on which the decision in *Lavender v. Minister of Housing and Local Government* makes plain, this suggestion is fraught with difficulty. (*Lavender* is discussed more fully at p.155).

The difficulty is well-illustrated by the case of *R. v. Port Talbot Borough Council ex parte Jones* (1988) where a councillor applied to her own council for a house. Decisions as to individual lettings were made by the chief housing officer, after consultation with the chairman and vice-chairman of the appropriate committee. After an unusually short time on the waiting list the councillor received an offer of a three bedroomed house, whereas, if the council's usual standards had been applied, her personal circumstances would have warranted a one or two bedroomed flat.

On the facts, Nolan J. found that the chief housing officer had been subjected to significant pressure from the chairman of the committee, who in turn had been motivated by two factors. First, the chairman thought that the applicant's status as a councillor meant that that a house would be more suitable than a flat, because she would need to receive members of the public at home. Secondly, the chairman thought that there was a need for the applicant to live in the ward which she represented, in order to establish a presence there before the next election. Nolan J. proceeded to find the decision unlawful on two grounds. The chairman's dominant role meant that the chief housing officer had not actually made his own decision in an authorized and lawful manner, and in any event relevant considerations had been ignored and irrelevant considerations had been taken into account.

Although any case involving the officer-in-consultation-with-a-member formula might seem likely to attract a challenge based on at least the first ground of the decision in the *Port Talbot* case, it does not follow that such a challenge will always succeed. A case in point is *Fraser v. Secretary of State for the Environment and the Royal Borough of Kensington and Chelsea* (1988), where planning enforcement notices were issued under a standing order which provided that, in cases of urgency, officers could "give such instructions as may be reasonable", subject to having obtained the written approval of an appropriate elected member. Upholding the legality of the enforcement notices, Nolan J. held that, on the facts, the officer had already formed his opinion before approaching the elected member, and therefore it was the officer and the officer alone who had made the decision.

At this stage it must be noted that critical consideration of the line of reasoning adopted in the *Kensington and Chelsea* case reveals a fundamental flaw. The short point is that, if the elected member is to have any effective role, he must at least have the power of veto. If this is so, it follows that in substance if not in form, the officer is making a recommendation to a committee consisting of a single member, and it is precisely this idea of a single member committee which was declared to be unlawful in the *Hillingdon* case.

The practical answer to the unlawfulness of a committee of one seems to be to establish urgency sub-committees to deal with matters arising between scheduled meetings. The delay and inconvenience involved in convening their meetings must, it seems, simply be accepted as the price of complying with the law.

In *Moffat v. Eden District Council* (1989) the appellant in the Court of Appeal was a member of the respondent district council. The council decided to create a working party to undertake a review of the council's structure and efficiency. The working party consisted of both members and officers but it did not include the appellant. One of the council's Standing Orders gave all members the right to attend, but not to speak, at meetings of committees and subcommittees of which they were not members. The appellant unsuccessfully sought to exercise this right in relation to the working party.

The appellant argued, *inter alia*, that s.101 of the Local Government Act 1972, as interpreted in the *Hillingdon* case prevented the council from delegating any of its functions to anything other than a committee, a subcommittee, an officer, or another local authority, and that therefore the working party was a committee of the council, and the Standing Orders gave him a right to attend its meetings.

On the appellant's application for judicial review, Webster J. held that the working party was not a committee or a sub-committee and that therefore the Standing Order was irrelevant.

The Court of Appeal held that although it was a function of the council to organize itself and to conduct its affairs in such a way as to be able to discharge its duties efficiently, it did not follow that delegation to a committee or a sub-committee was the only way of reviewing the best ways of discharging this function. The council was seeking advice rather than delegating anything, and the council's general power under s.111 of the 1972 Act, to do anything which is reasonably incidental or conducive to the discharge of the council's functions, covered the creation of the working party. (Section 111 of the 1972 Act is discussed at pp.25 *et seq.*).

In *R. v. Southwark London Borough Council ex parte Bannerman and Others* (1990) the local authority's scheme of delegation to officers provided that power to authorize the commencement of legal proceedings was vested in the Deputy Town Clerk on the recommendation of the relevant chief officer. An explanatory note to the scheme of delegation provided that "where authority to take decisions is given to the Chief Executive and Town Clerk or Chief Officer, the decision shall be taken in the name of (but not necessarily personally by) such officer."

A member of the Borough Valuer's staff, wrote to "the Head of Legal Services" giving instructions to obtain possession of certain property which was subject to squatting. He signed the instructions in his own name, under which there appeared the words "For Borough Valuer".

Possession proceedings were commenced but were then stayed pending an application for judicial review in order to determine the legality of the commencement of the proceedings.

On the application for judicial review the High Court considered, *inter alia*, the legality of decision of the member of staff and proceeded to dismiss the application and remove the stay on the possession proceedings. The court acknowledged that it is commonplace in both central and local government for decisions to be taken in the name of someone who is not in any meaningful sense the decision-maker. In such circumstances and in the absence of evidence of wrongdoing, the court will not investigate the internal organization of a department, but will assume that those who write letters on behalf of their superiors have the authority to do so. It follows that the proper analysis of the present facts was not that the Borough Valuer had delegated his authority to the member of staff, because he had not power to do so, but that the member of staff had made his decision in the name of the Borough Valuer, and this was lawful.

Section 101 does not enable a local authority to delegate the power to determine the size and composition of committees and sub-committees (see *R. v. Brent London Borough Council ex parte Gladbaum and Woods* (1990)).

D: The Legal Consequences of Lawful Delegation

Having discussed the situations in which delegation may be lawful, it is necessary to consider the legal consequences of lawful delegation.

The first point is that delegation consists of a sharing, rather than a transfer, of power. In *Huth v. Clarke* (1890) a local authority appointed an executive committee, which in turn appointed local sub-committees to deal with diseases of animals. When the sub-committees took no action under the Rabies Order 1887, the executive committee itself made appropriate regulations. Following a conviction for an offence against the regulations, the question arose as to whether the executive committee had retained the power to make the regulations. The High Court held that the power had been retained, because delegation involves giving the delegate authority to act on behalf of the delegator: it does not involve a transfer of all the delegator's powers.

Secondly, delegation can be revoked. In *Manton v. Brighton Corporation* (1951) a councillor had been appointed to three committees of the local authority. Following allegations of misconduct by the councillor, the local authority decided he should no longer serve on any of the committees. The High Court held that a local authority can revoke the authority of any of its committees as a whole, and therefore it could revoke the authority of individual committee members. For detailed provisions in relation to the removal of councillors from committees it is now necessary to consider ss.15 *et seq.* of the Local Government and Housing Act 1989. These provisions, which are outlined at pp.107-108, relate to the maintenance of political balance within local authorities, and do not affect the validity of the general proposition that delegation can be revoked.

In accordance with first principles, of course, revocation of authority must not be undertaken in such a way as to frustrate the legitimate expectations of third parties. (The doctrine of legitimate expectation is discussed at pp.189 *et seq.*)

Perhaps the most difficult point arising out of the law relating to delegation concerns the claim that lawful delegation has conferred retrospective validation. The case of *Ipswich Borough Council v. Webb* (1989) is instructive. The local authority had delegated to its Housing Renewal Sub-Committee sole power to determine all matters relating to, *inter alia*, houses in multiple occupation. One of the local authority's Senior Environmental Officers, having come to the conclusion that control orders should be made in respect of two houses in multiple occupation, drafted a letter to two councillors seeking authority to make the orders. The letter was signed by the local authority's Director of Environmental Health and sent to the councillors, both of whom were members of the Housing Committee but neither of whom were members of the Housing Renewal Sub-Committee. In due course, both members signified their agreement to the making of the orders, but before their agreement had been obtained, the orders had been made on the instructions of the Director of Environmental Health.

The owner of the properties appealed to the County Court, on the ground, *inter alia*, that the orders were made without lawful authority. After the appeal proceedings in the County Court had begun, the Housing Renewal Sub-Committee purported to ratify the decision to make the control orders. The owner succeeded in both the County Court and the Court of Appeal.

The Court of Appeal concluded that the facts disclosed an attempt to put right something which had been carried out by an unauthorized agent in a wholly wrong manner, and therefore the case did not involve either the retrospective correction of a formality which had not been observed, or the straightforward ratification of the act of an unauthorized agent who could properly have done what he had purported to do if he had had authority.

The key error was that the Director of Environmental Health had thought that he was acting on behalf of the two councillors whose authorization he had sought, and therefore as a matter of law his decision to make the control orders was their decision. The reality was that neither of the councillors had been given delegated powers to make such decisions, and therefore the making of the orders was unlawful. Furthermore, the purported ratification of the orders was ineffective not only because of the councillors' lack of power, but also because the legal rights of the owner of the property had been affected before the purported ratification.

Purchas L.J. specifically refused to consider whether, as a matter of general principle, retroactive delegation could be a lawful exercise of the s.101 power, preferring to say that each instance of delegation must be considered in the context of the powers which are delegated.

CHAPTER 11

FETTERING DISCRETION BY CONTRACT AND ESTOPPEL

A: Introduction to the Problem of Fettering by Contract

One aspect of the *Wednesbury* principle which has the potential to cause serious practical difficulty arises out of the exercise of the power to enter into contracts. The problem is quite simply one of predicting the court's reaction to a situation in which a public decision-maker chooses to enter into a contract. Will the court regard this as the perfectly proper exercise of discretion? Alternatively, will the court conclude that the exercise of present discretion is unlawful, because by committing himself to one particular course of conduct, the public decision-maker must necessarily be excluding some future options, if only on the basis that, for example, a single piece of property cannot be disposed of more than once? The leading cases are not always easy to reconcile with each other, but they must now be considered.

B: The Leading Cases on Contract

The classic case is *Ayr Harbour Trustees v. Oswald* (1883), where the trustees of the harbour had the power to purchase land compulsorily in connexion with their statutory function of maintaining and improving the harbour. Oswald owned a parcel of land adjoining the harbour, and the trustees wished to buy some of this land. The problem was that if the land which Oswald was to retain were to become landlocked its consequential loss of value would significantly increase the compensation which he would receive. Accordingly, in an attempt to reduce the price they would have to pay, the trustees offered to agree that they would not use the land they were acquiring in such a way as to prevent the retained land from having access to the harbour. Oswald objected to this, and the House of Lords upheld his objection.

The argument was that the trustees were under a duty to act for the benefit of the public, and in the future the public interest may require the use of the acquired land in such a way that Oswald's retained land would become cut off from the harbour. Therefore any purported agreement which was incompatible with the trustees' future performance of their public duty would be void.

The case of *Stourcliffe Estates v. Bournemouth Corporation* (1910) is, however, worth noticing by way of a caution against over-enthusiastic reliance on the principle contained in the *Ayr Harbour* case.

The facts were that the corporation bought a piece of land from the company and covenanted to use it in performance of its statutory functions to provide a pleasure ground and open space. There were also detailed covenants restricting the kind of building which the corporation could erect, such as bandstands and shelters.

The corporation then wanted to build public conveniences on the land, close to the boundary with other land which the company retained and which it intended to develop for other purposes. When the company objected, the corporation not only raised arguments on the detailed wording of the covenants, but also claimed that the restriction was void anyway, on the basis of the *Ayr Harbour* case.

The Court of Appeal held that the *Ayr Harbour* decision was irrelevant, because in the present case there was no incompatibility between the restriction on the use of the land and the performance of the statutory functions.

The public decision-maker was similarly unsuccessful in the case of *Dowty Boulton Paul Ltd. v. Wolverhampton Corporation* (1971). The facts were that the corporation owned an airfield, in respect of which it granted the company a contractual right to use the airfield for 99 years, or for as long as the corporation maintained the airfield, whichever was the longer. Subsequently, and well within the 99 year period, the corporation wanted to build a housing estate on the land. When the company sought to protect its position by way of an interlocutory injunction, the corporation argued that it was not bound by the contract, because otherwise there would be a fetter on its future exercise of discretion in relation to the land.

The court held that the rule against fettering discretion had no relevance to the facts. The correct analysis was that a statutory power had been validly exercised when the contractual right was granted. The fact that this inevitably reduced the scope of the corporation's options for the future did not make the contract objectionable. It will be noted, of course, that in this case the agreement in relation to the company's use of the airfield could not be said to be incompatible with the performance of any of the local authority's statutory duties.

Further support for the proposition that incompatibility is the key concept in these cases can be drawn from the decision of the Court of Appeal in *Windsor & Maidenhead Borough Council v. Brandrose Investments Ltd.* (1983). The facts were complicated and the law was less than straightforward, turning as it did to some extent upon the interpretation of the more obscure aspects of s.52 of the Town and Country Planning Act 1971.

Basically, however, the local planning authority entered into an agreement with the company relating to a scheme of development which included the demolition of some buildings. Prior to demolition taking place, the local planning authority used its statutory powers to designate the area as a Conservation Area. One consequence of this designation was that demolition required the local planning authority's consent. The question therefore arose as to whether the local planning authority was bound by its prior agreement to permit the demolition which was involved in the scheme of redevelopment covered by the s.52 agreement.

The court held that the local planning authority could not disable itself from using its statutory powers to designate Conservation Areas. The reasoning underlying this conclusion was complicated by the s.52 element, but a distinction was drawn between implementation of the local planning authority's basic planning policy, in the form of the Development Plan, and the pursuit of other planning objectives. How far this conclusion depends on the s.52 element is not clear from the judgment of the court. Nevertheless, irrespective of the s.52 point, the case can be seen as making some kind of sense at common law in any event, representing as it does a version of the incompatibility argument by distinguishing between major and fundamental matters on the one hand, and minor and peripheral matters on the other, with the result that lawful fettering can take place only in relation to the latter category.

The question of the contractual fettering of discretion came together with the question of the legality of political factors in decision-making in the case of *R. v. Hammersmith & Fulham London Borough Council ex parte Beddowes* (1987). The facts were that a Conservative-controlled local authority owned an estate consisting of several blocks of flats which it wished to see renovated and improved, with a view to the flats being sold to owner-occupiers. Lacking resources to enable it to achieve this objective itself, the local authority agreed to sell one of the blocks to a private developer, with the benefit of restrictive covenants. The effect of these covenants would be that all new lettings of flats on that part of the estate to be retained by the local authority would be by way of long leases at a premium. In other words, no ordinary council tenancies would be created in the future. Viewed in the round, therefore, this scheme enabled the local authority to raise the capital to renovate the premises which it retained, while the private developer could re-sell the flats which he had bought, and give his purchasers an assurance that the "quality of the neighbourhood" was improving. The scheme was, of course, politically highly contentious.

A council tenant on the estate sought judicial review to quash the local authority's decision to accept the private developer's offer to buy the block of flats. The Divisional Court dismissed the application, and the Court of Appeal upheld their decision. Briefly, the courts' conclusion was that the local authority's policy was rational and coherent, and therefore could not be characterized as *Wednesbury* unreasonable.

On the question of fettering discretion, the court said that the local authority's statutory power to dispose of land which was held for housing purposes carried with it an implied power to enter into covenants restricting the use of land which the local authority retained. The retained land was being held for the purpose of providing housing accommodation, and the local authority's policy that the accommodation should be made available on the basis of owner-occupation, rather than by way of council tenancies, was not inconsistent with that purpose. Furthermore, the present exercise of discretion was not rendered unlawful merely because the local authority, if subsequently constituted differently in party political terms, would find certain policy options were no longer available.

At the level of general principle, the court indicated that if a statutory power is honestly and reasonably exercised in pursuit of a statutory object, the exercise of the power could not be construed as an unlawful fetter on another power which existed for the same statutory purpose.

C: Introduction to the Problem of Fettering by Estoppel

Where the conduct of a public decision-maker does not amount to entering into a contract, it may nevertheless be possible to argue that the conduct is sufficient to raise an estoppel. Indeed, at first sight it may seem obvious that where a representation is made by, or on behalf of, a public body, in circumstances which would give rise to an estoppel if the situation were governed entirely by private law concepts, it may seem obvious that an estoppel should arise in the ordinary way. However, in some cases it may be that the statement relates to something which is *ultra vires* the public body. In such circumstances, allowing an estoppel to operate would amount to driving a coach and four through the doctrine of *ultra vires*, because the result would be to allow the public body to extend their powers by merely making an unlawful assertion to that effect. And yet, if the law accepts the legitimacy of this objection to recognizing an estoppel, the innocent representee suffers.

Two preliminary points may usefully be made. First, for the purposes of private law, there are various classifications of estoppel, such as *common law* estoppel, *equitable* estoppel, *issue* estoppel, and so on. However, Craig says:

"It may be best to regard estoppel as applied to public bodies as *sui generis*: it may refer to fact or intent, and may be suspensory or extinguish the right, depending upon the circumstances. The one constant is that there would be no reason to apply the doctrine unless the representee suffered detriment." (*Administrative Law*, 2nd edition, p.471 n.4.)

Useful though this comment appears to be in terms of reducing the analytical scheme of the topic to a single major heading, it does contain an element of oversimplification. The problem is that even in public law cases the courts continue to recognize a discrete area of *issue* estoppel within the doctrine of *res judicata*, which is, of course, that doctrine of public policy which requires finality in decision-making, and which some Judges and commentators seek to obscure beneath the Latin tag *interest rei publicae ut finis litium sit*.

A convenient statement of the elements of issue estoppel was provided by Lord Brandon in *The Sennar (No. 2)* (1985), cited with approval in a public law context by Millett J. in *Crown Estate Commissioners v. Dorset County Council* (1990):

"In order to create [an issue estoppel] three requirements have to be satisfied. The first requirement is that the judgment in the earlier action relied on as creating an estoppel must be (a) of a court of competent jurisdiction, (b) final and conclusive, and (c) on the merits. The second requirement is that the parties (or privies) in the earlier action ... and those in the later action in which that estoppel is raised as a bar, must be the same. The third requirement is that the issue in the later action ... must be the same issue as that decided by the judgment in the earlier action."

The court held that a decision of the Chief Commons Commissioner that certain land formed part of a highway, and therefore was not registrable as common land under the Commons Registration Act 1965, raised an issue estoppel which operated as a bar in the instant case involving the status of the same land.

Similarly, in *Thrasyvoulou v. Secretary of State for the Environment and Another* (1990) the House of Lords held that where there has been a successful appeal against an enforcement notice issued by a local planning authority, issue estoppel will operate to bar another enforcement notice in the same terms and in respect of the same alleged breach of planning control.

The second preliminary issue is that, in many cases which are alleged to involve estoppel in public law, a great deal of confusion can be avoided by taking care to give discrete consideration to two questions. The first question centres on whether the person making the representation had either actual or apparent authority to act on behalf of the decision-maker. If such authority did not exist, that is an end of the matter. On the other hand, if such authority did exist, or if the decision-maker itself made the representation (as could happen for example, where a local authority passes a resolution), the second question then arises in terms of whether the estoppel or the doctrine of *ultra vires* is to prevail.

D: The Leading Cases on Estoppel

The basic problem, and the generally prevalent judicial policy, are both well-illustrated by the Privy Council decision in *Maritime Electric Co. v. General Dairies Ltd.* (1937). The facts were that the electricity company had a statutory duty to charge a particular price for its electricity. Nevertheless, over a period of two years, the company actually charged one customer only 10% of the correct price. When the electricity company sued the customer for the balance of the price, the customer argued that an estoppel had arisen. Refusing to recognize an estoppel, the Privy Council emphasized the statutory duty aspect of the case. More particularly, Lord Maugham said:

> "Estoppel is only a rule of evidence ... [and] ... it cannot therefore avail ... to release the plaintiff from an obligation to obey such a statute, nor can it enable the defendant to escape from a statutory obligation of such a kind on his part."

Unfortunately, subsequent cases show a measure of judicial inconsistency. For example, in *Robertson v. Minister of Pensions* (1948), Robertson claimed a military pension on account of a war injury. The War Office wrote to him, telling him that his disability had been accepted as being attributable to military service. In fact, this decision should have been made by the Ministry of Pensions, which subsequently decided that Robertson's disability was not attributable to military service, and the pension appeal tribunal agreed.

Robertson successfully challenged this decision, on the basis that he had acted to his detriment in reliance on the War Office's representation, by, for example, refraining from obtaining independent medical evidence. Denning J. said:

> "In my opinion if a government department in its dealings with a

subject takes it upon itself to assume authority upon a matter with which it is concerned, he is entitled to rely upon it having the authority which it assumes. He does not know and cannot be expected to know, the limits of that authority."

Attractive though this extreme view may be from the point of view of the individual, it was soon authoritatively disapproved in *Howell v. Falmouth Boat Construction Co. Ltd.* (1951). The company repaired a boat owned by Howell. Wartime restrictions which were then in force required a licence to be obtained so that control could be exercised over the use of scarce materials. The company obtained an oral licence first, followed by a written one. When Howell failed to pay for the work, and the company sued him, Howell asserted that, in the absence of a valid licence, the work was illegal, and argued that no action can be brought to enforce an illegal contract. The company argued that it was entitled to rely on the licensing officer's apparent authority to issue an oral licence.

It was held, on the facts, that there was a valid licence anyway, on the basis that the written licence operated retrospectively. But for the present purposes, the interest of the case lies in the judicial comments on the estoppel point. In the Court of Appeal, Denning L.J. repeating his view in *Robertson*, held in favour of the company. The House of Lords upheld this result, as a matter of the interpretation of the relevant licensing provisions, but they disagreed with Denning L.J. on the estoppel point. Lord Simonds said:

"I know of no such principle in our law nor was any authority for it cited. The illegality of the act is the same whether or not the actor has been misled by an assumption of authority on the part of a government officer however high or low in the hierarchy."

Lord Normand said:

"It is certain that neither a minister nor any subordinate officer of the Crown can by any conduct or representation bar the Crown from enforcing a statutory prohibition or entitle the subject to maintain that there has been no breach of it."

The law developed through a series of cases involving ss.43 and 53 of the Town and Country Planning Acts 1947 and 1971 respectively (see now s.64, Town and Country Planning Act 1990). These sections allowed a person to obtain a binding determination from the local planning authority when he is uncertain whether what he proposes to do will fall within the legal definition of *development*, and if so, whether it will require planning permission. The questions raised in such cases are often highly technical, and therefore even before s.101 of the Local Government Act 1972 introduced a general power for local authorities to delegate their functions (see pp.164 *et seq.*), there was a widespread practice for determinations under ss.43 and 53 to be dealt with by officers.

In *Southend-on-Sea Corporation v. Hodgson (Wickford) Ltd.* (1961) the local authority's surveyor had told the company that no planning permission would be needed for the use of certain premises as a builders' yard, because there was an established use right. The company bought the premises in reliance on this statement. The local authority subsequently took enforcement action, alleging that the company's use of the premises constituted a breach of planning control. The High Court held that the case was indistinguishable from *Maritime Electric*, on the basis that the local authority had a discretion in relation to enforcement action, and that the public interest required the exercise of this discretion should not be fettered by an estoppel.

The pendulum swung the other way in *Wells v. Minister of Housing and Local Government* (1967). Wells applied for planning permission for the erection of a structure. The local authority's engineer wrote back to the effect that the proposed development would have the benefit of deemed planning permission under the General Development Order, so the application did not need to be determined. Wells then decided to erect a larger structure, assuming that the General Development Order would cover this also. However, following the erection of the structure, Wells' neighbours complained, and the local authority served an enforcement notice alleging breach of planning control. The question therefore was whether an estoppel operated against the local planning authority.

The Court of Appeal held that there was no representation in *respect of the larger structure*, which was the one which was actually erected, and therefore , on the facts of the case, Wells lost. Nevertheless, in terms of principle, the court acknowledged that there was a long-established and widespread practice of dispensing with formal applications for, and formal issues of, s.43 determinations. In other words, this case was seen as involving matters of form rather than of substance, which explains Lord Denning M.R.'s comment:

"A public authority cannot be estopped from doing its public duty, but I do think it can be estopped from relying on technicalities; and this is a technicality ... I take the law to be that a defect in procedure can be cured, and an irregularity can be waived, even by a public authority, so as to render valid that which would otherwise be invalid. I hold, therefore, that the letter [saying that there was deemed planning permission] was a valid determination under s.43 ... I put it on the ground that the planning authority waived any formal application and determined the matter straight away. Another way of putting it would be to say that the application for planning permission contained an implied invitation to the planning authority to make a determination under s.43, if they thought fit to do so."

Despite such a clear statement of principle from the Master of the Rolls, the other members of the court were divided. Davies L.J. was "in complete agreement" with Lord Denning M.R., but Russell L.J. was not:

"The local planning authority is not a free agent to waive statutory requirements in favour of (so to speak) an adversary: it is the guardian of the planning system."

The principle established by the majority of the Court of Appeal in *Wells*, was also applied in *Lever (Finance) Ltd. v. Westminster Corporation* (1970) where the company had planning permission for a group of houses. The company wanted to change the layout, and accordingly it asked the planning officer for permission to change the position of one house. He had mislaid the file, and, thinking the change was immaterial, he agreed to the re-siting of the house. In fact, the new position meant that the house would be significantly closer to existing properties on adjoining land. When the house was partly built in the revised position, the neighbours objected. The planning officer suggested that if the company applied for planning permission for the new siting, he would recommend the committee to grant it. An application was made, but the committee rejected both the officer's advice and the application. The company then submitted another application, in which the design of the house was altered in order to reduce the extent to which its neighbours would be prejudiced. This application was rejected and the committee resolved to take enforcement action in respect of what it saw as a breach of planning control.

The company successfully challenged the enforcement action in both the High Court and the Court of Appeal. Lord Denning M.R. said:

"If an officer, acting within the scope of his ostensible authority, makes a representation on which another acts, then a public authority may be bound by it, just as much as a private concern would be."

The case-law was in this somewhat confused state, with some fundamental statements in favour of public authorities, but with some significant apparent exceptions being seen in the context of Planning Law, when the problem came before the Court of Appeal in *Western Fish Products Ltd. v. Penwith District Council* (1981).

The company bought a disused factory which had an established use right for the production of fertilizer from fishmeal and other ingredients. The company wanted to use the building for the manufacture of fish-oil and fishmeal, and for the preparation and packing of fresh fish for human consumption. This proposal would involve the repair of old buildings and the construction of new ones. Thinking that the existing use rights covered the proposals, the company wrote accordingly to the planning officer. He wrote back, asking for details of the floor area previously given to the activities on the site. This information was provided, and the planning officer then wrote to the applicant, saying "the limits of the various parts of the commercial undertaking as now existing appear to be established."

The company then started work, and the planning officer asked it to submit an application for planning permission. An application was submitted and refused. Nevertheless, the company continued with the work. An enforcement notice was served. The company tried to appeal to the Secretary of State, but it was out of time. Application was then made to the court for a declaration that the local authority was estopped either from denying that planning permission was needed, and/or from refusing to grant it, and/or from taking enforcement action.

The Court of Appeal held that, quite apart from the law, the facts disclosed two reasons why no estoppel arose. First, there was an insufficient representation, because all the planning officer had said was that the existing buildings could continue to be used. Secondly, it appeared to the court that the company would have proceeded anyway, whatever the planning officer had said. Thus the essential elements of representation and reliance were both missing.

However, leaving aside the detailed facts of the case, the real significance of *Western Fish* lies in its interpretation of both *Wells* and *Lever*. Giving the judgment of the Court of Appeal, Megaw L.J. took the view that *Wells* contains both a general proposition of Administrative Law and a narrow proposition of Planning Law.

The general proposition is that where a procedural irregularity is waived, it cannot subsequently be relied upon.

The narrow proposition is that every application for planning permission includes an implied application for what is now a s.64 determination, so that if the local planning authority think that planning permission is not needed, they can simply say so, without requiring the applicant to submit a formal application for a determination. But this is not to say that applications for determinations can always be made informally. Indeed the correct position is that even where an officer is expressly authorized to deal with applications for determinations, any determination which he issues will be void unless there is either a formal application in writing, or an implied application within an application for planning permission.

Speaking of *Lever*, Megaw, L.J. said:

"For an estoppel to arise there must be some evidence justifying the person dealing with the planning officer for thinking that what the officer said would bind the planning authority. Holding an office, however senior, cannot, in our judgment, be enough by itself. In the *Lever (Finance) Ltd* case there was evidence of a widespread practice amongst planning authorities of allowing their planning officers to make immaterial modifications to the plans produced when planning permission was given. Lever (Finance) Ltd's architect presumably knew of this practice and was entitled to assume that the practice had been authorized by the planning authorities in whose areas it was followed ... Whether anyone dealing with a planning officer can safely assume that the officer can bind his authority by anything he says must depend on all the circumstances. In the *Lever (Finance) Ltd* case ... Lord Denning M.R. said: 'Any person dealing with them [i.e. officers of a planning authority] is entitled to assume that all necessary resolutions have been passed.' This statement was not necessary for the conclusion he had reached and purported to be an addendum. We consider it to be *obiter*; with all respect, it stated the law too widely."

Megaw L.J. also said:

"If a planning authority waives a procedural requirement relating to any application made to it for the exercise of its statutory powers, it may be estopped from relying on the lack of formality. Much, however, will turn on the construction of any statutory provisions setting out what the procedure is to be. *Wells v. MHLG* is an example [of this]."

If regard is had to the facts of the case, it is apparent that, strictly speaking, the observations of the Court of Appeal in *Western Fish* are themselves *obiter*. However, there seems to be little doubt that those observations represent the current state of the law.

Even Lord Denning M.R. appeared to come round to an acceptance of the orthodox position, as indicated by his *obiter* comment in *Co-Operative Retail Services Ltd. v. Taff-Ely Borough Council* (1979):

> "Representative bodies ... should not be bound by mistakes made by ... people in the office - when the result would be to damage the interests of the public at large."

E: Alternatives to Estoppel

Finally, in those cases where it is impossible to establish an estoppel against a public decision-maker, it may nevertheless be possible to base a challenge on the presumption of regularity or the doctrine of legitimate expectation, which are discussed at pp. 17-19, and 189 *et seq.* respectively.

However, even at this stage it is worth saying that dealing with estoppel-type situations in terms of the doctrine of legitimate expectation is largely a terminological change rather than a conceptual one. This is apparent from *R. v. Jockey Club ex parte RAM Racecourses Ltd.* (1990), where Stuart-Smith L.J. and Simon Brown J. said that if an application were to succeed on the basis of legitimate expectation, the following matters would need to be established, namely that there had been a clear and unambiguous representation; that the applicants were within a class of persons entitled to rely on the representation, even though it was not made directly to them, or that it was reasonable for them to rely on it; that the applicants did rely on the representation; that the applicants' reliance on the representation was to their detriment; and that there was no overriding interest, arising from their duties and responsibilities which entitled the respondents to change their policy to the detriment of the applicants.

These comments contain an element of overstatement in one important respect. As the facts of *GCHQ* (1984) make clear, an explicit representation is not an essential ingredient in the creation of a legitimate expectation. In this case, the House of Lords held that the long-standing practice of consulting trades' unions before changing the conditions of service of their members had created a legitimate expectation that such consultation would precede such changes. The fact that, in all the circumstances of the case, the interests of national security were held to override the legitimate expectation does not detract from the basic principle.

It will be apparent that the only substantive consequence of speaking in terms of legitimate expectation rather than estoppel is that the question of the authority of the person making the representation fades into the background, to be replaced by a consideration of the legitimacy of the expectation which the representation creates. In some cases, of course, this may be the crucial issue.

On the whole, however, the doctrine of legitimate expectation does nothing to deal with the fundamental difficulty which bedevils the law on estoppel, namely the prospect of illicit exercises of power becoming legally effective.

CHAPTER 12

NATURAL JUSTICE - THE REQUIREMENT OF FAIRNESS

A: Introduction

It would be difficult to dispute the characteristically perceptive comment of Sir Robert Megarry V-C in *McInnes v. Onlsow-Fane* (1978):

> "Justice is far from being a 'natural' concept - the closer one goes to a state of nature, the less justice does one find."

Nevertheless the common law has long used the phrase "natural justice" to indicate those requirements of procedural fairness, which Harman L.J., in *Ridge v. Baldwin* (1963), characterized as "fair play in action."

Over the years there have been significant fluctuations with regard to both the types of decision covered by this principle, and the characteristics which the decision-making process must possess if it is to be lawful. More precisely, the Victorian era saw a well-developed body of law in this area, and this continued to be true into the early part of the twentieth century. Thereafter the courts became increasingly reluctant to intervene, and the doctrine of natural justice went into decline.

The emergence of the modern law dates from the decision of the House of Lords in *Ridge v. Baldwin*, where the House of Lords indicated that any decision-making process which affects the rights of subjects must comply with the requirements of natural justice. This proposition has since been extended still further to include the protection of *legitimate expectations* as well as rights.

Even more recently, a tendency to speak in terms of *fairness* rather than *natural justice* has emerged. In *GCHQ* (1984) Lord Diplock suggested that *fairness* should be the generally preferred usage, while Sir Robert Megarry V-C had expressed the more sophisticated view that natural justice should be reserved for cases with a judicial flavour, whereas *fairness* is more appropriate in cases of administrative decision-making (*McInnes v. Onslow-Fane* (1978)). However, there is no uniformity of usage, nor should it be assumed that fairness is a distinct concept. As Wade says:

> "There is no difference between natural justice and 'acting fairly' ...

they are alternative names for a single but flexible doctrine whose content may vary according to the nature of the power [which the decision-maker is exercising] and the circumstances of the case." (*Administrative Law*, 6th edition, 1988, p.524.)

R. v. Wandsworth London Borough Council ex parte P (1989) provides a useful example of the way in which the courts can invoke the principles of natural justice in order to give a remedy in a situation which would otherwise have been non-justiciable. Following allegations that a woman on the local authority's approved list of foster mothers had sexually abused a child, the Director of Social Services decided to remove her name from the list. Although the foster mother protested on the basis that she had been given no opportunity to respond to the allegations against her, the appropriate sub-committee of the local authority endorsed the Director's decision.

On an application for judicial review, the High Court held that complaints based on the assessment of an individual's suitability as a foster mother were non-justiciable. Nevertheless, the court proceeded to grant the application on the basis that in the absence of an emergency situation, it was an elementary principle of natural justice that the applicant should have been told what was alleged against her in sufficient detail to enable her to respond effectively. Her rights, however, would stop short of an entitlement to call witnesses, or to see the local authority's casenotes and other documentation.

The Court of Appeal disposed of similar difficulties in *R. v. Harrow London Borough Council ex parte D* (1990), holding that in principle social services' case conferences dealing with suspected non-accidental injury to children are subject to judicial review. However the court recognized that a decision as to whether to place a child's name on an "at risk" register involves balancing protection of the child with fairness to any adult who may be suspected of having caused the injury. Furthermore, the difficulty and delicacy of this decision-making process are such that decision-makers should be allowed to perform their task without looking over their shoulders all the time for possible intervention by the court. The court concluded, therefore, that judicial review should be reserved for exceptional cases involving points of principle which are of general application. In routine cases, where the only criticism made relates to some individual aspect of procedure, leave to apply for judicial review should be refused.

The relationship between judicial review and natural justice has not always been clear. The source of the confusion is that for many years the courts felt that the ideas of fairness which had been developed in the context of public-decision-makers, should be imported into certain other types of cases, even though those cases were at least arguably within the realm of what is now regarded as being private law.

In *R. v. Jockey Club ex parte RAM Racecourses Ltd.* (1990) Simon Brown J. offered a perceptive comment on this historical phenomenon by listing a number of cases, namely *Eastham v. Newcastle United Football Club Ltd.* (1963), *Nagle v. Feilden* (1966), *Breen v. Amalgamated Engineering Union* (1971), and *McInnes v. Onslow-Fane* (1978), and then going on to say:

> "Had [these cases] arisen today and not some years ago, [they] would have found a natural home in judicial review proceedings. As it was, considerations of public policy forced the courts to devise a new private law creature: a right in certain circumstances to declaratory judgments without any underlying cause of action. But clear recognition of the true, essentially public law, nature of these cases is to be found in the judgment of Lord Denning M.R. in *Breen's* case itself, and I for my part would judge it preferable to develop these principles in future in a public law context than by further distorting private law principles."

Another illustration of the wide-ranging nature of natural justice emerges from *R. v. Secretary of State for the Environment ex parte Davidson* (1990) where, in the context of an appeal on a point of law under s.246 of the Town and Country Planning Act 1971, Nolan J. could see

> "no reason why a denial of natural justice could not be perfectly properly raised as an error of law."

For the purpose of identifying the principles of natural justice, therefore, it seems clear that no distinction need be drawn between statements contained in cases brought by way of judicial review and those brought by other means.

B: The Variable Content of Natural Justice

Although there is a sense in which the whole of the judicial review can be said to be safeguarding the interests of fairness, two matters are usually identified as constituting the central elements of the modern law of natural justice.

First, the courts will impose different requirements in different circumstances. As Tucker L.J. said in *Russell v. Duke of Norfolk* (1949):

"[The requirements of natural justice] must depend on the circumstances of the case, the nature of the inquiry, the rules under which the tribunal [sc. the decision-maker] is acting, the subject-matter that is being dealt with, and so forth."

A typically open-ended statement of the potential requirements of natural justice may be found in *R. v. Army Board of the Defence Council ex parte Anderson* (1991), where the High Court said that a forum of last resort dealing with an individual's fundamental statutory rights must adopt procedures which would achieve a high standard of fairness. More particularly, it was insufficient merely to act in good faith.

However, the decision in *Ward v. Bradford Corporation* (1972) makes it clear that natural justice does not require the provision of any avenue of appeal against a decision.

Secondly, the flexible requirements which constitute the doctrine of natural justice are very widely applicable. Megarry J. offered an extreme view in *Gaiman v. National Association for Mental Health* (1970):

"It may be that there is no simple test, but there is a tendency for the court to apply the principles [of natural justice] to all powers of decision unless the circumstances suffice to exclude them."

This comment must, of course, be read in context. The requirements of natural justice are usually restricted to cases involving public law, along with certain other areas such as some aspects of the conduct of clubs, trades' unions and professional or quasi-professional bodies. In these cases, even though the relationships involved may originate in the private law of contract, the law may nevertheless require fairness in decision-making, especially in the context of decisions which affect the individual's opportunity to earn a living. As Woolf L.J. said in *R. v. Derbyshire County Council ex parte Noble* (1990), which is discussed more fully at p.74:

"It should not be assumed that because ... this is a case where judicial review is not available, it follows automatically that the principles of natural justice do not apply."

It is clear that even where statute or delegated legislation has prescribed a detailed procedural scheme, the courts may still be prepared to add further procedural requirements in the interests of fairness. A cautious version of this principle was formulated by Lord Reid in *Wiseman v. Borneman* (1969):

"For a long time the courts have, without objection from Parliament, supplemented procedure laid down in legislation where they have found this to be necessary ... But before this unusual kind of power is exercised it must be clear that the statutory procedure is insufficient to achieve justice and that to require additional steps would not frustrate the apparent purpose of the legislation."

The case of *R. v. Birmingham City Council ex parte Ferrero Ltd.* (1991) provides an example of the court refusing to impose an additional requirement that the local authority should consult the manufacturer of chocolate eggs containing plastic toys before issuing an order suspending the sale of the eggs. One child had already choked to death on one of the toys, and the court took the view that the local authority had been under a duty to act quickly in the interests of the safety of other children. The performance of this duty would have been frustrated by the imposition of an additional requirement of consultation.

C: Legitimate Expectation

Since the scope of the modern law has been significantly extended by the introduction of the doctrine of legitimate expectation, it may be helpful at this stage to consider this doctrine in rather more detail.

According to Lord Diplock in *GCHQ* (1984) the precise terminology is important:

"I prefer ... to call [this] kind of expectation ... a 'legitimate expectation' rather than a 'reasonable expectation', in order thereby to indicate that it has consequences to which effect will be given in public law, whereas an expectation or hope [of] some benefit or advantage ..., although it might well be entertained by a 'reasonable man', would not necessarily have such consequences ... 'Reasonable' furthermore bears different meanings according to whether the context in which it is being used is that of private law or public law. To eliminate confusion it is best avoided in the latter."

In *Re Liverpool Taxi Owners' Association* (1972) the local authority proposed to increase the number of taxi cab licences which it issued. The cab *owners* wanted the number of licences to remain static, but the cab *drivers* wanted the number to be increased to enable them to compete more effectively with mini-cabs. The corporation told the cab owners that full consultation would precede any decision on the question of an increase. Thereafter, the corporation again began to think in terms of an increase, but the chairman of the relevant committee said that no increase would take place before the corporation had obtained Private Act powers to control mini-cabs. When the corporation was advised that the chairman's undertaking was not binding, the cab owners applied for judicial review to prevent the increase from taking place. Having lost in the High Court, they succeeded in the Court of Appeal, which held that full consultation was required. The court also held that the chairman's undertaking should be honoured, unless - as was not the case here - it conflicted with the performance of a statutory duty.

In situations such as the *Liverpool Taxi* case there is no doubt that there has been a representation. Other cases may be less clear. In *R. v. Secretary of State for the Home Department ex parte Patel* (1991) the High Court had to consider the effect of certain stamps which were in an immigrant's passport when he left the United Kingdom. The *leave to remain* stamp was followed by one which read:

"This will apply, unless superseded, to any subsequent leave the holder may obtain after an absence from the United Kingdom with the period limited as above."

Another stamp stated:

"The holder is exempt from requiring a visa if returning to the United Kingdom to resume earlier leave before September 30, 1989."

The High Court held that these stamps were relevant only to the exercise of discretion as to whether or not to allow the immigrant to re-enter the country, and that they did not constitute representations giving rise to a legitimate expectation that re-entry would be permitted.

On the other hand, a comparatively informal situation was held to create a legitimate expectation in *R. v. Enfield London Borough Council ex parte T. F. Unwin (Roydon) Limited* (1989). A local authority suspended one of its contractors in consequence of a private transaction between the contractor and one of the local authority's employees. The High Court held that because the contractor had been on the authority's approved list for a long time, and there had been no previous complaints which would justify removal from the list, the contractor had a legitimate expectation of fair treatment over and above the specific provisions as to the giving of reasons contained in s.20 of the Local Government Act 1988.

Disputes as to whether a genuinely held expectation is also legitimate will be resolved by reference to an objective test. In *R. v. Swale Borough Council and Another ex parte Royal Society for the Protection of Birds* (1990) the applicant for judicial review claimed, *inter alia*, to have had a legitimate expectation that it would be consulted during the decision-making process on a complex scheme of land reclamation. The difficulty arose over a misunderstanding between the parties as to precisely which decision would be preceded by consultation.

Having had no difficulty in holding that a promise of consultation creates a legitimate expectation, the High Court went on to hold that where there is a genuine and reasonable misunderstanding of the kind in question, the court must adopt the position of the reasonable bystander.

Even more specifically, in *R. v. South Somerset District Council ex parte DJB (Group) Ltd.* (1989) the High Court held that where a local authority adopts a policy as to the exercise of its discretion to prosecute for a certain type of offence, and a member of the public, being aware of that policy, breaches the law in circumstances which according to the policy will not result in prosecution, the individual's expectation of not being prosecuted cannot be said to be legitimate.

The concept of legitimate expectation is particularly significant in certain situations which involve licensing. In *McInnes v. Onslow-Fane* (1978), the plaintiff had had a chequered career in professional boxing. He had held licences as a trainer, a manager and a master of ceremonies - all of which had been taken from him as a result of misconduct. He then applied five times for a manager's licence. On the sixth application he asked for an oral hearing and notification of what was to be held against him. His application was refused, without an oral hearing, and without prior notification of what was being held against him.

Sir Robert Megarry V-C held that, in principle, the court could intervene, because the case involved the plaintiff's liberty to work. However, the court would not intervene on the present facts, because having lost his previous licences, and having made a series of unsuccessful applications, the plaintiff could do no more than hope for a licence, and could certainly not expect to be granted one. His only entitlement was to be dealt with honestly, without bias or caprice. The judge seems to have thought it important that, in his opinion, the refusal did not necessarily cast a slur on the plaintiff. He also thought it important that, if the Board told him what was being held against him, he would be able to use this in litigation against the Board, whereas the public interest required that a body such as the Board, which was responsible for maintaining high standards in an area which could easily become degraded and corrupt, should not be hampered by the prospect of unnecessary litigation.

It is important to note that the situation giving rise to the instant case was distinguished from the situation which exists where an existing licence is being revoked. In the latter situation the judge recognized the existence of a right to receive notice of the allegations and to be afforded a fair hearing, because the proceedings would constitute a threat to existing rights. However, Sir Robert Megarry V-C also recognized an intermediate category of case, where an existing licence falls due for renewal. In such circumstances it could be said that the applicant could have a legitimate expectation of, but not a right to, a renewal.

Since the case-law clearly emphasizes the width of the range of possibilities which may subsist within the general heading of fairness, it is now appropriate to consider each of the possible elements which the court may require.

D: The Right to a Hearing - *Audi Alteram Partem*

1. The Hearing Need Not Be Oral

Despite the obvious implication of the term hearing, it is well-established that orality is not an essential ingredient. In *Local Government Board v. Arlidge* (1914) a public inquiry had been held through the medium of an oral hearing before an inspector, who had then made a report in the light of which the actual decision had been made. One of the grounds of challenge was that the the objector had not been allowed an oral hearing before the true decision-maker. The argument failed, because the House of Lords accepted that the practical realities of public administration will often prevent the actual decision-maker from conducting an oral hearing. Lord Haldane L.C. said:

> "The Minister at the head of the Board is directly responsible to Parliament like other Ministers. The volume of work entrusted to him is very great ... Unlike a judge in a court, he is not only at liberty but is compelled to rely on the assistance of his staff. When, therefore, the Board is directed to dispose of an appeal, that does not mean that any particular official of the Board is to dispose of it."

A useful summary of the principles relating to the requirement of orality was given in *R. v. Army Board of the Defence Council ex parte Anderson* (1991). The High Court thought it was well-established that regard should be had to the subject-matter and circumstances of the case, and in particular whether there were substantial issues of fact, which were central to the issue to be determined, and which could not be satisfactorily resolved on the available written evidence. The court also said that the decision whether or not to allow cross-examination would usually be inseparable from the decision whether or not to allow an oral hearing, but cases may arise where it would be possible to allow an oral hearing simply in order to receive submissions.

Where an oral hearing is permitted, its duration may be important. In *R. v. Portsmouth City Council ex parte Gregory and Mos* (1990) the High Court was dealing with an application for judicial review arising out of disciplinary proceedings brought by a local authority against two of its members who were alleged to have breached the National Code of Local Government Conduct. Some of the meetings which investigated the complaints were very protracted, and in due course the High Court commented that the interests of justice require that proceedings do not go on for too long each day

2. The Need for Notice of the Hearing

The case of *Glynn v. Keele University* (1971) indicates not only that notice must be given but also that the notice must be effective. Glynn, a student at the University, had been sunbathing on the campus in the nude. The Vice-Chancellor instituted disciplinary proceedings, and notice of those proceedings was sent to the student at his University address. However, when the notice was received he had already left for the long vacation, and the proceedings took place in his absence. The court held that the disciplinary proceedings were quasi-judicial because they were fundamental to the applicant's position as a student at the University, and therefore that the requirements of natural justice applied. Moreover, the lack of effective notice meant that those requirements had not been observed. However, at a practical level, the student failed as a result of the exercise of the court's discretion. The judge said:

"I do not think the mere fact that he was deprived of throwing himself on the mercy of the Vice-Chancellor ... is sufficient to justify setting aside a decision which was intrinsically a perfectly proper one."

Although this comment runs counter to the basic emphasiz on the quality of the decision-making process rather than on the correctness of the decision itself, it does provide a useful reminder of the discretionary nature of the remedies.

In cases of ineffective notice where the fault cannot be laid at the door of the decision-maker, the position may be different. Perhaps the most obvious situation is where the individual's lawyer is at fault. In *Al-Mehdawi v. Secretary of State for the Home Department* (1989). The respondent to an appeal by the Home Secretary was an Iraqi student who had been granted repeated extensions of his leave to stay in the United Kingdom, until eventually a further extension was refused. The Home Secretary then gave the respondent notice that he was to be deported.

The respondent's solicitors gave notice of appeal, but when they tried to notify the respondent they sent notification of the date of the hearing to the wrong address. The result was that the respondent never received the notification. His solicitors did nothing further, so the respondent did not appear at the hearing and was not represented. The adjudicator proceeded on the basis of the documents which he had in front of him, and dismissed the appeal. The solicitors wrote to notify the respondent of the time within which any further appeal should be made, but again they sent this notification to the wrong address.

In the High Court Macpherson J. held that the respondent had not been at fault and proceeded to quash the adjudication. The Court of Appeal upheld this decision, but the House of Lords saw the matter differently, holding that there is no procedural impropriety or breach of natural justice where a person has been deprived of the opportunity of a hearing as a result of the default of his own legal advisers.

Even if effective notice is given, it is clear that the notice itself must be fair in terms of each of the following matters: *the substance of the notice; the amount of time allowed between the notice and the hearing;* and *the relationship between the notice and the final decision.*

Dealing first with the requirement that the substance of the notice must be fair, in *Sloan v. General Medical Council* (1970) the Privy Council dealt with a "trap" charge, or in other words a charge which will inevitably produce a finding of guilt, irrespective of the view of the facts taken by the decision-maker.

Dr. Sloan had a religious objection to abortion with the result that when he was consulted by pregnant women wishing to have illegal abortions, he administered a general anaesthetic, and on their regaining consciousness, he told them that they had had abortions, even though they had not. By the time they found out that they were still pregnant, it was too late for safe abortions to be performed. Dr. Sloan's religious beliefs were thus satisfied at his patients' expense.

When disciplinary proceedings were taken against him, the charge was such that he was guilty of either performing illegal abortions if the tribunal thought he had actually done what he told the patients he had done, or lying to his patients if the tribunal thought he had not done what he told the patients he had done. In view of the nature of the charge, it is not surprising that the disciplinary tribunal found the charge was substantiated.

On appeal, the Privy Council strongly disapproved of the use of "trap" charges, but as there was no evidence on which the tribunal could have found him guilty of anything other than the charge of lying to his patients, there was no reason to think he had been prejudiced. The Privy Council therefore refused to grant a remedy.

Turning secondly to the requirement that the notice shall be fair in terms of the amount of time allowed between the notice and the hearing, the case of *R. v. Thames Magistrates' Court ex parte Polemis* (1974) is instructive. Oil was seen on the water near a ship in a London dock. At 10.30 a.m. on the day on which the ship was due to sail at 9.00 p.m., the ship's master received a summons to appear before the Magistrates' Court at 2.00 p.m. At 2.30 p.m. his solicitor applied for an adjournment. This application was refused, but the case was put back to 4.00 p.m., when, on a plea of Not Guilty, the master was convicted and fined £5,000. The conviction was quashed on the basis that the defendant had not had an adequate opportunity to present his case.

Turning thirdly to the requirement that the notice must be fair in terms of its relationship to the final decision, the leading case is *Trustees of the Maradana Mosque v. Mahmud* (1966). An independent school in Ceylon was subject to detailed control by the education authorities. More particularly, the trustees of the school were required to satisfy two conditions, namely prompt payment of teachers' salaries and the provision of adequate funding to maintain the general functioning of the school at a satisfactory level. The Minister of Education gave the trustees notice that he was considering taking the school over on the grounds of their failure to pay teachers' salaries promptly. The trustees made representations about this matter, but nevertheless the school was taken over. Subsequently, it transpired that one of the Minister's reasons for taking action was his dissatisfaction with the general level of funding.

The Privy Council quashed the Minister's decision on the ground that he had acted unlawfully, because the trustees had not been given an opportunity to respond to the allegations in their entirety.

3. Is There an Entitlement to Legal Representation?

There is no definitive answer to the question of whether there is an entitlement to legal representation. The courts sometimes draw a distinction between statutory bodies, to which the parties are subject as a result of the operation of law, and domestic bodies, to which the the parties are subject as a result of the exercise of their own freedom of choice. Admittedly, this distinction cannot be sustained in all cases, since in practical terms the freedom to pursue certain activities may depend on submission to the disciplinary jurisdiction of a non-statutory body, as shown by some of the regulatory body cases discussed at pp.66 *et seq.* Nevertheless, the distinction provides a useful starting point

Historically, the courts used the concept of agency to justify a right to legal representation before statutory bodies. In *R. v. St. Mary Abbott's Kensington Assessment Committee* (1891) the Court of Appeal held that a householder who objected to a valuation list need not attend in person to present his objection to the assessment committee, but could appoint an agent to appear on his behalf. Attractive though this approach is, the courts have subsequently been concerned to reject arguments that there is a universal entitlement to legal representation. In particular, the *Kensington* case has been distinguished on a number of occasions, with the most authoritative instance occurring in *R. v. Board of Visitors of the Maze Prison ex parte Hone* (1988), where a life prisoner had been refused legal representation when the Board of Visitors was dealing with a charge of assaulting a prison officer. Lord Goff, giving the judgment of the House of Lords, said that the *Kensington* case "was concerned only with the making of a communication to an administrative body."

Lord Goff went on to say:

"Everything must depend on the circumstances of the particular case ... it is easy to envisage circumstances in which the rules of natural justice do not call for representation, even though the disciplinary charge relates to a matter which constitutes in law a crime, as may well happen in the case of a simple asssault where no question of law arises and where the prisoner is capable of presenting his own case."

Lord Goff also considered art. 6(3) of the European Convention on Human Rights:

"Everyone charged with a criminal offence has the following minimum rights .... (c) to defend himself in person or through legal assistance of his own choosing."

Lord Goff concluded that this article does not provide an entitlement in disciplinary proceedings, even where the allegation concerned was a criminal offence as well as a disciplinary one.

In *R. v. Board of Visitors of H.M. Remand Centre Risley ex parte Draper* (1988) the High Court held that there is no need for representation where an allegation has a simple factual basis.

In the context of domestic bodies, where an individual has chosen to enter into a contract or some similar arrangement, part of which involves his submission to a disciplinary jurisdiction, it may be argued that the parties can easily incorporate into their agreement a provision relating to the availability of legal representation, if they so wish. According to this argument, therefore, if the agreement is silent on the matter there will be a presumption against legal representation. On the other hand, it can be argued that reasonable people might assume that a right to legal representation is so obviously a part of fairness that any specific provisions relating to it would be otiose. In practice, the courts do not appear to have followed either of these lines of argument with any consistency.

In *University of Ceylon v. Fernando* (1960) disciplinary proceedings were brought against a student arising out of an allegation of cheating in an examination. The Privy Council held that because the University's rules of procedure for disciplinary proceedings gave no right to cross-examine witnesses, it followed that there was no right to legal representation. In passing, it may be noted that the Privy Council's reasoning is quite unsupportable, because expertise in cross-examination is only one of the skills which a lawyer-advocate may be expected to possess. The real, if rather odd, explanation for the decision seems to have been that the Privy Council did not regard the allegation as being particularly serious.

In *Pett v. Greyhound Racing Association (No. 1)* (1968) there was an inquiry into allegations that a greyhound trainer's dogs had been doped. The rules of the National Greyhound Racing Club, which licensed trainers, did not allow legal representation. On the preliminary question of the availability of legal representation, the Court of Appeal held that there was a presumption in favour of legal representation because the allegation was a serious matter affecting the trainer's reputation and livelihood. However, when the matter came to a full trial as *Pett v. Greyhound Racing Association (No. 2)* (1969), Lyell J. held that in all the circumstances the presumption in favour of representation did not apply, because it was not necessary in order to ensure the adequate dispensation of justice.

An assessment of the authority of the two *Pett* cases is complicated by the fact that in *No. 2* Lyell J. was strongly influenced by the decision in *Fernando*, which had not been cited in the Court of Appeal in *No. 1*. From the point of view of authority, the flawed reasoning in *Fernando* and the technically non-binding nature of Privy Council decisions complicate the matter still further.

It may be thought that the courts emerged with rather more credit from the case of *Enderby Town Football Club v. Football Association* (1971). The Rutland County Football Association conducted an inquiry into the affairs of Enderby Town, and concluded that there had been gross negligence in the administration of the club. The club appealed to the Football Association, whose rules provided that legal representation may be allowed in appeal proceedings. In the present case, however, the Football Association refused to allow the club to be legally represented. The Court of Appeal held that if the club wanted to raise points of law the best place to do so would be a court of law, where in the present situation a declaration could be an appropriate remedy. On the other hand, if the club chose to submit to the Association's jurisdiction, it followed that they must submit to the Association's rules.

4. The Right to a Hearing in Open-and-Shut Cases

Respondents sometimes seek to resist applications for judicial review on the ground that there would have been no point in offering a hearing, because there could be only one outcome to the matter anyway, irrespective of anything which could have been said on behalf of the applicant. The courts generally reject this argument, with the classic formulation of that rejection being found in the judgment of Megarry J. in *John v. Rees* (1969):

> "As everybody who has anything to do with the law well knows, the path of the law is strewn with examples of open and shut cases which, somehow, were not; of unanswerable charges which, in the event, were completely answered; of inexplicable conduct which was fully explained; of fixed and unalterable determinations that, by discussion, suffered a change."

Moreover, even where the only possible outcome genuinely is that someone will be held to be at fault, a hearing may still serve a useful purpose. In *R. v. Smith ex parte Harris* (1844), a vicar dismissed the parish clerk for conducting himself in front of the congregation in a manner which was "indecent and unbecoming". The question arose as to whether the vicar had been entitled to dispense with a hearing on the basis that he had personally witnessed the objectionable behaviour. The court held that there should have been a hearing, if only to give the clerk the opportunity to produce some mitigation.

Similarly, in *Ridge v. Baldwin* (1963), Lord Reid emphasized that even if the Chief Constable was obviously unfit to retain office, he might still have been able to produce sufficient mitigation to justify the Watch

Committee in deciding to let him resign, thereby preserving pension rights which would be lost on dismissal.

Although at the level of principle a hearing should be provided even in open-and-shut cases, it is worth remembering that in purely practical terms, the respondent's failure to provide a hearing may not avail the applicant anything because of the discretionary nature of the remedies, as illustrated by the cases of *Glynn* and *Sloan* (see pp.193 and 194 respectively).

5. Must the Decision-Maker Conduct the Hearing?

Some challengers seek to argue that although a hearing has taken place, the real decision-maker was not involved in it. This argument was dealt with in general terms by the House of Lords in *Arlidge* (see p.160), but the case of *R. v. Army Board of the Defence Council ex parte Anderson* (1991) is also worth noticing.

The facts relevant to the present point were that a soldier alleged he had been the victim of racial discrimination. The allegations were considered at various levels within the army. Eventually, the matter came before the Army Board, which proceeded without an oral hearing. More particularly, the two members of the Board dealing with the matter proceeded to consider various documents, and to form their conclusions, without meeting each other, although the second member was aware of the first member's conclusion before he reached his own conclusion.

The High Court granted an application for judicial review, holding, *inter alia*, that the Board, operating as a single adjudicating body, should have considered all the relevant evidence and contentions before reaching its conclusions.. More particularly, it was unsatisfactory that the members should consider the papers and reach their conclusions individually, and perhaps, as in the present case, with one member reaching his conclusion after having received the final views of another member.

E: The Rule Against Bias - *Nemo Iudex in Sua Causa*

1. Introduction

The idea that fairness requires an absence of bias on the part of the decision-maker may seem to be self-evident. The difficulty arises at the practical level of deciding what actually constitutes bias.

One preliminary point which must be emphasized is that although in ordinary usage it may well be uncomplimentary of someone to say that he is biased, this will not necessarily be so in the present context. Thus in *R. v. Barnsley Licensing Justices ex parte Barnsley & District Licensed*

Victuallers' Association (1960) Devlin L.J. said:

> "Bias is or may be an unconscious thing and a man may honestly say that he was not actually biased and did not allow his interest to affect his mind, although, nevertheless, he may have allowed it unconsciously to do so."

Similarly, in the Irish case of *R. (De Vesci) v. Queen's County Justices* (1908) Lord O'Brien C.J. said:

> "By bias I understand a real likelihood of an operative prejudice, whether conscious or unconscious."

2. The Tests for Identifying Bias

Traditionally, English law has known two tests for identifying bias, namely *reasonable suspicion* of bias, and *real likelihood* of bias. The extent to which these two tests actually signify different situations is a matter for further comment, but before that comment may be sensibly made the leading cases must be surveyed, and for this purpose the two tests will be considered in turn.

The case of *R. v. Sussex Justices ex parte McCarthy* (1923) arose out of a road traffic accident following which two sets of proceedings were instituted against the defendant: a civil action for damages and a prosecution for dangerous driving. At the criminal hearing, the clerk to the justices was a partner of the solicitor who was acting for the plaintiff in the civil matter. Although the two cases were procedurally and conceptually quite distinct, it would nevertheless be true that a conviction before the Magistrates would enhance the plaintiff's chances of success in the claim for damages. Quashing the conviction in the Magistrates' Court, Lord Hewart C.J. said:

> "It is not merely of some importance but is of fundamental importance that justice should not only be done, but should manifestly and undoubtedly be seen to be done."

An extreme example of this approach may be found in *R. v. Smethwick Justices ex parte Hands* (1980) where proceedings had been brought in the Magistrates' Court under the statututory nuisance provisions of the Public Health Act 1936. The essence of the matter was whether design defects in a particular council house meant that its condition was likely to harm the health of the occupiers. The husband of one of the magistrates had been a member of the local authority which owned the house, and, at the time the house was built, he had been chairman of the committee which was responsible for its building and subsequent maintenance. At the time of the case, however, he was no longer a member of the local authority. The High Court held that there had been a breach of the rule against bias, because the presence of that particular magistrate on the bench would look wrong to anyone who knew of her link with the former chairman of the committee.

Although the *McCarthy* emphasiz that even the appearance of injustice is sufficient to constitute a breach of fairness may seem a useful element in promoting the maintenance of high quality decision-making processes, there is clearly a danger that emphasizing appearances may lead to neglecting realities. It is on this basis that the courts have sometimes applied the alternative test of real likelihood of bias.

In *R. v. Camborne Justices ex parte Pearce* (1954) a County Council brought a prosecution under the Food and Drugs Act. The Clerk to the Justices, who was a member of the County Council, sat as the clerk of the court. The High Court held that although it would be better for the court to have been clerked by a member of the clerk's staff, nevertheless there was no real likelihood of bias, and therefore the magistrates' decision would not be quashed. Slade J. said:

"While indorsing and fully maintaining the integrity of the principle reasserted by Lord Hewart C.J., [in *McCarthy*] this court feels that the continued citation of it in cases to which it is not applicable may lead to the erroneous impression that it is more important that justice should appear to be done than that it should in fact be done. In the present case this court is of the opinion that there was no real likelihood of bias."

Matters become more complicated with the case of *Metropolitan Properties Co. (F.G.C.) Ltd. v. Lannon* (1968), which has given rise to a degree of subsequent judicial confusion. The facts were that a solicitor, who was the chairman of a Rent Assessment Committee, lived with his father in a flat. His father, who was the tenant of the flat, was in dispute with the landlords over his rent. Furthermore, the solicitor had acted for other people against the landlord. Then the Rent Assessment Committee had to deal with rents payable in respect of flats in another block, which was owned by a company which was associated with the company which owned the chairman's father's flat. The Court of Appeal quashed the committee's decision. Dankwerts L.J. and Edmund-Davies L.J. were both content to apply the reasonable suspicion test, saying respectively:

"A person subsequently hearing of these matters might reasonably feel doubts, I think, of the chairman's impartiality."

And:

"I cannot bring myself to hold that a decision may properly be allowed to stand even although there is a reasonable suspicion of bias on the part of one or more members of the adjudicating body."

Matters become more complicated when attention is turned to the judgment of Lord Denning M.R., who said:

"In considering whether there was a real likelihood of bias, the court does not look at the mind of the justice himself or at the mind of the chairman of the tribunal or whoever it may be, who sits in a judicial capacity. It does not look to see if there was a real likelihood that he would, or did in fact, favour one side at the expense of the other. The court looks at the impression which would be given to other people. Even if he was as impartial as could be, nevertheless if right-minded persons would think that, in the circumstances, there was a real likelihood of bias on his part, then he should not sit. And if he does sit, his decision cannot stand. Nevertheless, there must appear to be a real likelihood of bias. Surmise or conjecture is not enough. There may be circumstances from which a reasonable man would think it likely or probable that the justice, or chairman, as the case may be, would, or did, favour one side unfairly at the expense of the other. The court will not inquire whether he did, in fact, favour one side unfairly. Suffice it that reasonable people might think he did. The reason is plain enough. Justice must be rooted in confidence; and confidence is destroyed when right-minded people go away thinking: 'The judge was biased'."

The less than lucid quality of this passage has not escaped the attention of Judges in later cases, with *Hannam v. Bradford City Council* (1970) and *R. v. Altrincham Justices ex parte Pennington* (1975) being particularly significant.

In *Hannam* the governors of a school maintained by the council wanted to dismiss a teacher. The system was that the council could prevent the dismissal if they so wished, but unless they actively opposed it, the dismissal would take place. Three out of the ten members of the committee which decided not to oppose the dismissal were governors of Hannam's school, although none of them had attended the governors' meeting which decided in favour of dismissal in the first place. The County Court judge applied the test of whether "a reasonable man would say that a real danger of bias existed."

In due course, the Court of Appeal held that the rule against bias had been breached. According to Sachs L.J:

"[*Lannon* shows] somewhat of a swing back towards the principle enunciated in the *Sussex Justices* case ... For my part, I doubt whether in practice materially different results are produced by the 'real likelihood of bias' test ... or that adopted by the County Court judge. If there is such a difference, I uphold the latter."

Widgery L.J. said:

"I, like Sachs L.J., am satisfied that there was a real likelihood of bias in this case ... [and] ... whichever of the tests adumbrated in [*Lannon*] is properly to be applied in this case, the plaintiff has made out his allegation."

Cross L.J. said:

"To my mind, there really is little (if any) difference between the two tests ... If a reasonable person, who has no knowledge of the matter beyond knowledge of the relationship which subsists between some members of the tribunal and one of the parties, would think that there might well be bias, then there is in his opinion a real likelihood of bias. Of course, someone else with inside knowledge of the characters of the members in question might say: 'Although things don't look very well, in fact there is no real likelihood of bias.' But that would be beside the point, because the question is not whether the tribunal will in fact be biased, but whether a reasonable man with no inside knowledge might well think that it might be biased."

In *Pennington* the magistrates convicted the applicant of selling short weight vegetables to two schools in Cheshire. The chairman of the magistrates was a member of the County Education Committee and was a governor of two schools. Although the charges related to neither of the schools to whose governing body the chairman belonged, the applicant did also supply vegetables to those schools.

The High Court quashed the convictions because of the magistrate's active connexion with the victims of the offences, saying that she should have either disqualified herself, or at least drawn attention to her connexion with the case, so that the parties could either consent or object to her continuing to sit. On the question of the test for bias, Lord Widgery C.J.

said:

> "It is not altogether clear to me how the matter was left in *Lannon's* case so far as which of [the] two tests was the correct one."

His Lordship also commented that the two tests "are often overlapping."

It is understandable that Lord Denning's judgment in *Lannon* should have caused subsequent judicial confusion. However, a sympathetic reading of that judgment may go some way towards resolving the difficulty. The key lies in understanding that Lord Denning began by considering the standpoint from which the existence or non-existence of bias is to be assessed. In this context he adopted the objective perspective of the contemporaneous reasonable man, as distinct from both the subjective perspectives of the decision-maker and the person actually affected by the decision, and the *ex post facto* perspective of reasonableness in the eyes of the reviewing court. Lord Denning then progressed to the other limb of the question, namely what constitutes bias?

A much-quoted formulation of the test for bias emerged from *R. v. Liverpool Justices ex parte Topping* (1983). The High Court quashed a conviction imposed by magistrates who were aware of other charges outstanding against the defendant. Ackner L.J. said that the correct test was:

> "Would a reasonable and fair-minded person sitting in court and knowing all the relevant facts have a reasonable suspicion that a fair trial for the applicant was not possible?"

The question of the correct formulation of the test for bias has arisen in a number of cases where local planning authorities have granted planning permission where it was in their own interests to do so.

In *Steeples v. Derbyshire County Council* (1984) the local authority wished to develop an amusement park. It entered into a contract with a company, whereby the company would manage the park and the local authority would take all reasonable steps to obtain planning permission for the development. The local authority was to be liable in damages if planning permission was not forthcoming. The County Council then granted itself planning permission.

Webster J., taking the view that a reasonable person, knowing of the contract, would say that there was a real likelihood of bias, said:

> "Which of [the] tests is to be applied may depend ... on the nature of

the decision-making body in question. Where the body is a judicial tribunal it may be that any doubt that justice is seen to be done is enough ... At the other end of the scale, where the body is primarily administrative, it may be that its decisions are invalid (when they are in fact fair) only when they actually appear to be unfair ... For the purposes of the present case ... I shall apply the test of likelihood."

A similar situation arose in *R. v. Sevenoaks District Council ex parte Terry* (1985) where a developer had made proposals for a piece of land which the local authority owned, and had offered £600,000 for a lease of the land. The local authority accepted the offer and then granted planning permission. A ratepayer asked the court to quash the planning permission on the basis that the local authority had fettered its discretion in relation to the determination of the application for planning permission. The High Court held that the real question was whether the local authority had acted in such a way that it was clear that the proper exercise of discretion was impossible. Answering this question in the negative, the court upheld the planning permission.

One of the most helpful solutions to the problem raised by the conflicting tests emerged in *R. v. St. Edmundsbury District Council ex parte Investors in Industry* (1985). The local authority applied to itself for planning permission authorizing the development of a piece of its own land as a supermarket. It then decided not to proceed with the application, but agreed to let the land to Sainsburys, subject to Sainsburys obtaining planning permission. Six other applications for planning permission were received for other supermarkets in the area. Sainsburys' application was granted and the others were all refused.

One of the unsuccessful applicants for planning permission challenged the Sainsbury decision on various grounds, arguing that it looked wrong, whilst conceding that in fact the decision was unbiased. Upholding the planning permission, the High Court said that the only question was whether the council had genuinely and impartially exercised its discretion. Furthermore, Stocker J. suggested that there was no real difference between the two tests for bias anyway, because a reasonable man does not reasonably suspect the existence of something unless there is a real likelihood of its existence.

Although the decision which was being challenged in *St. Edmundsbury* was towards the administrative end of the judicial-administrative spectrum, the principle formulated by Stocker J. possesses such obvious logic that it deserves to be more widely adopted. The fact that judicial psychology may always be such that the courts will quash decisions with a judicial flavour more readily than those which are merely administrative, should not be allowed to obscure the issue at the level of principle.

The planning cases clearly involve the decision-maker's financial advantage. It is appropriate at this stage, therefore, to consider cases involving pecuniary interest generally.

3. Bias and Pecuniary Interests

The classic case is *Dimes v. Grand Junction Canal Co.* (1852), where the parties had been involved in a long series of cases between 1831 and 1853. On three occasions the Lord Chancellor, Lord Cottenham, was on the bench. Dimes subsequently discovered that Lord Cottenham held shares in the company. The House of Lords held that this was a breach of natural justice, even though no-one would seriously think that the Lord Chancellor's judgment had been affected. In other words this was an early example of the need for justice to be seen to be done.

Similarly, in *R. v. Rand* (1866) the justices authorized a local authority to take water from certain streams without the owners' permission. Two of the justices were trustees of bodies which had lent money to the local authority. Although the court held that on the facts there was no bias because there was no benefit to the justices, Blackburn J. made the following statement of principle:

"There is no doubt that any direct pecuniary interest, however small ... does disqualify a person from acting as a judge in the matter."

The point is further reinforced by *R. v. Gaisford* (1892), where a Vestry Meeting decided to order the defendant to remove rubbish which he had deposited on the highway. When he failed to comply with this order, a court consisting of two justices ordered the rubbish to be removed and sold, with the proceeds being applied for the repair of the highway. One of the justices involved had proposed the original motion at the Vestry Meeting. The court quashed the justices' decision, partly on the ground of reasonable suspicion of bias arising out of the proposing of the motion in the Vestry Meeting, and partly because, in their capacity as ratepayers, the justices had an interest in reducing the cost of highway maintenance. On this latter point, A.L. Smith J. said:

"The fact that a man has even the slightest pecuniary interest operates to disqualify him from adjudicating upon a case."

This judicial attitude persisted well into the twentieth century. In *R. v.*

Hendon Rural District Council ex parte Chorley (1933) a purchaser agreed to buy land from a vendor, subject to the local authority's approval of the purchaser's proposals for the use of the land. An estate agent acting in the transaction not only had a clear interest in the sale proceeding to completion, but was also a member of the local authority. When the purchaser's proposals came before the local authority, the estate agent voted in favour of approving them. In due course the High Court quashed the approval.

However, there is also some evidence that the courts may take a more relaxed view of such cases. As early as the end of the nineteenth century the court was disinclined to see bias where an official of a union which was in dispute with an employers' association was convicted of disorderly conduct as the result of a prosecution which was initiated by an official of the employers' association. Three of the justices who were parties to the decision to convict held shares in ships which were insured by an organization which was a member of the employers' association (see *R. v. McKenzie* (1892)).

Similarly, in *R. v. Secretary of State for Trade ex parte Anderson Strathclyde plc* (1983) the Secretary of State for Trade had referred a takeover bid to the Monopolies Commission, who recommended that the bid should not be allowed to proceed. Because the Secretary of State had a small shareholding in the bidding company he arranged for a Minister of State to make the actual decision as to whether the Commission's recommendation should be accepted. The court said that even if the Secretary of State had made the decision himself, his shareholding could not be said to have vitiated the decision unless it was shown to have influenced him.

It may be that some further evidence of relaxation can be discerned in *R. v. Mulvihill* (1989). The appellant had been convicted of conspiracy to rob banks and building societies. The Crown Court judge who presided at the trial failed to disclose the fact that he owned 1650 shares in one of the banks. The Court of Appeal had to decide whether this shareholding constituted a breach of the rule against bias.

The court held that the judge had had no direct pecuniary interest in the outcome of the criminal proceedings, and therefore the principle of automatic disqualification did not apply. Although the remainder of the judgment must, therefore, strictly be regarded as *obiter*, it is significant to note that Brooke J., giving the judgment of the court, drew a distinction between the role of the judge in a jury trial, and the role of a lay justice:

"A lay justice ... is one of the primary decision-makers in summary proceedings in a magistrates' court; and although [the judge] had to make direct decisions on the admissibility of evidence during the course of trials within a trial, we do not consider that the hypothetical reasonable bystander would reasonably suspect that it was not possible for him to reach a fair decision because of the existence of his shareholding."

It is not clear from *Mulvihill* whether lay magistrates are in a different position from Judges sitting with juries simply because they are the primary decision-makers, or whether it is their lay status which is crucial. An argument could certainly be made in support of the latter proposition, on the basis that the public may well have little confidence in a lay magistrate's ability to distance himself from the facts of his personal finances.

However, if the lay status of the magistracy really is the basis of the reasoning in *Mulvihill*, it follows that the decision would not apply to a stipendiary magistrate, nor to a judge sitting in the County Court and finding himself in a position similar to Lord Cottenham's in *Dimes*. On the other hand, of course, if it is status as a primary decision-maker which counts, both stipendiary magistrates and Judges in the County Court would be covered by *Mulvihill*.

In passing, it is worth noticing that the court in *Mulvihill* endorsed the correctness of the test in *R. v. Liverpool Justices ex parte Topping* (1983), which is quoted at p.204.

A variety of specific provisions have been enacted by way of additions to the common law on pecuniary interests, notably ss.94 *et seq.* of the Local Government Act 1972 creating criminal sanctions, and reg.14 of the Education (School Government) Regulations 1987. Such provisions may prohibit any or all from attending, speaking or voting at a meeting. Any breach of provisions such as these appears to taint an ensuing decision with illegality to the extent that it is void, without the court investigating the extent to which the wrongful participation actually influenced the decision (*R. v. Justices of Hertfordshire* (1845)).

This decision was followed by the Court of Appeal in the private law case of *Noble v. Inner London Education Authority* (1984) where a teacher claimed to have been validly appointed by the authority following a favourable recommendation from the governors. One governor who had participated had been disqualified from doing so, and the recommendation was by a majority of one. Stephenson and Purchas L.JJ., with Griffiths L.J. dissenting, took the view that the recommendation was void, and therefore the consequential decision must also be void.

In *Bostock and Others v. Kay and Others* (1989) the Court of Appeal considered the position of teachers who were also governors when the question of converting a school into a City Technology College arose. The relevant provisions were contained in the Education (School Government) Regulations 1987.

The court held that when the governing body of a school was considering whether the school should be converted into a City Technology College, a governor who was also a teacher at the school had a direct pecuniary interest in the matter because, if the City Technology College comes into existence those teachers who join its staff are likely to be paid more than teachers at other establishments, and those teachers who do not join its staff may receive redundancy payments. Furthermore, the fact that the creation of the City Technology College depended on the completion of other stages in the decision-making process was not sufficient to make the prospects of receiving either higher salaries or redundancy payments too vague or remote.

It followed, therefore, that a governor who was also a teacher at the school should have declared an interest, and withdrawn from the meeting at which the matter was being discussed (unless the governing body permitted him to remain), and should also have refrained from speaking and voting while the matter was being discussed.

This case was distinguished in *R. v. Governors of Small Heath School ex parte Birmingham City Council* (1990), where the change in the school's status involved opting out of local authority control and becoming grant-maintained under the Education Reform Act 1988. The court said that in this situation the only necessary changes were that the cost of maintaining the school was transferred from the local education authority to the Secretary of State for Education and Science, with a consequential increase in autonomy for the governing body. This contrasted with the transition to a City Technology College, where the old school ceased to exist and a new institution took its place. It followed that the disqualifying provisions of the 1987 Regulations did not apply to meetings of the governing body at which the proposed change of status was considered.

An aspect of the case of rather wider interest arose when the court proceeded to consider the proper attitude of the Court of Appeal where the High Court has held that an application for judicial review succeeded on the facts and the law, but has nevertheless exercised its discretion to withhold relief.

In these circumstances the Court of Appeal was not entitled to override the exercise of the High Court's discretion on the basis that it was plainly wrong if the illegality arose only in respect of an intermediate stage of decision-making, without having any direct result on the final decision itself, and the illegality consisted of improper participation in a meeting, provided that three conditions are satisfied. The first condition is that those who participated improperly could have disseminated their views outside the meeting in any event. The second condition is that the arithmetic of the voting at the meeting must show that the votes which were improperly cast were not determinative of the issue. Finally, there must have been no objection at the meeting itself in respect of the improper participation.

The school governors cases were reviewed by the High Court in *R. v. Governors of Bacon's School ex parte Inner London Education Authority* (1990). The facts involved a meeting of the governors of a school at which a proposal to create a City Technology College was discussed, and in which a disqualified governor took part. Another meeting followed in which he did not take part, but which nevertheless made the same decision as the earlier one.

On the facts, the court took the view that the disqualification was highly technical, and that the breach of the relevant regulations had occurred in good faith. The court also concluded that in fact the decision of the first meeting had almost certainly not been affected by the illegality. In the light of a concession that on the authorities the decision of the first meeting was *ultra vires*, the court's attention centred on the question of the exercise of its discretion in relation to the final decision. Deciding to withhold a remedy, Simon Brown J., with whom Stuart-Smith L.J. agreed, said:

> "It would not be right routinely to refuse relief in cases involving breaches of the regulations merely because of the probability that such a breach will not in fact have affected the decision in question. That would be to ignore the long-term public interest in providing a sanction for these regulations and thereby protecting the integrity of the decisions of school governors generally. But it would be equally wrong to regard the regulations as sacrosanct and their strict enforcement as an absolute imperative in all situations. There is a countervailing public interest in the children's future and in not frustrating the governors' wishes where, as here, these are clearly discernible."

One thing is clear: the courts have at their disposal a number of verbal formulations relating to bias. Furthermore, it is difficult to avoid the conclusion that, within very broad parameters, in any given case they will choose whichever formulation most easily enables them to reach a conclusion which is consistent with their sense of justice.

F: Miscellaneous Aspects of Bias

1. Introduction

The simplicity of the proposition that no-one should be a judge in his own cause can be deceptive. Four questions arise sufficiently frequently to merit discussion.

The first is whether there is unity of identity between the initiator of a decision-making process and someone who is subsequently involved in that process, usually as an adjudicator. Secondly, there is the situation which arises where the initiator is clearly not the same person as the adjudicator, but is nevertheless present with the adjudicator while the latter is considering the case. Thirdly, in the case of multi-member decision-makers the question may arise whether the participation of one member tainted with bias is sufficient to taint the whole decision-making body. Finally, the facts of life generally, and political reality in particular, both indicate that many decision-makers will have already taken a position on the subject-matter under consideration, thus causing obvious difficulties if a strict test of bias is to be applied.

2. The Problem of Unity of Identity

In *Leeson v. General Medical Council* (1890) the managing body of the Medical Defence Union decided to bring disciplinary proceedings against Dr. Leeson. The proceedings were heard by the General Medical Council, which struck him off. Two of the twenty-nine members of the General Medical Council also belonged to the Medical Defence Union, but neither of them belonged to its governing body. A majority in the Court of Appeal held that there was no breach of natural justice, because in substance, the accuser and the adjudicator were not the same person.

The decision of the Court of Appeal in *McGoldrick v. Brent London Borough Council* (1987) illustrates the need for careful analysis of the facts in cases where it is alleged that there is overlapping identity between those who may loosely be termed "prosecutors" and "judges". The local education authority employed the respondent as the headteacher of a school. Under the terms of her contract of employment she was subject to the authority's disciplinary code and to the articles of government of her school.

The disciplinary code clearly envisaged a dichotomy between the authority, including its committees and sub-committees, on the one hand, and management, in the form of the Director of Education and his staff on the other. The articles of government provided a procedure for the governing body to make recommendations to the authority in disciplinary cases, and also provided for the authority to take disciplinary action itself, even in the absence of any recommendation from the governing body.

The headteacher was alleged to have made a racist remark to an administrative assistant within the office of the Director of Education. As a result of this allegation she was suspended from duty by the authority's Education Officer (Schools), and the matter was referred to the governing body of her school. After a full hearing, the governing body decided that there was no evidence to substantiate the allegation, and recommended immediate re-instatement. The authority then convened an *ad hoc* disciplinary sub-committee of the Education Committee, which declined to accept the governing body's recommendation, and resolved to hold a full hearing of the case.

The High Court granted the headteacher's application for a declaration that the findings of the governing body were binding on the authority, but the Court of Appeal reversed this decision.

The Court of Appeal conceded that at first sight it looked as if the headteacher, having been tried by the governing body, was then to be tried again by the authority, and that in the second set of proceedings the authority would be both "prosecutor" and "judge". However, on closer analysis, the Court of Appeal said that the role of the governing body was analogous to that of the justices in committal proceedings, and that in the second set of proceedings the dichotomy between the authority and its management, as envisaged by the disciplinary code, would manifest itself in reality, with management taking the role of "prosecutor" and the authority, acting through its sub-committee, taking the role of "judge".

Despite the convolutions of cases such as *McGoldrick*, and the questions of degree presented by cases such as Leeson, the majority of cases will present no problems of identity. However, even without this complication, the second question can still arise, namely whether natural justice has been breached where "prosecutors" are present with "judges" during the decision-making process.

2. "Prosecutors" Being Present With "Judges"

The problem is typified by *Cooper v. Wilson* (1937) where a police officer was dismissed by his Chief Constable. The officer appealed to the local authority's Watch Committee. The Chief Constable was present while the committee considered the matter, but he took no part in its deliberations. The court held that there had been a breach of natural justice.

Similarly, in *R. v. Barnsley Metropolitan Borough Council ex parte Hook* (1976) a committee of the local authority decided to ban a market trader for life from trading in their market, following a complaint that he had urinated in a side-street one evening when the public conveniences were closed. The trader was given the opportunity of presenting his case to a sub-committee, but the market manager, who had referred the complaint to the committee in the first place, gave evidence to the sub-committee in the absence of the trader, and was present while the sub-committee was deliberating.

When the sub-committee decided to uphold the original decision, the High Court refused an application for certiorari on the ground that the decision was purely administrative. However, the Court of Appeal allowed an appeal, holding not only that certiorari was available because the decision affected the trader's rights, but also that there had been a breach of natural justice.

The strictness of the courts' traditional view can also be illustrated by *R. v. Leicestershire Fire Authority ex parte Thompson* (1978) where a fireman was subject to disciplinary proceedings before a committee. There was a history of ill-feeling between him and the chief fire officer. While the committee were deliberating as to sentence they called in the chief fire officer to ask for advice on the implications of the various sentencing options open to them. The chief fire officer gave the advice, but took no part in the sentencing decision itself. The court held that the mere presence of the chief fire officer was sufficient to justify quashing the committee's decision.

On the other hand, it is interesting to note, although difficult to assess the significance of, *R. v. Chief Constable of South Wales ex parte Thornhill* (1987). The facts arose out of the police disciplinary procedure, under which deputy chief constables have responsibility for the conduct of disciplinary investigations, while chief constables adjudicate in any disciplinary proceedings which result from those investigations.

The appellant was a police officer who had been the subject of disciplinary proceedings. During an adjournment of the disciplinary hearing, while the chief constable was deliberating on his decision, the deputy chief constable attended on the chief constable in relation to urgent business which required the chief constable's personal attention, but which had no connexion with the disciplinary proceedings. The appellant saw the deputy chief constable go into the chief constable's room, but he did not know the purpose of the visit.

The chief constable found the charges proved and decided that the appellant should be dismissed from the force.

The Court of Appeal, taking what it considered to be a realistic approach, upheld the High Court's dismissal of an application for judicial review. More particularly, the work of the police force had to continue while the disciplinary proceedings were being conducted, and in any event the evidence disclosed that there had been no actual injustice, because the deputy chief constable had taken no part in the determination of the disciplinary proceedings.

On the question of the appearance of injustice, the Court of Appeal took the view that such an appearance would arise only from the fact that the appellant knew that it was the deputy chief constable who had entered the room where the chief constable was deliberating, and if the reason for the deputy chief constable's attendance had been explained to the appellant at that stage, even the possibility of an appearance of injustice could not have arisen.

3. Is the Participation of One Person Tainted with Bias Sufficient to Taint the Whole Decision-Making Body?

It is at least implicit in most of the cases discussed above that the participation of one person tainted with bias is sufficient to taint the whole decision-making body. However, it is possible to argue that an extension of the principle in *Leeson v. General Medical Council* (see p.211), would enable the court to disregard bias on the part of a very small proportion of the membership of a multi-member decision-maker, such as a large local authority exercising a licensing function.

Furthermore, in *Nell v. Longbottom* (1894) the court embarked on a process of assessing the legality of a number of individual votes in order to strike down those which were bad in order to recompute the arithmetic of an election to a mayoralty, rather than merely declaring the whole election to be void. Similarly, the court mentioned the potential relevance of arithmetical considerations in the *Small Heath School* case (see p.209).

4. Does Bias Exist Where the Decision-Maker has an Established Position in Relation to the Subject-Matter?

Decision-makers often have pre-conceived ideas of desirable outcomes, many of which may have been endorsed by the electoral process. Clearly, therefore, the disqualification of such decision-makers on the ground of bias may strike at the very basis of elected government.

In *R. v. Reading Borough Council ex parte Quietlynn Ltd.* (1987) a three-member panel dealing with applications for sex shop licences consisted of two members from the Conservative group and one from the Labour group. The Conservative group as a whole had previously decided that it was opposed to sex shops generally, and one of the Conservative members of the panel was a particularly outspoken opponent of such establishments.

Dealing with an application for judicial review following the unanimous refusal of a number of applications, Kennedy J. indicated that, even in the context of a process which he characterized as being quasi-judicial, the test applicable in the magistrates' courts was inappropriate (see *Topping*, which is mentioned at p.204). The judge went on to say:

> "Every councillor is to some extent a communicator ... whose function it is to formulate and to express views on subjects of local interest such as the licensing of sex establishments. It would be astonishing if by doing his job as a communicator he were to disqualify himself from taking part in deciding something which Parliament has left to local authorities to decide."

However, the judge did comment that as a matter of practice it would be desirable for local authorities to refrain from appointing individuals with strongly pre-conceived views to such small decision-making panels.

A similar suggestion about the desirability of introducing an independent decision-maker, albeit in another context, was made in *R. v. Portsmouth City Council ex parte Gregory and Mos* (1990), which is discussed further at p.193.

In certain circumstances there may be an overlap between this topic and the requirement of consultation, which is discussed fully in chapter 9.

G: Natural Justice in Multi-Stage Proceedings

It will be common for final decisions to be the result of several decision-making stages. The most obvious example will be a hearing at first instance followed by an appeal, but various other possibilities also exist. The most common problem which arises is whether a breach of natural justice at an early stage can be cured by compliance at a later stage.

At least where an appeal is concerned, the obvious difficulty is that if a subsequent curative effect is permitted, the consequence will be the practical denial of the right of appeal, since if the initial hearing is void, the appeal will be the only effective hearing. Accordingly, in the trades' union expulsion case of *Leary v. National Union of Vehicle Builders* (1970) Megarry J. stated as a general rule:

> "A failure of natural justice in the trial body cannot be cured by a sufficiency of natural justice in an appellate body."

Despite the evident good sense of this comment, in *Calvin v. Carr*

(1979), which concerned the disciplinary procedures of the Australian Jockey Club, the Privy Council indicated that it is an overstatement. Lord Wilberforce said:

"No clear and absolute rule can be laid down on the question whether defects in natural justice appearing at an original hearing, whether administrative or quasi-judicial, can be 'cured' through appeal proceedings. The situations in which this issue arises are too diverse, and the rules by which they are governed so various, that this must be so. There are, however, a number of typical situations as to which some general principle can be stated. First there are cases where the rules provide for a re-hearing by the original body, or some fuller or enlarged form of it. This situation may be found in relation to social clubs. It is not difficult in such cases to reach the conclusion that the first hearing is superseded by the second, or, putting it in contractual terms, the parties are taken to have agreed to accept the decision of the hearing body, whether original or adjourned ... At the other extreme are cases where, after examination of the whole hearing structure, in the context of the particular activity to which it relates (trade union membership, planning, employment, etc.), the conclusion is reached that a complainant has the right to nothing less than a fair hearing at the original and at the appeal stage ... these may very well include trade union cases, where movement solidarity and dislike of the rebel or renegade may make it difficult for appeals to be conducted in an atmosphere of detached impartiality and so make a fair trial at the first - probably branch - level an essential condition of justice."

Lord Wilberforce went on to say:

"[There is an intermediate category of cases where] those who have joined in an organization or contract should be taken to have agreed to accept what in the end is a fair decision, notwithstanding some initial defect."

In these cases:

"It is for the court, in the light of the agreements made, and in addition having regard to the course of proceedings, to decide whether, at the end of the day, there has been a fair result, reached by fair methods, such as the parties should fairly be taken to have accepted when they joined the association. Naturally, there may be instances when the defect is so flagrant, the consequences so severe, that the most perfect of appeals or re-hearings will not be sufficient to produce a just result. Many rules (including those now in question) anticipate that such a situation may arise by giving power to remit for a new hearing. There may also be cases when the appeal process is itself less than perfect: it may be vitiated by the same defect as the original proceedings: or short of that there may be doubts whether the appeal body embarked on its task without predisposition or whether it had the means to make a fair and full inquiry, for example where it has no material but a transcript of what was before the original body. In such cases it would no doubt be right to quash the original decision. These are all matters (and no doubt there are others) which the court must consider ...

"While flagrant cases of injustice, including corruption or bias, must always be firmly dealt with by the courts, the tendency in their Lordships' opinion in matters of domestic disputes should be to leave these to be settled by the agreed methods without requiring the formalities of judicial processes to be introduced."

Support for the *overall fairness* criterion may be derived from *Lloyd v. McMahon* (1987). Liverpool City Council had substantially delayed the making of a rate for the financial year 1985-86, as part of a campaign against the operation of central government's policy on local government finance.

The auditor, who proceeded on purely documentary evidence, made findings which were adverse to certain members of the council's controlling group, and issued a certificate against those members, alleging wilful misconduct resulting in loss. He neither offered the members an oral hearing, nor was he asked to do so. In appeal proceedings in the High Court, the members were offered an oral hearing, but they declined it.

In the Court of Appeal the members argued, *inter alia*, that the auditor's procedure had been unfair and that the appeal to the High Court had not cured the unfairness. The Court of Appeal dismissed the appeal, holding that although the auditor had been entitled to begin his proceedings without an oral hearing, when it became apparent that his conclusions were to be based on impugning the credibility and good faith of the members, he should have offered them an oral hearing. However, the members had been offered an oral hearing in the High Court, where the proceedings had been by way of re-hearing, and therefore if the auditor's proceedings and the appeal to the High Court were viewed as a whole, there was no unfairness.

The House of Lords held that there had been no obligation on the auditor to offer an oral hearing, although if one had been requested it would have been desirable to accede to the request. However, there was no reason to suppose that the auditor would have refused such a request if it had been made, therefore he had not acted unfairly. Nevertheless, if there had been unfairness, the fact that the High Court had had very wide powers, including the power to quash the auditor's decision and substitute its own, meant that the appellate process could have cured the unfairness.

The *overall fairness* approach was also taken in *R. v. Secretary of State for Transport ex parte Gwent County Council* (1987). The Secretary of State had statutory power to levy tolls on users of the Severn Bridge. The statute provided that any increases in the tolls must be preceded by a public inquiry. Accordingly, when the Secretary of State was minded to increase the tolls, he arranged for a public inquiry. The inquiry was informed that it was government policy for the total cost of providing estuarial crossings to be borne by their users, with no cost at all falling on the general public. Objectors at the public inquiry wished to challenge this policy, but were faced with the difficulty that in *Bushell v. Secretary of State for the Environment* (1980), where the House of Lords had held that in these circumstances natural justice did not require an inquiry to entertain challenges to government policy.

The inspector who conducted the inquiry noted the objections and summarized them in his report to the Secretary of State, but he also expressed the view that the evaluation of government policy was not within his remit. The Secretary of State issued a decision-letter increasing the tolls.

Although the High Court granted judicial review on the basis that the inspector's failure to evaluate the objections amounted to a procedural impropriety, which was not cured when the Secretary of State made the final decision, the Court of Appeal allowed an appeal. According to the Court of Appeal, the crucial question was whether the objectors had been treated unfairly. On the facts it was clear that the Secretary of State had considered the objections but had concluded that they did not justify a departure from the established policy.

The decision of the Court of the Court of Appeal in *R. v. Governors of Small Heath School ex parte Birmingham City Council* (1990), which is discussed at p.209, is also relevant here to the extent that the illegality had arisen only at an intermediate stage of decision-making, without having directly affected the final result.

Finally, in *R. v. Legal Aid Area No.8 (Northern) Appeal Committee ex parte Angell and Others* (1991) the High Court said that it was undesirable that an official whose decision is being appealed should investigate and comment upon material for the benefit of an appeal committee.

H: Specific Situations where Compliance with Natural Justice is Not Required

1. Necessity

In some situations the only possible decision-maker may have an interest in the subject-matter. This point was made in *Dimes v. Grand Junction Canal*, which is discussed further at p.206, where the Lord Chancellor had to sign an order or enrolment before the case could progress from the Vice-Chancellor to the House of Lords. Although his interest in the company disqualified him from hearing the appeal, the order of enrolment was not affected, because:

> "[In] a case of necessity ... the objection of interest cannot prevail."

The *Dimes* situation must, however, be carefully distinguished from those cases where the decision-maker who is subject to bias may merely be the obvious one, and not the only possible one. In *R. v. Portsmouth City Council ex parte Gregory and Mos* (1990), which is also discussed at p.193, the applicants were two councillors who were disciplined by the council of which they were members, on the basis that they had breached the National Code of Local Government Conduct. One member of the committee which investigated the matter and made recommendations had previously said to an officer of the local authority that one of the councillors was obviously guilty.

The High Court held, *inter alia*, that the membership of the committee was such that a reasonable and fair-minded person would have concluded that a fair trial was not possible. At the level of general principle, the court went on to say that, in a small community such as a local authority, the interests of justice may require the appointment of a wholly independent judge if influential senior members are to receive what is seen to be a fair trial when charged with serious misconduct.

2. Waiver

A person who is entitled to object to a biased decision-maker will be allowed to waive his right to do so, in which case he cannot subsequently seek to impugn the ensuing decision. He will be deemed to have waived his right to object if he allows the hearing to continue without protest even though he knows of the bias (see *R. v. Nailsworth Licensing Justices ex parte Bird* (1953)). However, an individual without the benefit of legal representation may be held not to have waived his right to object if he knows of the facts giving rise to the bias, but does not know of his entitlement to object (see *R. v. Essex Justices ex parte Perkins* (1927)).

This is justified on the basis that a person cannot waive rights of which he is unaware.

3. Statutory Exclusion

Parliament may, of course, expressly exclude the application of some or all of the elements of natural justice. These situations will be rare, and when they do arise they will usually be limited to an exclusion of the rule against bias. Furthermore, such provisions will be construed strictly.

In *R. v. Lee ex parte Shaw* (1882) the Public Health Act 1875 provided that no justice of the peace should be deemed to be incapable of acting under the statute by reason of being a member of a local authority. This provision was held to be irrelevant where the justice of the peace in question was not merely a member of the local authority but had concurred in the decision to bring the proceedings upon which he subsequently adjudicated in his magisterial capacity. However, in *R. v. Pwllheli Justices ex parte Soane and Others* (1948), where there was a similar statutory provision, it was held that mere presence at - as distinct from active participation in - a meeting which authorizes proceedings will not disqualify a justice of the peace from subsequently adjudicating when the case comes to court.

4. The Legislative Process

In *Bates v. Lord Hailsham of St. Marylebone* (1972) the court was faced with a challenge to the legality of the process of making delegated legislation affecting solicitors' remuneration. Megarry J. said:

> "I do not know of any implied right to be consulted or make objections, or any principle upon which the courts may enjoin the legislative process at the suit of those who contend that insufficient time for consultation and consideration has been given."

The position could, of course, be different if there was non-compliance with statutory procedural requirements, as may be the case with delegated legislation (see e.g. the *Aylesbury Mushrooms* case, discussed at p.21).

Furthermore, and without prejudice to the general correctness of *Bates*, the *GCHQ* case (1984), which is discussed further at p.182, is authority for the proposition that it would now be open to the court in an appropriate case to hold that a legitimate expectation of consultation had been created, even in the absence of any express requirement.

APPENDIX

The material contained in parts A and B of this Appendix is copyright and is reproduced by kind permission of Her Majesty's Stationery Office.

PART A

RULES OF THE SUPREME COURT, ORDER 53

Applications for Judicial Review

Cases appropriate for application for judicial review (O.53, r.1)
1.–(1) An application for-
    (a) an order of mandamus, prohibition or certiorari, or
    (b) an injunction under section 30 of the Act restraining a person from acting in any office in which he is not entitled to act,
        shall be made by way of an application for judicial review in accordance with the provisions of this Order.
    (2) An application for a declaration or an injunction (not being an injunction mentioned in paragraph (1)(b) may be made by way of an application for judicial review, and on such an application the Court may grant the declaration or injunction claimed if it considers that, having regard to-
    (a) the nature of the matters in respect of which relief may be granted by way of an order of mandamus, prohibition or certiorari,
    (b) the nature of the persons and bodies against whom relief may be granted by way of such an order, and
    (c) all the circumstances of the case,
it would be just and convenient for the declaration or injunction to be granted on an application for judicial review.

Joinder of claims for relief (O.53, r.2)
2.–On an application for judicial review any relief mentioned in rule 1(1) or (2) may be claimed as an alternative or in addition to any other relief so mentioned if it arises out of or relates to or is connected with the same matter.

Grant of leave to apply for judicial review (O.53, r.3)
3.–(1) No application for judicial review shall be made unless the leave of the Court has been obtained in accordance with this rule.

(2) An application for leave must be made ex parte to a judge by filing in the Crown Office-

    (a) a notice in Form No. 86A containing a statement of

        (i)   the name and description of the applicant,

        (ii) the relief sought and the grounds upon which it is sought,

        (iii) the name and address of the applicant's solicitors (if any) and

        (iv) the applicant's address for service; and

    (b) an affidavit which verifies the facts relied on.

(3) The judge may determine the application without a hearing, unless a hearing is requested in the notice of application, and need not sit in open court; in any case, the Crown Office shall serve a copy of the judge's order on the applicant.

(4) Where the application for leave is refused by the judge, or is granted on terms, the applicant may renew it by applying-

    (a) in any criminal cause or matter, to a Divisional Court of the Queen's Bench Division;

    (b) in any other case, to a single judge sitting in open court or, if the Court so directs, to a Divisional Court of the Queen's Bench Division:

Provided that no application for leave may be renewed in any non-criminal cause or matter in which the judge has refused leave under paragraph (3) after a hearing.

(5) In order to renew his application for leave the applicant must, within 10 days of being served with notice of the judge's refusal, lodge in the Crown Office notice of his intention in Form No. 86B.

(6) Without prejudice to its powers under Order 20, rule 8, the Court hearing an application for leave may allow the applicant's statement to be amended, whether by specifying different or additional grounds or relief or otherwise, on such terms, if any, as it thinks fit.

(7) The Court shall not grant leave unless it considers that the applicant has a sufficient interest in the matter to which the application relates.

(8) Where leave is sought to apply for an order of certiorari to remove for the purpose of its being quashed any judgment, order, conviction or other proceedings which is subject to appeal and a time is limited for the bringing of the appeal, the Court may adjourn the application for leave until the appeal is determined or the time for appealing has expired.

(9) If the Court grants leave, it may impose such terms as to costs and as to giving security as it thinks fit.

(10) Where leave to apply for judicial review is granted, then-

    (a) if the relief sought is an order of prohibition or certiorari and the Court so directs, the grant shall operate as a stay of the proceedings

to which the application relates until the determination of the application or until the Court otherwise orders;

(b) if any other relief is sought, the Court may at any time grant in the proceedings such interim relief as could be granted in an action begun by writ.

Delay in applying for relief (O.53, r.4)

4.–(1) An application for leave to apply for judicial review shall be made promptly and in any event within three months from the date when grounds for the application first arose unless the Court considers that there is good reason for extending the period within which the application shall be made.

(2) Where the relief sought is an order of certiorari in respect of any judgment, order, conviction or other proceeding the date when grounds for the application first arose shall be taken to be the date of that judgment, order, conviction or proceeding.

(3) The preceding paragraphs are without prejudice to any statutory provision which has the effect of limiting the time within which an application for judicial review may be made.

Mode of applying for judicial review (O.53, r.5)

5.–(1) In any criminal cause or matter, where leave has been granted to make an application for judicial review, the application shall be made by originating motion to a Divisional Court of the Queen's Bench Division.

(2) In any other such cause or matter, the application shall be made by originating motion to a judge sitting in open court, unless the Court directs that it shall be made-

(a) by originating summons to a judge in chambers; or

(b) by originating motion to a Divisional Court of the Queen's Bench Division.

Any direction under sub-paragraph (a) shall be without prejudice to the judge's powers under Order 32, rule 13.

(3) The notice of motion or summons must be served on all persons directly affected and where it relates to any proceedings in or before a court and the object of the application is either to compel the court or an officer of the court to do any act in relation to the proceedings or to quash them or any order made therein, the notice or summons must also be served on the clerk or registrar of the court and, where any objection to the conduct of the judge is to be made, on the judge.

(4) Unless the Court granting leave has otherwise directed, there must be at least 10 days between the service of the notice of motion or summons and the hearing.

(5) A motion must be entered for hearing within 14 days after the grant of leave.

(6) An affidavit giving the names and addresses of, and the places and dates of service on, all persons who have been served with the notice of motion or summons must be filed before the motion or summons is entered for hearing and, if any person who ought to be served under this rule has not been served, the affidavit must state that fact and the reason for it; and the affidavit shall be before the Court on the hearing of the motion or summons.

(7) If on the hearing of the motion or summons the Court is of opinion that any person who ought, whether under this rule or otherwise, to have been served has not been served, the Court may adjourn the hearing on such terms (if any) as it may direct in order that the notice or summons may be served on that person.

Statements and affidavits (O.53, r.6)

6.–(1) Copies of the statement in support of an application for leave under rule 3 must be served with the notice of motion or summons and, subject to paragraph (2), no grounds shall be relied upon or any relief sought at the hearing except the grounds and relief set out in the statement.

(2) The Court may on the hearing of the motion or summons allow the applicant to amend his statement, whether by specifying different or additional grounds or relief or otherwise, on such terms, if any, as it thinks fit and may allow further affidavits to be used if they deal with new matters arising out of an affidavit of any other party to the application.

(3) Where the applicant intends to ask to be allowed to amend his statement or to use further affidavits, he shall give notice of his intention and of any proposed amendment to every other party.

(4) Any respondent who intends to use an affidavit at the hearing shall file it in the Crown Office as soon as practicable and in any event, unless the Court otherwise directs, within 56 days after service upon him of the documents required to be served by paragraph (1).

(5) Each party to the application must supply to every other party on demand and on payment of the proper charges copies of every affidavit which he proposes to use at the hearing, including, in the case of the applicant, the affidavit in support of the application for leave under rule 3.

Claim for damages (O.53, r.7)

7.–(1) On an application for judicial review the Court may, subject to paragraph (2), award damages to the applicant if-

(a) he has included in the statement in support of his application for leave under rule 3 a claim for damages arising from any matter to which the application relates, and

(b) the Court is satisfied that, if the claim had been made in an action begun by the applicant at the time of making his application, he could have been awarded damages.

(2) Order 18, rule 12, shall apply to a statement relating to a claim for damages as it applies to a pleading.

Application for discovery, interrogatories, cross-examination etc. (O.53, r.8)

8.–(1) Unless the Court otherwise directs, any interlocutory application in proceedings on an application for judicial review may be made to any judge or a master of the Queen's Bench Division, notwithstanding that the application for judicial review has been made by motion and is to be heard by a Divisional Court.

In this paragraph "interlocutory application" includes an application for an order under Order 24 or 26 or Order 38, rule 2(3) or for an order dismissing the proceedings by consent of the parties.

(2) In relation to an order made by a master pursuant to paragraph (1) Order 58, rule 1, shall, where the application for judicial review is to be heard by a Divisional Court, have effect as if a reference to that Court were substituted for the reference to a judge in chambers.

(3) This rule is without prejudice to any statutory provision or rule of law restricting the making of an order against the Crown.

Hearing of application for judicial review (O.53, r.9)

9.–(1) On the hearing of any motion or summons under rule 5, any person who desires to be heard in opposition to the motion or summons, and appears to the Court to be a proper person to be heard, shall be heard, notwithstanding that he has not been served with notice of the motion or the summons.

(2) Where the relief sought is or includes an order of certiorari to remove any proceedings for the purpose of quashing them, the applicant may not question the validity of any order, warrant, commitment, conviction, inquisition or record unless before the hearing of the motion or summons he has lodged in the Crown Office a copy thereof verified by affidavit or accounts for his failure to do so to the satisfaction of the Court hearing the motion or summons.

(3) Where an order for certiorari is made in any such case as is referred to in paragraph (2) the order shall, subject to paragraph (4) direct that the proceedings shall be quashed forthwith on their removal into the Queen's Bench Division.

(4) Where the relief sought is an order of certiorari and the Court is satisfied that there are grounds for quashing the decision to which the application relates, the Court may, in addition to quashing it, remit the matter to the court, tribunal or authority concerned with a direction to reconsider it and reach a decision in accordance with the findings of the Court.

(5) Where the relief sought is a declaration, an injunction or damages and the Court considers that it should not be granted on an application for judicial review but might have been granted if it had been sought in an action begun by writ by the applicant at the time of making his application, the Court may, instead of refusing the application, order the proceedings to continued as if they had been begun by writ; and Order 28, rule 8, shall apply as if, in the case of an application made by motion, it had been made by summons.

Saving for person acting in obedience to mandamus (O.53, r.10)

10. No action or proceeding shall be begun or prosecuted against any person in respect of anything done in obedience to an order of mandamus.

Proceedings for disqualification of member of local authority (O.53, r.11)

11.–(1) Proceedings under section 92 of the Local Government Act 1972 must be begun by originating motion to a Divisional Court of the Queen's Bench Division, and, unless otherwise directed, there must be at least 10 days between the service of the notice of motion and the hearing.

(2) Without prejudice to Order 8, rule 3, the notice of motion must set out the name and description of the applicant, the relief sought and the grounds on which it is sought, and must be supported by affidavit verifying the facts relied on.

(3) Copies of every supporting affidavit must be lodged in the Crown Office before the motion is entered for hearing and must be supplied to any other party on demand and on payment of the proper charges.

(4) The provisions of rules 5, 6 and 9(1) as to the persons on whom the notice is to be served and as to the proceedings at the hearing shall apply, with the necessary modifications, to proceedings under the said section 92 as they apply to an application for judicial review.

Consolidation of applications (O.53, r.12)

12. Where there is more than one application pending under section 30 of the Act, or section 92 of the Local Government Act 1972, against several persons in respect of the same office, and on the same grounds, the Court may order the applications to be consolidated.

Appeal from judge's order (O.53, r.13)

13. No appeal shall lie from an order made under paragraph (3) of rule 3 on an application for leave which may be renewed under paragraph (4) of that rule.

Meaning of 'Court' (O.53, r.14)

14.–In relation to the hearing by a judge of an application for leave under rule 3 or of an application for judicial review, any reference in the Order to 'the Court' shall, unless the context otherwise requires, be construed as a reference to the judge.

PART B

SUPREME COURT ACT 1981, SECTION 29

Orders of mandamus, prohibition and certiorari

29.–(1) The High Court shall have jurisdiction to make orders of mandamus, prohibition and certiorari in those classes of cases in which it had power to do so immediately before the commencement of this Act.

(2) Every such order shall be final, subject to any right of appeal therefrom.

(3) In relation to the jurisdiction of the Crown Court, other than its jurisdiction in matters relating to trial on indictment, the High Court shall have all such jurisdiction to make orders of mandamus, prohibition or certiorari as the High Court possesses in relation to the jurisdiction of an inferior court.

(4) The power of the High Court under any enactment to require justices of the peace or a judge or officer of a county court to do any act relating to the duties of their respective offices, or to require a magistrates' court to state a case for the opinion of the High Court, in any case where the High Court formerly had by virtue of any enactment jurisdiction to make a rule absolute, or an order, for any of those purposes, shall be exercisable by order of mandamus.

(5) In any enactment-
(a) references to a writ of mandamus, of prohibition or of certiorari shall be read as references to the corresponding order; and
(b) references to the issue or award of any such writ shall be read as references to the making of the corresponding order.

SUPREME COURT ACT 1981, SECTION 30

Injunctions to restrain persons from acting in offices in which they are not entitled to act

30.–(1) Where a person not entitled to do so acts in an office to which this section applies, the High Court may-
  (a) grant an injunction restraining him from so acting; and
  (b) if the case so requires, declare the office to be vacant.
  (2) This section applies to any substantive office of a public nature and permanent character which is held under the Crown or which has been created by any statutory provision or royal charter.

SUPREME COURT ACT 1981, SECTION 31

Application for judicial review

31.–(1) An application to the High Court for one or more of the following forms of relief, namely-
  (a) an order of mandamus, prohibition or certiorari;
  (b) a declaration or injunction under subsection (2); or
  (c) an injunction under section 30 restraining a person not entitled to do so from acting in an office to which that section applies,
shall be made in accordance with rules of court by a procedure to be known as an application for judicial review.
  (2) A declaration may be made or an injunction granted under this subsection in any case where an application for judicial review, seeking that relief, has been made and the High Court considers that, having regard to-
  (a) the nature of the matters in respect of which relief may be granted by orders of mandamus, prohibition or certiorari;
  (b) the nature of the persons and bodies against whom relief may be granted by such orders; and
  (c) all the circumstances of the case, it would be just and convenient for the declaration to be made or the injunction to be granted, as the case may be.
  (3) No application for judicial review shall be made unless the leave of the High Court has been obtained in accordance with rules of court; and the court shall not grant leave to make such an application unless it considers that the applicant has a sufficient interest in the matter to which the application relates.

(4) On an application for judicial review the High Court may award damages to the applicant if-

    (a) he has joined with his application a claim for damages arising from any matter to which the application relates; and

    (b) the court is satisfied that, if the claim had been made in an action begun by the applicant at the time of making his application, he would have been awarded damages.

(5) If, on an application for judicial review seeking an order of certiorari, the High Court quashes the decision to which the application relates, the High Court may remit the matter to the court, tribunal or authority concerned, with a direction to reconsider it and reach a decision in accordance with the findings of the High Court.

(6) Where the High Court considers that there has been undue delay in making an application for judicial review, the court may refuse to grant-

    (a) leave for the making of the application; or

    (b) any relief sought on the application, if it considers that the granting of the relief sought would be likely to cause substantial hardship to, or substantially prejudice the rights of, any person or would be detrimental to good administration.

(7) Subsection (6) is without prejudice to any enactment or rule of court which has the effect of limiting the time within which an application for judicial review may be made.

PART C

EXTRACTS FROM THE EUROPEAN CONVENTION FOR THE PROTECTION OF HUMAN RIGHTS AND FUNDAMENTAL FREEDOMS

The provisions of this Convention have not been incorporated into English law. They may, however, be of persuasive authority.

Article 1
The High Contracting Parties shall secure to everyone within their jurisdiction the rights and freedoms defined in section I of this Convention.

SECTION I

Article 2
1. Everyone's right to life shall be protected by law. No one shall be deprived of his life intentionally save in the execution of a sentence of a court following his conviction of a crime for which this penalty is provided by law.

2. Deprivation of life shall not be regarded as inflicted in contravention of this Article when it results from the use of force which is no more than absolutely necessary:
    (a) in defence of any person from unlawful violence;
    (b) in order to effect a lawful arrest or to prevent the escape of a person lawfully detained;
    (c) in action lawfully taken for the purpose of quelling a riot or insurrection.

Article 3
No one shall be subjected to torture or to inhuman or degrading treatment or punishment.

Article 4
1. No one shall be held in slavery or servitude.
2. No one shall be required to perform forced or compulsory labour.
3. For the purpose of this Article the term 'forced or compulsory labour' shall not include:

(a) any work required to be done in the ordinary course of detention imposed according to the provisions of Article 5 of this Convention or during conditional release from such detention;

(b) any service of a military character or, in case of conscientious objectors in countries where they are recognized, service exacted instead of compulsory military service;

(c) any service exacted in case of an emergency or calamity threatening the life or well-being of the community;

(d) any work or service which forms part of normal civic obligations.

Article 5

1. Everyone has the right to liberty and security of person.

No one shall be deprived of his liberty save in the following cases and in accordance with a procedure prescribed by law:

(a) the lawful detention of a person after conviction by a competent court;

(b) the lawful arrest or detention of a person for non-compliance with the lawful order of a court or in order to secure the fulfilment of any obligation prescribed by law;

(c) the lawful arrest or detention of a person effected for the purpose of bringing him before the competent legal authority on reasonable suspicion of having committed an offence or when it is reasonably considered necessary to prevent his committing an offence or fleeing after having done so;

(d) the detention of a minor by lawful order for the purpose of educational supervision or his lawful detention for the purpose of bringing him before the competent legal authority;

(e) the lawful detention of persons for the prevention of the spreading of infectious diseases, of persons of unsound mind, alcoholics or drug addicts, or vagrants;

(f) the lawful arrest or detention of a person to prevent his effecting an unauthorized entry into the country or of a person against whom action is being taken with a view to deportation or extradition.

2. Everyone who is arrested shall be informed promptly, in a language which he understands, of the reasons for his arrest and of any charge against him.

3. Everyone arrested or detained in accordance with the provisions of paragraph 1(c) of this Article shall be brought promptly before a judge or other officer authorized by law to exercise judicial power and shall be entitled to trial within a reasonable time or to release pending trial. Release may be conditioned by guarantees to appear for trial.

4. Everyone who is deprived of his liberty by arrest or detention shall be entitled to take proceedings by which the lawfulness of his detention shall be decided speedily by a court and his release ordered if the detention is not lawful.

5. Everyone who has been the victim of arrest or detention in contravention of the provisions of this Article shall have an enforceable right to compensation.

Article 6

1. In the determination of his civil rights and obligations or of any criminal charge against him, everyone is entitled to a fair and public hearing within a reasonable time by an independent and impartial tribunal established by law. Judgement shall be pronounced publicly but the press and public may be excluded from all or part of the trial in the interest of morals, public order or national security in a democratic society, where the interest of juveniles or the protection of the private life of the parties so require, or to the extent strictly necessary in the opinion of the court in special circumstances where publicity would prejudice the interests of justice.

2. Everyone charged with a criminal offence shall be presumed innocent until proved guilty according to law.

3. Everyone charged with a criminal offence has the following minimum rights:

    (a) to be informed promptly, in a language which he understands and in detail, of the nature and cause of the accusation against him;

    (b) to have adequate time and facilities for the preparation of his defence;

    (c) to defend himself in person or through legal assistance of his own choosing or, if he has not sufficient means to pay for legal assistance, to be given it free when the interests of justice so require;

    (d) to examine or have examined witnesses against him and to obtain the attendance and examination of witnesses on his behalf under the same conditions as witnesses against him;

    (e) to have the free assistance of an interpreter if he cannot understand or speak the language used in court.

Article 7

1. No one shall be held guilty of any criminal offence on account of any act or omission which did not constitute a criminal offence under national or international law at the time when it was committed. Nor shall a heavier penalty be imposed than the one that was applicable at the time the criminal offence was committed.

2. This Article shall not prejudice the trial and punishment of any person for any act or omission which, at the time when it was committed, was criminal according to the general principles of law recognized by civilized nations.

Article 8

1. Everyone has the right to respect for his private and family life, his home and his correspondence.
2. There shall be no interference by a public authority with the exercise of this right except such as is in accordance with the law and is necessary in a democratic society in the interests of national security, public safety or the economic well-being of the country, for the prevention of disorder or crime, for the protection of health or morals, or for the protection of the rights and freedoms of others.

Article 9

1. Everyone has the right to freedom of thought, conscience and religion; this right includes freedom to change his religion or belief, and freedom, either alone or in community with others and in public or private, to manifest his religion or belief, in worship, teaching, practice and observance.
2. Freedom to manifest one's religion or beliefs shall be subject only to such limitations as are prescribed by law and are necessary in a democratic society in the interests of public safety, for the protection of public order, health or morals, or for the protection of the rights and freedoms of others.

Article 10

1. Everyone has the right to freedom of expression. This right shall include freedom to hold opinions and to receive and impart information and ideas without interference by public authority and regardless of frontiers. This Article shall not prevent States from requiring the licensing of broadcasting, television or cinema enterprises.
2. The exercise of these freedoms, since it carries with it duties and responsibilities, may be subject to such formalities, conditions, restrictions or penalties as are prescribed by law and are necessary in a democratic society in the interests of national security, territorial integrity or public safety, for the prevention of disorder or crime, for the protection of health or morals, for the protection of the reputation or rights of others, for preventing the disclosure of information received in confidence, or for maintaining the authority and impartiality of the judiciary.

Article 11

1. Everyone has the right to freedom of peaceful assembly and to freedom of association with others, including the right to form and to join trade unions for the protection of his interests.
2. No restrictions shall be placed on the exercise of these rights other than such as are prescribed by law and are necessary in a democratic society in the interests of national security or public safety, for the prevention of disorder or crime, for the protection of health or morals or for the protection of the rights and freedoms of others. This Article shall not prevent the imposition of lawful restrictions on the exercise of these rights by members of the armed forces, of the police or of the administration of the State.

Article 12

Men and women of marriageable age have the right to marry and to found a family, according to the national laws governing the exercise of this right.

Article 13

Everyone whose rights and freedoms as set forth in this Convention are violated shall have an effective remedy before a national authority notwithstanding that the violation has been committed by persons acting in an official capacity.

Article 14

The enjoyment of the rights and freedoms set forth in this Convention shall be secured without discrimination on any ground such as sex, race, colour, language, religion, political or other opinion, national or social origin, association with a national minority, property, birth or other status.

Article 15

1. In time of war or other public emergency threatening the life of the nation any High Contracting Party may take measures derogating from its obligations under this Convention to the extent strictly required by the exigencies of the situation, provided that such measures are not inconsistent with its other obligations under international law.
2. No derogation from Article 2, except in respect of deaths resulting from lawful acts of war, or from Articles 3, 4 (paragraph 1) and 7 shall be made under this provision.
3. Any High Contracting Party availing itself of this right of derogation shall keep the Secretary-General of the Council of Europe fully informed

of the measures which it has taken and the reasons therefor. It shall also inform the Secretary-General of the Council of Europe when such measures have ceased to operate and the provisions of the Convention are again being fully executed.

Article 16
Nothing in Articles 10, 11, and 14 shall be regarded as preventing the High Contracting Parties from imposing restrictions on the political activity of aliens.

Article 17
Nothing in this Convention may be interpreted as implying for any State, group or person any right to engage in any activity or perform any act aimed at the destruction of any of the rights and freedoms set forth herein or at their limitation to a greater extent than is provided for in the Convention.

Article 18
The restrictions permitted under this Convention to the said rights and freedoms shall not be applied for any purpose other than those for which they have been prescribed.

PROTOCOL 1

ENFORCEMENT OF CERTAIN RIGHTS AND FREEDOMS NOT INCLUDED IN SECTION I OF THE CONVENTION

Article 1
Every natural or legal person is entitled to the peaceful enjoyment of his possessions. No one shall be deprived of his possessions except in the public interest and subject to the conditions provided for by law and by the general principles of international law.

The preceding provisions shall not, however, in any way impair the right of a State to enforce such laws as it deems necessary to control the use of property in accordance with the general interest or to secure the payment of taxes or other contributions or penalties.

Article 2
No person shall be denied the right to education. In the exercise of any functions which it assumes in relation to education and to teaching, the State shall respect the right of parents to ensure such education and

teaching in conformity with their own religious and philosophical convictions.

Article 3
The High Contracting Parties undertake to hold free elections at reasonable intervals by secret ballot, under conditions which will ensure the free expression of the opinion of the people in the choice of the legislature.

PROTOCOL 4

PROTECTING CERTAIN ADDITIONAL RIGHTS

Article 1
No one shall be deprived of his liberty merely on the ground of inability to fulfil a contractual obligation.

Article 2
1. Everyone lawfully within the territory of a State shall, within that territory, have the right to liberty of movement and freedom to choose his residence.
2. Everyone shall be free to leave any country, including his own.
3. No restrictions shall be placed on the exercise of these rights other than such as are in accordance with law and are necessary in a democratic society in the interests of national security or public safety, for the maintenance of 'order public', for the prevention of crime or for the protection of the rights and freedoms of others.
4. The rights set forth in paragraph 1 may also be subject, in particular areas, to restrictions imposed in accordance with law and justified by the public interest in a democratic society.

Article 3
1. No one shall be expelled, by means either of an individual or of a collective measure, from the territory of the State of which he is a national.
   2. No one shall be deprived of the right to enter the territory of the State of which he is a national.

Article 4
Collective expulsion of aliens is prohibited.

INDEX